"MAY THIS BOOK BE THE BEGINNING OR CONTINUATION OF A LIFETIME OF READING ENJOYMENT."

Nancy and Ed Vojtik

A Visual Guide to the History, Language, & Practice of Fashion

FASHION DESIGN, REFERENCED

A Visual Guide to the History, Language, & Practice of Fashion

FASHION DESIGN, REFERENCED

Alicia Kennedy & Emily Banis Stoehrer
with Jay Calderin

Rockport Publishers
100 Cummings Center, Suite 406L
Beverly, MA 01915

rockpub.com • rockpaperink.com

© 2013 Rockport Publishers

First published in the United States of America in 2013 by
Rockport Publishers, a member of Quayside Publishing
Group
100 Cummings Center
Suite 406-L
Beverly, Massachusetts 01915-6101
Telephone: (978) 282-9590
Fax: (978) 283-2742
www.rockpub.com

10 9 8 7 6 5 4 3 2 1
ISBN: 978-1-59253-677-1

Digital edition published in 2013
eISBN: 978-1-61058-201-8

Library of Congress Cataloging-in-Publication Data
available

Printed in China

Book Concept and Art Direction
Alicia Kennedy

Design
Jonathan Hanahan and Chris Grimley for over,under

Timeline Drawings
Lynn Blake and Charles Neumann

Life of a Garment Drawing, page 196
Michael Alexander Guran

Technical Drawings
Chris Grimley (color), Kyle Jonasen (silhouettes and
details), and Celine Larkin (stitches)

Cover Image
Photographs from Hussein Chalayan's Spring/Summer
2007 collection by Pierre Verdy, AFP, Getty Images.

Images: p. 3, sketch from Bellezza, 1947; p. 4, photo of Maison Martin Margiela, Spring/Summer 2009, by Karl Prouse,
Catwalking, Getty Images; p. 9, Lasell's Gibson Girl, 1896,
printed with permission of the Winslow Archives, Lasell
College, Auburndale, Massachusetts.

VANNA

About This Book

In 2006 Hussein Chalayan, working with tech innovators 2D:3D, encapsulated eleven decades of fashion in a suite of breathtaking animatronic dresses that morphed from one era into another. Our cover splices together two moments in one such evolution (from Dior to Rabanne) and is meant to evoke fashion's constant referencing and transformation of its history and aesthetic language while looking into the future.

Our book approaches fashion design from the perspective of connectivity. It unfolds how fashion is imagined, produced, and disseminated within larger social, economic, and cultural systems. We have avoided traditional chapters in favor of entries that can be read individually or as part of an entire cycle. To borrow a metaphor from another discipline, we offer this volume as a kind of tasting menu, our suggestions for a progression of morsels to help the reader cultivate an informed and discerning palette.

We must note a few limitations: Fashion design today continues to be dominated by its Western roots and by a focus on women's clothing, which our book reflects. Moreover, some designers whose work we value appear here only briefly or not at all, simply because we could not affordably source the images.

Given fashion's relentless pace and the speed at which information is now transmitted, predicting its future has become exponentially harder. Nonetheless, it is our hope that both students of fashion and connoisseurs of design will find in these pages a path through the complexity of the industry's operations to the substance behind the style, and along the way, discover the extraordinary practitioners who have fashioned the changing perceptions of the world out of thread and cloth.

Alicia Kennedy

Acknowledgments

Like any endeavor in fashion, this book evolved as a team effort. Alicia and Emily researched and developed material; Alicia wrote Fundamentals, Principles, and Practice, while Jay contributed much of Dissemination. We had many conversations and, along the way, we had the support of many friends and colleagues.

Thanks, above all, to Michael Guran, who housed and fed us and lent us his expert eye and skilled hand.

At Rockport, Winnie Prentiss believed in the project from the start and we are deeply grateful for her continued support. Betsy Gammons, as always, offered a calm presence amid the storm of details and deadlines.

Long-time collaborator Chris Grimley, together with Jonathan Hanahan, realized the vision for this book with grace. Aiding them were three other members of the over,under family, Kyle Jonasen, Danielle LaFountaine, and Kelly Smith.

Celine Larkin contributed the wonderful suite of stitches. Charles Neumann began our timeline and Lynn Blake so ably stepped in to complete the history.

Lisa Kessler gave us portraits and photographic advice. For generously sharing images, we would like to thank designers Fukoko Ando, Lynne Bruning, Natalie Chanin, Diana Eng, Carla Fernández, Marie Galvin, Katiti Kironde, Carlos Mansilla, Maggie Orth, and Nara Paz; photographers Tracy Aiguier, Claire Zellar Barclay, Joel Benjamin, and Andie Guran; Philippa Katz of Barleycorn Antique Prints, Jeanie Quirk of Sudbury Antique Exchange, Marilyn Negip of Brennan Library at Lasell College, Charles Cross and Alfred Fiandaca, Kim Pashko, and an anonymous collector. Our appreciation, as well, to Cora Hawks at Rockport, Moira Heffernan at Getty Images, and Lyndsay Black at firstVIEW.

Our thanks to Teresa Calabro, Katie Ernest, and Hilary Ritter, for pitching in early in the process, and to Betty Ahearn, Laird Borrelli, Julian Clark, Fred Dennis, Robert Frye, James Hannon, Henry Horenstein, Cynthia Kozdeba, Mark Stoehrer, and Trisha Wilson-Nguyen for kindnesses along the way.

to the Class of '96 with all good wishes from C.D. Gibson 96
Easter 1895

In memory of Alicia McGrory Kennedy Struble, for first lessons

Defining Fashion

Fashion eludes easy definition. Broadly, fashion can be understood as shifting styles of dress—that is, specific combinations of silhouettes, textiles, colors, details, and fabrications—embraced by groups of people at a particular time and place. Such styles may be projected by a designer or emerge from the street. Fashion can also be viewed as the entire system of innovation, production, marketing, dissemination, and adoption. Fashion is both a creative endeavor and a product; or, put another way, it is an aesthetic practice that produces useful, and sometimes lucrative, objects. On the one hand, a craft or an art form; on the other, a multibillion-dollar worldwide business.

Fashion's reach, of course, goes far beyond the chain of activities that result in *objets de la mode*. Dating at least to the late Middle Ages with the rise of the city and early capitalism, fashion was redefined in the second half of the nineteenth century with the spread of industrialization and the birth of the modern couturier, and again in the late twentieth century with increasing levels of democratization and globalization. Along this trajectory, fashion has operated as cultural construction, social performance, spectacle, class identification, self-expression, and lifestyle articulation. A consumer of history enmeshed in its own time, fashion, like all design, can also be read as an attempt, however fleeting, to predict and shape the future.

Fundamentals

To grasp the fundamentals of the fashion industry means looking at the systems by which it operates, the centers of its activities, and its stylistic formulations. Fashion, as a system of dress that functions beyond utilitarian needs and serves as a marker of identity, has a long history. In the mid-nineteenth century, however, two developments—the establishment of the haute couture salons and the first mass production of apparel—created a framework for fashion that would hold sway for the next hundred years. Twice since, fashion culture has undergone significant shifts: with the rise of boutiques and young designers of ready-to-wear in the 1960s and 1970s and with the globalization and speeding up of fashion in the 1990s. Where fashion takes place is key. The dominant system has been a Western, Paris-centric, one. As new centers began to emerge in the twentieth century, their particular voices expanded and enriched the image of fashion; designers also arrived in Paris with a distinctly non-Western approach to how clothes could be made and worn. By the new millennium, the production and marketing of fashion had spread across the globe (even if many fashion practices in the far reaches remained unexamined). Another important consideration is how an aesthetic is conceived. By the 1960s, the consumer of fashion was changing and a proliferation of style subcultures entered into the fashion cycle. Today, in essence, fashion is the articulation of a lifestyle.

An Illustrated Timeline of Fashion

Drawings by Lynn Blake and Charles Neumann

By 1500

In northern Europe, exaggerated hennins (conical and beehive-shaped women's hats) and poulaines (long, pointed men's shoes) have become the first garments to serve no purpose outside of fashion. • The rise of the city allows fashion to flourish; the urban street provides a theatre in which dress and adornment convey wealth and status. Italy is the primary producer of silk fabrics and England rules the wool trade. • Men dominate the fashion scene. The essential garment is the doublet: a slightly padded, short overshirt derived from the quilted lining worn under armor. Usually ending at the waist, with sleeves attached or unattached, in the early 1500s it is especially filled out in the shoulders and upper arms. Completing the look are hose and codpiece.

1501

Catherine of Aragon introduces the Spanish farthingale, a type of hoopskirt, to the English court on her marriage to Prince Arthur.

1532

Niccolò Machiavelli publishes *The Prince*, in which he advocates the skillful use of dress to assert one's power and social status. The trendsetting Francis I, who rules France from 1515 to 1547, frequently expresses his authority by challenging members of his court to adopt his unique style.

By 1550s

At court and among the land-owning classes, women are wearing corsets, possibly embraced in reaction to the emergence of fashionable dress among the guild members, traders, and merchants who constitute a growing European middle class.

1558–1603

Though royal courts throughout Europe drive fashion forward, none take dress to greater extremes than that of Elizabeth I in England. The queen promotes an especially opulent style: Luxurious materials like silk brocade and cut velvet are richly ornamented with lace, pearls, and precious jewels and decorated with intricate patterns of stitching and gold and silver embroidery. • The fashionable silhouette becomes increasingly restrictive. The farthingale expands, as does the ruff, a wide pleated collar worn by men and women. Stiffened with wire or starch (introduced in 1560), ruffs can be made to stand up to twelve inches (30 cm) away from the neck.

Late 1500s–early 1600s

The trend toward elaborate ornamentation reaches its apogee. The doublet, heeled shoes, and the cuffs of the courtier's kid gloves are embroidered to match. His wide standing collar, called a whisk, is made of reticella, a delicate cutwork lace. His heavily decorated trunk hose, or breeches, are set off by the poms on his garters. His stockings are adorned with intricate gold embroidery at the ankles and his shoes with large rosettes.

1600s

Throughout Europe, fashions tend to diverge along religious and political lines, with the more lavish styles worn by those who favor the Catholic Church and a strong monarchy and the more restrained styles worn by those who support Protestantism and a more representative government.

1607

Jamestown is settled in the Virginia colony.

1610–1715

Baroque

1620–60

Fashions become more natural. Waistlines rise and the padding disappears from both doublets and bodices, enabling the wearer to move more easily. Women prefer bodices that follow the contours of their body and adopt less rigid stomachers and skirts. Men exchange their starched ruffs for collars of soft linen and lace; they wear their hair longer, under soft-brimmed hats, and don looser breeches. • Artists such as Wenceslaus (Václav) Hollar and Abraham Bosse create fashion plates that spread the news of fashion change throughout Europe.

1642–49

English Civil War

1660

Charles II is restored to the throne of England after eleven years in exile at the French court; in 1666 he introduces the vest to men's fashion.

1661-83

Louis XIV, together with his minister of finance, Jean-Baptiste Colbert, positions France as an economic superpower based on the production and trade of luxury goods such as silk and lace. The French begin their reign as arbiters of refined taste and all things fashionable.

1672

In Paris, Jean Donneau de Visé publishes *Le Mercure Galant*, the first newspaper to report on fashion. Lasting only two years in its first incarnation, it returns in 1678 as a monthly supplement covering style and is marketed to women, especially in the provinces and abroad. Its success establishes the idea of the fashion magazine.

1680-1710

The forerunner of the men's three-piece suit is introduced, comprising a long jacket known as a justaucorps, *a vest, or waistcoat, and breeches.*

1682

The French court moves from Paris to Versailles, where the king busies his nobles by mandating a strict code of elegant dress to be displayed at countless balls and fêtes. Stiff, heavy textiles and lavish ornamentation characterize the look.

1705-15

Ensuring the success of the king's revival of the silk-weaving industry in Lyon, fashionable garments such as the *robe volante*, *robe á la française*, and *robe a l'anglaise* showcase wide expanses of pattered silk. Frequently depicted by the painter Antoine Watteau, the large pleats of the robe volante flow down the back of the gown from the shoulders to the hem.

1715-74
Rococo

1745-64

Madame de Pompadour, mistress to Louis XV, becomes an arbiter of style, favoring pastel colors and decorative ribbons adorning the stomacher.

1770

Austrian princess Marie Antoinette arrives at Versailles, bringing Paris fashion to the more traditional court. Her savvy marchande de mode, Rose Bertin, creates a taste for elaborate trimmings and extravagant headdresses.

1776-83
American Revolution

1778-88

Le Galerie des Modes et du Costume Français is published, one of a number of pre-Revolutionary magazines to promote French fashion throughout Europe. In the numerous magazines to follow during and after the Revolution, the latest styles reflect the political and social climate.

1780-90
Naturalism

1783

Elisabeth Vigée-Lebrun's portrait of Marie Antoinette wearing a chemise á la reine, a muslin dress similar to an undergarment, goes on display at the Paris Salon. The people of France are outraged.

1789-99
French Revolution

1790-1820
Neoclassicism

1790s

The *merveilleuses* and *incroyables* take to the streets of Paris, sparking the first antifashion movement. *Merveilleuses* crop their hair *à la victim.*

1790-1890
Dandyism

1795

The first bespoke tailors occupy London premises on what will become known as Savile Row.

Late 1700s-early 1800s

The dandy aesthetic for an austere color palette, restrained style, and impeccable tailoring begins to dominate men's fashion.

1804

Napoleon and his stylish wife, Joséphine, are crowned emperor and empress of France. Fashionable society adopts the diaphanous gown of the *merveilleuse* with its low décolletage and high empire waistline.

1811-20

During the English Regency, the Prince of Wales befriends George "Beau" Brummell, the dandy *par excellence.*

1817

By the early nineteenth-century, Marie Antoinette's revolutionary dress has become established fashion. The English version of the style is accessorized more modestly with a fichu or a spencer jacket.

1820-50

Romanticism

1830

The Bourbon monarchy is restored in France. ● The first American magazine to include fashion plates, *Godey's Lady's Book*, is published in Philadelphia.

1830s

In a move away from classicism, styles become more exaggerated, with an emphasis on the sleeve. The Romantic ideal is feminine and delicate.

1837

Princess Victoria becomes Queen of England. Her marriage to her cousin Albert in 1840 starts the trend for white wedding dresses.

1842

Peterson's Magazine begins publication.

1846

Elias Howe invents the lockstitch sewing machine. Mass production of some clothing becomes feasible.

1849

Newspaper editor Amelia Bloomer begins to advocate in *The Lily* for a woman's right to control her own wardrobe.

1850s-1880s

Artistic and Aesthetic dress movements react against the mainstream taste for crinolines and bustles as well as mass production.

1851

Thousands flock to the Crystal Palace in Hyde Park during the Great Exhibition to view displays of the latest technological advances of the Industrial Revolution. ● Isaac Singer introduces the first sewing machine scaled to domestic use.

1852

Napoleon III comes to power in France. ● Le Bon Marché, the world's first modern department store, opens in Paris.

1854-56

Japan, forced to open up to Western trade, asserts itself as a major fashion influence on Europe.

1855

Empress Eugénie, wife of Napoleon III, and members of her court become important tastemakers. Franz Xaver Winterhalter's portraits show the wide silhouette created by multiple stiff horsehair petticoats known as crinolines.

1856

William Henry Perkins discovers the first synthetic dye, known as Perkins Purple.

1857

The Spanish invention of the caged crinoline, made of steel-wire hoops, allows the fashionable silhouette to become lighter; consequently, skirts widen further. ● Otis installs the first commercial passenger elevator, in the E. V. Haughwout department store in New York.

1858

English dressmaker Charles Frederick Worth establishes the first couture house in Paris. His clients soon encompass European royalty, stage actresses, demimondaines, and American heiresses.

1861–65

American Civil War

1861

Prince Albert dies. Royal servants are required to dress in mourning for eight years; Queen Victoria will wear full mourning until her own death in 1901.

1865–70

The half-crinoline, flat in front and springing away from the body in back, becomes popular.

1867

The first issue of *Harper's Bazar* is published in New York.

1868

Worth and other couturiers establish the Chambre Syndicale de la Couture Parisienne.

1870–78

The bustle makes its first appearance. Its fullness comes from draping the back of the garment at the natural waist over a small steel-wire foundation.

1873

In San Francisco, Levi Strauss patents durable cotton pants with riveted pockets.

1878–83

The bustle either disappears or is worn with a long-waisted cuirass bodice that falls over the hips, creating a slim silhouette.

1883

Gabrielle "Coco" Chanel is born in France.

1883–90

The bustle morphs into an extreme shape: a padded shelf that protrudes from the mid-back. Fabrics become heavier and more ornately decorated.

1884

Liberty & Co. in London, having sold textiles from Asia since 1875, opens a dress department that features loose-fitting tea gowns. • French chemist Hilaire de Charbonnet, Comte de Chardonnay, patents a cellulose-based fabric known as artificial silk, which he begins manufacturing seven years later.

1886

In Tuxedo Park, New York, the tailless, boxier dinner jacket is introduced as an alternative to the traditional tailcoat worn with black tie.

1895–1914

Belle Époque

1890–1910

The New Woman, personified by the Gibson Girl, can transform herself from a spirited figure sporting a shirtwaist and jacket to a well-bred young lady attired in a frothy evening gown.

Late 1890s–1907

The straight-front corset creates the illusion of a soft hourglass silhouette. The popularity of tight-lacing the steel stays to produce a wasp waist thrusts the bosom forward and the hips backward, giving rise to the name S-curve or S-bend corset.

1892

The first issue of *Vogue* is published.

1895

As women become more active, a craze for cycling popularizes the bifurcated skirts gathered at the ankle known as bloomers. • The Montgomery Ward catalog introduces the term "ready-to-wear."

1898

Britain's first escalator is installed in Harrods in Knightsbridge. Within two years, "inclined elevators" will be incorporated into department stores in New York and Philadelphia, including Bloomingdale's.

1900

The Paris Exposition Universelle marks the first public representation of haute couture as a French profession, showcasing the designs of the houses of Worth, Doucet, Paquin, Chéruit, Redfern, and Callot Soeurs. • Cloak makers in New York City form the International Ladies' Garment Workers' Union to lobby for better working conditions. By the end the decade, membership in the ILGWU, which includes male and female workers, will surge as a result of two successful mass strikes: the Uprising of 20,000 in 1909 and the Great Revolt of 1910.

1900–10

Women's fashion eases into the twentieth century with little change from the previous decade. Tailored but feminine suits and separates define daywear. Hats are oversized and heavily trimmed.

1903

Paul Poiret founds his couture house at 5 rue Auber in Paris.

1904–5

Russo-Japanese War

1905

Herminie Cadolle, inventor of the *bien-être*, a two-piece undergarment exhibited at the Exposition Universelle, is selling the upper half, which supports the breasts by means of shoulder straps, independent of the corset at the waist. • American businessman Condé Nast purchases the society magazine *Vogue*.

1905–7

The Fauves, a loosely assembled group of painters, exhibit work notable for its expressive combinations of vibrant color. Raoul Dufy will later design bold textiles for Poiret and the leading French silk manufacturer, Bianchini-Ferier.

1907

Madeleine Vionnet, while working as a *modéliste* at the House of Doucet, creates a collection of lingerie-inspired dresses presented on braless, barefoot models, becoming the first fashion designer to liberate women from the corset. The *vendeuses* refuse to show her designs.

1907

Spanish-born artist and inventor Mariano Fortuny designs the Delphos, a tea gown of minutely pleated silk inspired by the ancient Greek chiton. The soft, liquid garment molds to the curves of the body and allows for unrestricted movement. Using a technique and device that he patents in 1909, Fortuny will produce variations on the dress over the next four decades.

1907–10

The fashionable silhouette becomes gradually straighter, reviving the empire line. Although less constrictive at the waist, it is slimmer at the hips, obliging many women to adopt the new tubular corsets. The style achieves its narrowest expression in Poiret's short-lived, and aptly named, hobble skirt of 1910.

1909

Serge Diaghilev's Ballets Russes explodes upon the Paris scene. Léon Bakst's sets and costumes for *Schéhérazade* in 1910 inspire a vogue for an idealized, exotic orientalism in the decorative arts throughout Europe and the Americas that lasts well into the 1920s.

1910

In Austria, the Wiener Werkstätte establishes its textile department and, the following year, its fashion department; the aesthetic is exuberant in both color and design. • In the United States, *Women's Wear Daily*, the first fashion industry trade paper, is founded.

1911

A fire at the Triangle Shirtwaist Company in New York kills 146 sweatshop workers, mostly immigrant girls, who are locked into the factory building. Outrage at the horrific deaths leads to improvements in garment workers' safety, wages, and hours, but sweatshops will continue to play a central role in the economics of the ready-to-wear industry.

1911

Chinese Revolution

1911

Dressed as a sultan, Paul Poiret throws a lavish 1,002nd Night costume ball at which his wife, Denise, debuts his Persian-inspired harem pants and hoop-skirted "lampshade" tunic. In 1913, he interprets the costume for his fashion collection. The Sorbet ensemble's tunic, with its kimono neckline and slightly higher waist, is meant to be worn with a brassiere not a corset; the petal skirt is a step forward from Poiret's hobble, allowing its wearer to move more freely while maintaining the illusion of a narrow hem.

1912

Vionnet opens her couture house on the rue de Rivoli in Paris. • The *Gazette du Bon Ton* and *Journal des Dames et des Modes* begin publication.

1913

In North America, Gideon Sunback introduces a "hookless fastener" with interlocking teeth, later known as the zipper.

1914-18

World War I

1914

Giacomo Balla publishes *Il vestito antinetrale*, a futurist manifesto for menswear that exhorts men to abandon their mundane clothing in favor of dynamic, expressive, and modifiable clothing suitable to the energy and forward thrust of the twentieth century. • Caresse Crosby (aka Mary Phelps Jacob) patents the first modern brassiere. Soft and lightweight, it gains wide acceptance among women whose figures conform to the boyishly slim ideal. • Men's clothing workers form the Amalgamated Clothing Workers of America (ACWA).

1914

Irene Castle, style icon and half of the famous dance duo with her husband Vernon, cuts her hair short, immediately popularizing throughout America the bobbed locks introduced in Paris in 1909.

1914-18

Haute couture continues in Paris on a smaller scale, with many male couturiers joining the army. • Deployed by the military to produce standardized uniforms, clothing manufacturers improve their operations and increase production capabilities, leaving them well situated to address the postwar market for high-quality but affordable ready-to-wear.

1914-18

Commissioned by the British War Office, Burberry transforms its waterproofed gabardine coat for new requirements in combat, adding epaulets, D-rings, and straps. The company offers to make a complete officer's kit—uniform, cap, and coat—within four days. After the war, women as well as men adopt what frontline soldiers have come to call the trench coat.

1916

Recognizing that each country has its own unique tastes, Condé Nast founds *British Vogue*, to be followed by *French Vogue* in 1920.

1917

Russian Revolution

Post-1917

Many of the White Russians forced to immigrate after the revolution end up in Paris, where some female nobles, and even royalty, become *vendeuses mondaines* in various couture houses.

1918

By the end of World War I, a more relaxed attitude prevails for clothing. Fashionable women, increasingly educated and working, need their clothing to perform throughout the day and choose ease, function, and simplicity over formality and opulence.

1919

The Eighteenth Amendment to the U.S. Constitution, prohibiting the manufacture or sale of liquor, is ratified and goes into effect the next year. Prohibition does not end until 1933.

1920

The Nineteenth Amendment to the U.S. Constitution gives women the right to vote.

1920s

A distinctive historicizing style takes hold in the early 1920s as an alternative to the garçonne look that will define the decade. Jeanne Lanvin, known for her coordinated mother/daughter dresses, will also produce variations on the romantic robe de style. Worn for afternoon tea dances and evening parties, it is characterized by a low waist and an almost panniered skirt that exaggerates the hips.

Early 1920s

Women adopt the close-fitting cloche hat, set low on the brow over a sleek short bob. Popular until 1933 by when it becomes looser, the cloche reinforces the streamlined dropped-waist silhouette of the 1920s, which hangs from the shoulders in a line uninterrupted by the curves of the body.

1920–26

Wimbledon and French Championships star Suzanne Lenglen epitomizes the ideal woman: youthful and physically fit in Jean Patou's sleeveless, above-the-knee tennis attire. Designers are creating active wear for active women who swim, ski, ride, fish, golf, drive, sail, and fly planes.

1921

Coco Chanel, whose couture house at 31 rue Cambon opened in 1919, launches Chanel No. 5. It becomes the best-selling perfume in the world, and within a decade, numerous other Parisian couturiers will introduce their perfumes.

1922

Archaeologist Howard Carter discovers and starts excavating the tomb of the pharaoh Tutankhamun in Egypt's Valley of the Kings. The resultant Egyptomania spreads to the design of clothing and accessories.

1923

Haute couturiers, including Vionnet, Poiret, Lanvin, Chéruit, and Worth, form an anticopyist society, the Association pour la Défense des Arts Plastiques et Appliqués. All dresses made by Vionnet now carry a label with her signature and an imprint of her thumb. • Basketball star Chuck Taylor's signature appears on the Converse All-Star basketball shoe.

1923–28

Artist Sonia Delaunay creates "simultaneous" fabrics in abstract geometric patterns, first for a Lyon manufacturer, then for her own Atelier Simultané. Her fashions integrate construction and decoration.

1924

Oxford University outlaws the wearing of knickers on campus. In response, male students begin to sport oversized trousers later known as Oxford Bags. These extremely wide pants can measure as much as 40 inches (1 m) at the hem.

1925

African American performer Josephine Baker steps on stage at the Théâtre des Champs-Élysées, where she finds immediate success. Known to roam the streets with her pet cheetah, Chiquita, "La Baker" brings sexuality, humor, and exoticism to Parisian nightlife. • Delaunay opens a boutique with the furrier Jacques Heim at the Exposition Internationale des Arts Décoratifs et Industriels Modernes. The Paris fair acquaints the world with a streamlined, geometric aesthetic called *style moderne*, later termed art deco.

1926

Coco Chanel introduces her "little black dress." Chanel's designs embody both la garçonne—a slim boyish figure in easy, modern garments borrowed from menswear—and a pauvreté de luxe, elevating a simple silhouette and simple material, such as wool jersey, through fine tailoring and couture details.

1926

Waldo S. Semon discovers vinyl.

1926–27

First-ranked tennis player René Lacoste begins wearing an embroidered alligator on his shirt, a symbol of his nickname on the court. In 1933, with André Gillier, president of the largest French knitwear-manufacturing firm, he will begin to mass-produce the shirt.

1927

Hemlines are at their shortest. Fashionable women wear theirs just above the knee. The flapper wears hers short enough to reveal her garters when dancing the Charleston, as caricatured by the illustrator John Held in Life *magazine.*

1928

Hemlines become asymmetrical and longer. • The Ente Nazionale della Moda (ENM) is founded to unify the Italian fashion industry, from design houses to textile mills to manufacturers. • While British women over thirty who meet certain property qualifications have been enfranchised since 1918, the Representation of the People Act now grants all women the right to vote on the same terms as men.

1929

The New York Stock Exchange collapses on 29 October. The economic downturn to which the stock market crash contributes will affect the industrialized nations for a decade to come. • In November, Federated Department Stores is incorporated, linking the financial interests of four prominent U.S. department stores: Abraham & Straus of Brooklyn, Filene's of Boston, F&R Lazarus of Columbus, Ohio, and Bloomingdale's of New York.

Late 1920s–early 1930s

In resort towns the world over, from Palm Beach to Biarritz, women don the loose trousers known as beach pajamas. At the beach, men and women are fashion equals, showing a similar amount of skin while sunbathing, now a widespread practice.

1930

Marlene Dietrich appears in white tie and tails in Josef von Sternberg's film Morocco. The look, with its associations of male sexual autonomy, would become a favorite for her. Throughout the 1930s, women will emulate stars like Dietrich and Katherine Hepburn, who are often photographed in custom-made menswear trousers and suits.

1931

In France, the Protection Artistique des Industries Saisonniers (PAIS) is formed to fight against copyists. In the United States, the following year, the Fashion Originators Guild, a trade association of garment designers, manufacturers, and retailers, puts sanctions into place to protect the original work of American designers. Despite the guild's effectiveness in stemming design piracy, in 1941 the U.S. Supreme Court will find that its practices violate the Sherman Antitrust Act. • *Apparel Arts* is founded. A men's fashion magazine published for the trade, it will become the sartorial bible for the middle-class American male.

By 1931

The effects of the Great Depression emerge in a more conservative approach to fashion. For day, the look is tidy and ladylike, with skirts at midcalf; coordinated but nonmatching separates allow for multiple outfits. The planar silhouette of the 1920s gives way to a leaner, more natural shape: Women's suits and dresses are carefully tailored, and often belted, to define the waist and follow closely over a slim bottom.

By 1931

Eveningwear marks a return to womanly glamour. Whether Madame Grès's intricate Grecian draperies or Vionnet's fluid bias cut, evening dresses skim along and cling to the curves of the female body. Floor length, with exposed backs or décolletage, these gowns are sophisticated and, unlike the ornately beaded dresses of the 1920s, uncluttered.

1932

Dorothy Shaver, vice president of Lord & Taylor, establishes the American Designers' Movement program to promote American fashion, showcasing, by name, the work of young designers like Elizabeth Hawes, Muriel King, and Clare Potter. • In July, the first color photograph, by Edward Steichen, appears on the cover of *Vogue*. • MGM costumer Adrian designs a puffed-sleeved white cotton organdy gown for Joan Crawford to wear in the film *Letty Lynton*. Macy's department store sells over 500,000 replicas nationwide. Hollywood costumes, often covered by fashion magazines, will exert a strong influence on fashion throughout the 1930s and early 1940s. • The University of Southern California commissions Jockey to develop an inexpensive undergarment for their football team that will absorb sweat and protect skin against chafing. The modern T-shirt is born.

1933–47

Couturière Elsa Schiaparelli is among the first to move fashion's focus to a strong-shouldered silhouette. Wide shoulders will remain a fashion staple until after the Second World War.

Mid-1930s

A new, large-torsoed silhouette emerges in menswear. Popularized by Savile Row tailor Frederick Scholte, the London, or drape cut, suit allows its wearer greater ease. Extra fabric in the shoulders and armholes, light padding in the shoulders, and a narrower waist create vertical folds or drapes front and back that are seen to enhance a man's figure. Trousers, by mid-decade, begin to taper at the bottom.

By the mid-1930s

Garments such as knickerbockers and plus fours are being reserved for hiking and the golf course. Men like the Duke of Windsor continue to wear traditional English sportswear, and even women find a way to incorporate this style into their sporting wardrobes.

1935

Scientists at DuPont, led by Wallace Hume Carothers, develop nylon. The synthetic fiber is stronger and more abrasion-resistant than, but similar in appearance to, silk (increasingly difficult to obtain from Japan). The company markets the new material for full-fashioned hosiery and by 1939 will begin the commercial production of nylon stockings, which go on sale nationally in May 1940 only to be withdrawn as nylon is diverted to military use.

1937

The Duke of Windsor abdicates the British throne to marry the twice-divorced American socialite Wallis Simpson. The austere gray-blue gown that American couturier Mainbocher designs for their wedding becomes the most widely copied dress of the decade.

Late 1930s

Bold colors and prints replace the minimal look that has defined the early years of the decade. The prevailing streamlined shape begins to give way to a more exaggerated silhouette. In Paris, designers show fuller skirts reaching just below the knee—a practical length that, without the fullness, will remain in fashion for day dresses throughout the war years ahead.

1939–45

World War II

Late 1939

Madeleine Vionnet closes her house as the Nazis invade the country. Before shuttering her couture house, Chanel pays homage to France with a red, white, and blue collection. • In a short-lived return to the wasp waist, Balenciaga's Infanta gown echoes seventeenth-century Spanish court costume and Mainbocher presents evening dresses that require a structured foundation garment. Horst P. Horst photographs Mainbocher's corset as *Vogue* magazine shuts down its Paris office. • Southern textile workers found the Textile Workers Union of America (TWUA).

1937

New York–based couturier Charles James holds his first showing in Paris. • Spanish couturier Cristóbal Balenciaga delivers his debut collection in his Paris salon.

1938

In what will become an annual event, *Vogue* devotes an entire issue to American fashion. • Claire McCardell, working for Townley Frocks, introduces an unfitted long-sleeved trapeze dress that can be worn belted or loose. Dubbed the Monastic Dress, it will prove such a success that fighting its knock-offs will for a time drive the manufacturer out of business.

1939–40

The National Bureau of Home Economics of the U.S. Department of Agriculture conducts the first large-scale scientific study of women's body measurements. Technicians record fifty-nine different measurements each for approximately 15,000 volunteers.

1938

The Exposition Internationale du Surréalisme opens in Paris in January. Schiaparelli works with a number of surrealist artists in the mid- to late 1930s, channeling their ideas into provocative surfaces and ornamentation for her clothing designs. For her Spring/Summer 1938 Circus Collection, she collaborates with Salvador Dalí, who transforms one of his 1936 paintings into a trompe l'oeil of flayed flesh on an evening dress.

1940–44

Nazi troops occupy Paris.

1940

Seizing the chance to position New York as an international fashion capital, garment manufacturers and the ILGWU join forces for the first time to form the New York Dress Institute, later known as the Couture Group. • Recognizing that the war will disrupt dispatches from Paris, publicist Eleanor Lambert takes over the Best-Dressed List and reintroduces it through the Dress Institute, with a decidedly American slant.

1940–46

Wartime shortages and restrictions produce women's fashions that are slimmer and more economical. Practicality rules and tailored suits and sportswear dominate. Skirts hover near the knee, blouses are simply cut and paired with square-shouldered jackets. Shoes sport wooden or cork platforms, while heavily embellished belts and hats provide some novelty. Women doing war work don practical trousers, jumpsuits, and overalls, bundling their hair into caps and snoods. Military looks, like the short Eisenhower jacket, find popularity.

1941

In the U.K. the Civilian Clothing Act, later termed the Utility Clothing Scheme, limits the use of textiles, leather, and rubber. The following year, the British Board of Trade will enlist the new Incorporated Society of London Fashion Designers (couturiers Edward Molyneux, Hardy Aimes, Norman Hartnell, Digby Morton, and Victor Stiebel, among others) to create clothes that are both law abiding and attractive. The designs selected for mass production bear the CC41 label.

1941

The Nazis set up a textile rationing system in occupied France. As president of the Chambre Syndicale de la Couture, Lucien Lelong prevents the Germans from moving the industry to Berlin or Vienna and obtains rationing exemptions for the main couture houses. When Madame Grès and Balenciaga are forcibly shut down for exceeding their fabric allocations, other couturiers show solidarity by helping to finish their collections. • To maximize the number of shopping days before Christmas, Congress passes a law establishing Thanksgiving as the fourth Thursday of November. • The United States enters into World War II; Claire McCardell, Vera Maxwell, and Bonnie Cashin are immediately commissioned to design uniforms for the Women's Civilian Defense Corps.

1942

The U.S. War Production Board introduces Limitations Order (L-85) regulations, limiting natural fibers, rubber, and nylon and design elements such as collars, cuffs, pockets, as well as skirts of excessive length. Adrian, now a ready-to-wear designer, becomes known for the inventive way his woman's suits abide by these strict fabric restrictions.

1943

In January, Norman Norell receives the first Coty American Fashion Critics' Award; announced the year before to promote American design during the war, the Coty's will be given out until 1984. • To demonstrate that New York fashion can equal that of Paris, Lambert convinces fashion editors to attend the collections of American designers previously shown only to buyers. Thus is born New York Press Week, the precursor to New York Fashion Week. • The Centre d'Études Techniques des Industries de l'Habillement (CETIH) forms to help modernize the French fashion industry by upgrading machinery and standardizing production.

1943–44

Riots break out in Los Angeles, Detroit, Harlem, and Montreal between servicemen and zoot-suiters. Emerging from the culture of jazz and swing and by 1940 adopted primarily by socially disadvantaged African Americans and Mexican Americans, including gang members, the zoot suit expresses both youthful rebellion and cultural identification. It is the extreme form of the drape: Oversized jackets with exaggerated shoulders and full pegged trousers with high waists are worn with swagger and by 1942 in defiance of L-85 regulations. The press depicts the elaborate zoot as the uniform of unpatriotic malcontents, contributing to the racially motivated attacks on the street. (The Swing Kids in Germany and the Zazous in Occupied France, flaunting a variation on the style, have already become targets of the Nazis.)

1944

Suffrage is extended to women in France by the 21 April 1944 Ordinance of the French Provisional Government. • In New York, the Fashion Institute of Technology and Design, located above the High School of Needle Trades, opens to train American garment workers and designers. • *Seventeen* debuts, the first fashion magazine aimed at the teenaged girl.

1945

In Germany, Dr. Klaus Maertens creates a sturdy boot to wear after a skiing accident. • Two dress-related exhibitions open in New York: *Are Clothes Modern?* at the Museum of Modern Art and *American Fabrics and Fashions* at the Metropolitan Museum of Art.

Mid-1940s–1950s

A less restrictive, more functional silhouette dominates American sportswear, exemplified by the designs of Clare Potter, Tina Lesser, and Claire McCardell, whose hit Popover dress, debuting in denim in 1942, can be worn as a beach cover or a dress for entertainment at home—complete with matching oven mitt. The postwar generation newly settled in the suburbs adopts these casual separates, dresses, and playsuits.

1945

French fashion picks up where it left off with romantic silhouettes like Maggie Rouff's, in an abundance of fabric and exuberant prints. When the couture houses are discovered to have continued designing full skirts and wide puffy sleeves during wartime, couturiers justify their fabric use by explaining that less was available to the German army; moreover, they have kept the textile industry afloat.

1946

The bikini makes its first appearance in Cannes on the French Riviera; the name given by designer Louis Réard, referencing the nuclear bomb test on Bikini Atoll, takes hold, but it's Jacques Heim's more modest version that becomes popular. • In Italy, women achieve the right to vote.

1946–91

Cold War

1947

In February, Christian Dior shows his Corolle Collection, which Harper's Bazaar editor Carmel Snow dubs the "New Look." Defined by sloped shoulders, an articulated bust, a fitted waist, padded hips, and billowing skirts, the style in fact presents a nostalgic ideal of a femininity both delicate and lush. With this collection, Dior revives haute couture and reasserts Paris's dominance of fashion.

1947

Writing in *Vogue* on a theme she will develop two years later in *Le Deuxième Sexe*, Simone de Beauvoir describes how society constructs a view of feminine decorum that leads to women's oppression.

1947–57

The postwar baby boom leads to an increased interest in well-designed maternity clothing and, as the children grow up, an emerging market for junior fashions.

1948

The term *prêt-à-porter*, a direct translation of "ready-to-wear," comes into use in France. • Debuting in designer Sonja de Lennart's Capri Collection, a slim three-quarters-length pant with a short side slit will go on capture the imagination of sexy women everywhere.

1949

Chinese Communist Revolution

1950

The first suburban shopping mall opens in the Northgate district of Seattle, Washington.

1950–53

Korean War

Early 1950s

Paris once again sets the agenda for high fashion: Shape and volume will define the decade. After years of utilitarian clothing, Dior's ultrafeminine narrow-waisted look (which requires serious foundation garments) continues to resonate deeply with many women, though Balenciaga offers a semifitted alternative. In tailored suits or day dresses, below-the-knee skirts are either pencil slim or very full and held aloft by petticoats. Fashionable ensembles are polished and high maintenance, demanding perfectly chosen accessories (hats, gloves, handbags, and matching shoes). Coats are wide, tent or bell-like to accommodate the volume below. • Men's suits begin to narrow, with less padding in the shoulders. Often fabricated in dark charcoal, they give rise to the era of the man in the gray flannel suit.

Early 1950s

Blue jeans, associated with youth, freedom, and rock'n'roll, become widely popular. They also come to suggest alienation from the prevailing social conformity, as depicted in 1953 by Marlon Brando's outlaw biker in The Wild One *and two years later by James Dean's troubled teens in* East of Eden *and* Rebel without a Cause.

1951

Giovan Battista Giorgini organizes a pivotal fashion show in Florence. Moving to the Pitti Palace two years later, the event firmly establishes Italy on the international fashion circuit. • Dupont brings polyester, invented a decade earlier in England, to the U.S. clothing market.

By 1952

Salvatore Ferragamo in Italy and Roger Vivier in France introduce shoes with high daggerlike heels. Within years, the addition of thin steel rods allows heels to become even higher and the modern stiletto is born.

1953

Queen Elizabeth II wears a Norman Hartnell gown to her coronation in Westminster Abbey.

1953–56

Asserting themselves via a subversive dandyism, working-class youth in England appropriate the elitist style of the New Edwardians and combine it with the wide-shouldered American drape to create the quintessential Teddy Boy look: long boxy jacket with velvet or satin collars, waistcoat, drainpipe trousers, thick-soled brothel creepers, and a shoestring tie.

1954

Gabrielle Chanel emerges from retirement to debut her comeback collection of boxy softly tailored suits, in stark opposition to Dior's form-fitting designs. Rejected by the European press, the easy look is embraced by the Americans and will soon become a Chanel staple.

1954

Audrey Hepburns's elegant but understated wardrobe for the film *Sabrina*, designed by Hubert de Givenchy, marks the beginning of a decades-long collaboration. • The House of Schiaparelli closes in December.

By the mid-1950s

The economic prosperity of the postwar years allows for greater leisure time. Relatively affordable airfare and the new interstate highway system in the States encourage travel vacations. Casual clothing becomes lighter and easier to care for, and materials and motifs often reflect the sun-soaked climates of holiday destinations.

1955

Richard Avedon's inventive photograph *Dovima with Elephants* captures Yves Saint Laurent's first design for the House of Dior. • Claire McCardell appears on the cover of *Time* magazine. • Mary Quant opens Bazaar, an instantly hip boutique on King's Road, selling affordable ready-to-wear fashions to London youth.

Mid-1950s

Evenings require opulent dresses. Bodices are often strapless; skirts, whether floor or ballerina length, have sculptural volume.

1956

Philadelphia-born actress Grace Kelley marries Prince Rainier of Monaco in a dress designed by Paramount costume designer Helen Rose. • In London, John Stephen opens his seminal menswear boutique His Clothes, which moves the following year to Carnaby Street.

Mid- to late 1950s

A barrellike silhouette that cuts away from the body and flatters the ideal womanly figure, which Cristóbal Balenciaga pioneered in suits as early as 1951, achieves popularity. The supple, unfitted chemise, or sack dress, which Balenciaga, Dior, and Givenchy all show in 1957, reenergizes modernism in couture and anticipates the shift dress of the coming decade.

1956–67

To fight piracy, Balenciaga and Givenchy allow the press to view their designs only a day (rather than the traditional four weeks) before the delivery date to clients and buyers.

1957

Christian Dior dies; his young assistant, Saint Laurent, is appointed to head the couture house. His daring first collection will introduce a trapeze line that flares dramatically outward from fitted shoulders.

1958

Striking ILGWU members ensure that the union label appears in clothing made in the U.S.A. • The Camera Nazionale della Moda Italiana is founded to develop and promote the image of Italian fashion design worldwide. • Journalist Herb Caen coins the term *beatnik* to describe the American expression of the countercultural existentialist. Known in France as *rive gauche*, the look has filtered into fashions for both sexes: khaki chinos or slim dark trousers, leather jackets, duffle coats, fisherman's sweaters, black turtlenecks, and generally unadorned clothing.

Late 1950s

Despite Paris's dominance of the decade, New York has remained a fashion center, especially for sportswear and stylish but comfortable ready-to-wear that is cut to move with the body and that can go from day to evening with a change of accessories.

Late 1950s

Fashionable men adopt the lighter weight "continental" suit from Italy, which has a shorter, more fitted jacket with sharper shoulders.

1959

Pantyhose, developed separately by Ernest G. Rice and Allen Grant Sr., hit the market. • DuPont begins commercial production of its new highly elastic fiber, Spandex.

1959–75

Vietnam War

1960

The first birth control pill is approved for contraceptive use in the United States.

1960–63

Givenchy's designs for Hepburn's little black shift in Breakfast at Tiffany's *and Jacqueline Kennedy's sleeveless sheath dresses exemplify the taste for high modernism in fashion, an impeccable look predicated on simplicity.*

1961

To complement their slim-suited image, John Lennon and Paul McCartney purchase the Baba, shoemakers Anello & Davide's version of the elastic-sided, snug-fitting boot popular with young, moneyed Londoners. Cuban-heeled and ankle-high, with a center seam, the footwear becomes known as the Beatle boot.

1962

Valentino Garavani shows his first collection of elegant haute couture at the Pitti Palace, attracting the attention of the international social set. Emilio Pucci shows his first couture collection as well, but it is his weightless silk jersey dresses and resort-style sportswear in kaleidoscopic prints that will appeal to the decade's jet-setters.

Early 1960s

Demand grows for greater variety in menswear to keep pace with the changes in women's clothing. In London, now a fount of fashion ideas, the Peacock Revolution, as the style movement comes to be called, takes hold. Whether velvet suits or boldly patterned jackets, worn with flowing silk scarves and longer hair, the new male attire is, above all, flamboyant.

1963

At the helm of *Vogue*, Diana Vreeland coins the term "youthquake" to describe the impact of street style and youth culture on the fashion landscape, not the least of which is the increasing power of the young as a consumer class.

1964

The Twenty-Fourth Amendment to the U.S. Constitution is passed, guaranteeing African Americans the right to vote. • Marshall McLuhan proposes the world as a global village united by new media technologies. • Rudi Gernreich debuts the monokini, with its ample wool bottom and thin V-strap that reveals the breasts. Meant as a conceptual gesture, the topless bathing suit presciently suggests a new freedom for the body. Four months later Gernreich introduces the No-Bra Bra, whose tiny sheer triangles liberate the breasts from years of padding; it becomes an immediate bestseller.

1964–66

In Paris André Courrèges and Paco Rabanne look toward the Space Age, employing new materials and new geometries that push the boundaries of couture: In 1964 Courrèges presents a collection of streamlined pantsuits and short boxy dresses accessorized with glossy white boots. In 1966 Rabanne provokes with his 12 Unwearable Dresses collection of garments comprising chain mail, aluminum, and plastic plaques sold in a box and assembled by the customer.

1965

The dominant silhouette for dresses, skirts, and coats is a flared A-line. • Pioneering mod designer Mary Quant, who began to experiment with shorter hemlines in 1958, trademarking the term *mini*, offers a version that reaches mid-thigh. • American sportswear designer Anne Klein begins showing separates that women can combine to accommodate uneven figures and to wear with pieces from other seasons. • Neiman Marcus picks up the debut collection of Hanae Mori.

1966–67

Pop Art graphics pervade fashion, often on disposable garments made of cellulose tissue, a fad for a couple of years, but also in witty interpretations such as Geoffrey Beene's sequined evening gown based on a numbered football jersey.

1966

Pierre Cardin, who has been creating pop-inflected couture collections, resigns from the Chambre Syndicale to concentrate on ready-to-wear. He debuts Nehru jackets for men and begins to build his licensing empire. • Saint Laurent launches Rive Gauche, his luxury ready-to-wear line sold in a boutique of the same name. • Donyale Luna becomes the first African American model to appear on the cover of *Vogue*, the March British issue shot by David Bailey. • Countering the prevailing pop sensibility, the boutiques Granny Takes a Trip and I Was Lord Kitchner's Valet open in London, selling vintage clothing and old military uniforms.

1966

Yves Saint Laurent introduces a radical look for evening: trousers and a tuxedo jacket paired with a feminine blouse. Initially resisted in his couture collection, his ready-to-wear version of le smoking, *as the androgynous ensemble is called, proves an enormous success.*

1967

Ralph Lauren launches a line of wide men's ties.

1968

Balenciaga announces his retirement. • Two years after creating Bergdorf Goodman's first ready-to-wear collection, Halston launches his own fashion line. • Turned away for wearing pants, Paraphernalia designer Betsey Johnson marries John Cale at a civil ceremony in New York dressed in the matching tunic reappropriated as a micro-minidress. • Joseph Gerber invents the first automated cutting machine, revolutionizing the apparel industry.

1968

Student and labor revolts break out in Paris. Martin Luther King and Robert F. Kenedy are assassinated.

1969

Membership in the ILGWU peaks at nearly half a million garment workers. • The Gap is founded in San Francisco. • Tommy Hilfiger opens his first retail store in Elmira, New York. • In Tokyo, Rei Kawakubu starts designing under the name Commes de Garçons.

1969

The Woodstock music festival takes place in upstate New York, attracting half a million revelers. The three-day event becomes an emblem of the hippie movement, whose countercultural look—bellbottoms, long skirts, vests, flowing shirts, often with a homemade or psychedelic flavor—enters the fashion lexicon.

Early 1970s

Two trends within the late-1960s hippie aesthetic find high-fashion expressions: an ethnographic eclecticism and a nostalgic romanticism. Bill Gibbs, Ossie Clark with Celia Birtwell, Thea Porter, Giorgio Sant'Angelo, and Zandra Rhodes are among the inventive designers who experiment with combinations of color, pattern, and texture in styles borrowed from non-Western cultures (caftans, kimonos, turbans, tunics, gypsy skirts) and the pre- to late industrial eras.

Early 1970s

Louis Vuitton and Gucci introduce monogrammed handbags and apparel, awakening a lust for logos that will reach epic proportions in the 1990s.

Early 1970s

John Fairchild of *Women's Wear Daily* decrees it the year of the midi. The skirt length, hitting from below the knee to mid-calf, appeared in Paris in 1966 and piqued widespread interest in 1967 with Faye Dunaway's provocative portrayal of the gangster Bonnie Parker; but retailers encounter strong resistance to the fashion dictate. By the mid-1970s, hemlines will run the gamut from mini to maxi. ● Kenzo Takata opens his Jungle Jap boutique in Paris, showcasing playful separates in a riot of bright colors and strong prints. ● Dr. Miyoshi Okamoto invents the world's first microfiber, which his colleague Dr. Toyohiko Hikota transforms into washable Ultrasuede. Designers Vera Maxwell and Halston fall in love with the soft but durable new fabric so suited to the jet set.

1970–72

Hotpants, extremely short shorts, enjoy a fad, often worn with platform shoes and paired with maxicoats.

1971

Gabrielle "Coco" Chanel dies. ● Issey Miyake, after working at Givenchy and Geoffrey Beene, establishes his own design studio. ● Vivienne Westwood begins designing for Let It Rock, the new boutique she opens with Malcolm McLaren that caters to a Teddy Boy aesthetic. A popular hangout and distiller of subcultural styles, the shop will undergo numerous transformations and renamings: Too Fast to Live, Too Young to Die (1972), Sex (1974), Seditionaries—Clothes for Heroes (1976), and World's End (1980).

1972

President Nixon visits the People's Republic of China, opening trade between the two countries for the first time since the Chinese Revolution. ● David Bowie releases his *Ziggy Stardust* concept album. On tour, Bowie's androgynous persona, in costumes designed by Kansai Yamamoto, gives rise to British Glam, characterized by theatrical make-up, lamé jumpsuits, and glittery platform boots.

1972

Noting the ease and elegance of his work, Newsweek proclaims Halston America's premier designer. His versatile sportswear and glamorous minimalist gowns will make his name synonymous with 1970s style.

1973

The Fédération Française de la Couture, du Prêt-à-Porter des Couturiers et des Créateurs de Mode is formed, expanding the governing body of haute couture fashion to embrace ready-to-wear. ● The benefit fashion show Le Grand Divertissement à Versailles becomes an international sensation by opposing Paris's top couturiers—the House of Dior, Givenchy, Saint Laurent, Cardin, and Emanuel Ungaro—with five ready-to-wear designers representing New York—Halston, Anne Klein, Oscar de la Renta, Bill Blass, and Stephen Burrows. The event generates global acclaim for the simple elegance of the American fashions. The New Yorkers also break racial barriers when eight African American models walk their high-fashion runway.

1973

Diane von Furstenberg introduces her boldly printed jersey knit wrap dress. Easy for day and sexy enough for evening, its many iterations become enormous best sellers, putting her on the cover of Newsweek in 1976.

1974

In August, Beverly Johnson becomes the first African American to appear on the cover of American *Vogue*; the following year, she lands the cover of French *Elle*. ● Sonia Rykiel, designer of sensual, often monochromatic knitwear, experiments with reversed seams and undone hems, creating what she will call a "démodé" look.

1975

The first official ready-to-wear shows are held in Milan. ● After debuting his line of impeccably tailored but relaxed business suits for men, Giorgio Armani shows a similarly understated womenswear collection. ● Mary McFadden patents a unique method for pleating silk.

1976

The French company Lectra develops its first patternmaking and grading system. • American sportswear designer Willi Smith establishes WilliWear.

1976

Saint Laurent counters the dominance of ready-to-wear and sportswear with a folkloric look executed in rich fabrics and embellishments. His Russian collection for Fall/Winter 1976/77 features a return to the luxurious excesses of haute couture.

1976

Raw and abrasive, "Anarchy in the U.K." hits the airwaves, the first single by the Malcolm McLaren–managed Sex Pistols. Vivienne Westwood dresses the band in her Seditionaries collection, which brings together the subversive, antifashion elements of her earlier work: ripped sloganed T-shirts, biker jackets, and bondage wear. The look spreads rapidly as punk rockers improvise their own confrontational outfits.

1976–82

Gloria Vanderbilt jeans are launched in 1976, followed by Calvin Klein's, and the era of designer jeans is born. In 1980, Avedon shoots a suggestive commercial for Calvin Klein Jeans in which model/actress Brooke Shields avers that "nothing" comes between her and her Calvins.

1977

Diane Keaton's outfits in *Annie Hall*, designed by Ralph Lauren, inspire legions of women to don menswear. • First catching on in 1973 at the Parisian nightclub Le Sept, disco madness burns bright with the opening of the fashionable Studio 54 in New York and enters the global mainstream with the release of *Saturday Night Fever*. The glittery theatrical clothing—in gold lamé, UV-friendly white, and second-skin spandex—is meant to show off beautiful bodies in movement.

Late 1970s

Men adopt stylish three-piece suits in a multitude of colors, with wide lapels, flared trousers, and high-rise vests.

1978

Gianni Versace's new label features clothes that are well cut, colorful, and seductive. • To launch his scent Opium, Saint Laurent throws a lavish shipboard party in the New York harbor, ushering in a new era of designer fragrances.

1980

Richard Gere's American Gigolo *wardrobe of lean, unstructured suits and immaculate shirts cements Giorgio Armani's reputation as a designer of elegantly simple masculine chic and influences men's style throughout the decade.*

1980

Azzedine Alaïa debuts a ready-to-wear collection.

Early 1980s

The first body-scanning technologies, [TC]2 and Cyberware, begin development.

1981

MTV begins broadcasting music videos. • Westwood's first runway show, the historicist Pirate Collection, coincides with the peak of New Romanticism, a scene within London New Wave nightclubs like Blitz. Eccentric, extravagant, often sexually ambiguous, always highly individual, the clubgoers costume themselves for a star performance.

1981

Rei Kawakubo and Yohji Yamamoto bring an avant-garde perspective to Paris fashion. Their monochromatic, multilayered garments highlight the beauty of imperfections and shift attention away from the expected contours of the female form to accentuate overlooked parts of the body as well as the space between body and clothing.

1982

Jane Fonda releases a workout video in which she dresses in bright leotards, leggings, and leg warmers. The fitness craze popularizes aerobics and dancewear, and increasingly, brands like OMO Kamali produce collections based on activewear. • Calvin Klein introduces a line of men's underwear with the company logo neatly on the waistband. A provocative advertising campaign turns men's briefs into a desirable fashion item. Within a year, Klein will offer women a branded line of men's-style underwear.

1983

Karl Lagerfeld takes the helm at now-dusty Chanel. In typical iconoclastic fashion, his opening runway look, a long black dress worn by Inès de La Fressange, pays tribute to the house's namesake with a trompe l'oeil of embroidered costume jewelry. • Stephen Sprouse, who has been designing stage clothes for Debbie Harry of pop-punk band Blondie, collaborates with New York artist Keith Haring on a collection of neon-bright, graffitied outfits that explode with the energy of the downtown club scene (though the high cost of their production keeps them out of range of the club kids).

1984

Jean Paul Gaultier helps to launch the fashion for underwear as outerwear. His corset dress, with its back lacing and wittily exaggerated conical bra, is both sexy and celebratory.

1984

Invited to meet Margaret Thatcher at 10 Downing Street, designer Katharine Hamnett wears an oversized T-shirt that boldly declares public opposition to American missiles in the U.K.: "58% don't want Pershing." • Designers from Jean Paul Gaultier to David Holah and Stevie Stewart of Body Map show skirts for men.

By the mid-1980s

The enormous wealth generated for the financial elite under the Reagan administration creates a flamboyant social scene that indulges in ostentatious attire and big jewels. In addition to the Parisian couturiers, socialites frequently turn to designers, such as Bill Blass, Oscar de la Renta, Carolina Herrera, and Carolyne Roehm, who travel in their same circles. • Affluence has also begotten the "yuppie": an acquisitive breed of men and women who navigate their way in wide-shouldered power suits bearing designer labels.

By the mid-1980s

The "glamazon" marches down the runway: Provocateurs Thierry Mugler and Claude Montana give her ultraexaggerated shoulders, a nipped-in waist, and a supreme self-confidence that she will carry into the next decade.

1986

Mass-market Liz Claiborne, Inc., becomes the first company founded by a woman to reach the Fortune 500. • Singer sells its sewing division. • Perry Ellis, designer of spirited American sportswear, dies of AIDS.

1987

The "Antwerp Six"—Dirk Bikkembergs, Ann Demeulemeester, Walter Van Beirendonck, Dries Van Noten, Dirk Van Saene, and Marina Yee—showcase their designs in London at the British Design Show, establishing Belgium's place on the world fashion map. Graduates of Antwerp's Royal Academy of Fine Art, the six distinctive designers combine impeccable craftsmanship with inventive style. • The French fashion luxury goods conglomerate LVMH is formed between Louis Vuitton SA and the Moët Hennessey Christian Dior Group. • A worldwide stock market crash in October signals the end to a period of economic exuberance.

Late 1980s

The decade's preoccupation with a slim but toned figure gives rise to body-conscious, second-skin dressing. Azzedine Alaïa, now known as the "king of cling," produces some of the best. In supple leather or stretch fabrics like silk jersey and Lycra, with innovative crisscross seaming, his garments articulate a curvy female form.

1985

Donna Karan, having left Anne Klein to launch her own ready-to-wear business, gives working women an alternative to the conservative power suit. Her Seven Easy Pieces is a versatile and feminine wardrobe system that revolves around a jersey bodysuit. • Although numerous department stores nearby carry his lines, Ralph Lauren opens a freestanding shop on Madison Avenue to better present his total lifestyle concept; other American designers will soon follow suit with their own stores. • Nike Air Jordans (named for rising basketball star Michael Jordan) hit the streets with the added cachet of being banned by the NBA. Meanwhile, having propelled their preferred kicks to bestsellerdom, Run-DMC will raise them to cultural icon with their 1986 hit single "My Adidas." Buoyed by the athletic wave and the rise of hiphop, expensive specialty sneakers will become a sought-after fashion accessory and status symbol worldwide.

1986

At Patou, Christian Lacroix dazzles with a collection of ornate pouf dresses. Within a year, he will open the first new couture house since Saint Laurent's.

1989

Italian luxury leather firm Prada shows its first ready-to-wear line, with the founder's granddaughter Miuccia at the helm. Her disregard of seasonal styles, unconventional combinations of materials, and streamlined but feminine aesthetic quickly gains a following.

1990

Halston dies of AIDS. • Jean Paul Gaultier designs hundreds of outfits for Madonna's Blond Ambition tour, including a pink corset bodysuit that the pop singer pairs with black menswear trousers.

1990–91

Gulf War

Early 1990s

Postmodern pastiche becomes evermore present, exemplified by the sharp parodies of Franco Moschino and the sly high-low reworkings of Karl Lagerfeld.

Early 1990s

The supermodel transforms a cluster of models—Linda Evangelista, Christy Turlington, Naomi Campbell, Cindy Crawford, Claudia Schiffer, and Kate Moss, among them—into highly paid celebrities and household names.

1991

In the U.S., casual attire begins to be sanctioned in the corporate workplace. • The regenerated cellulose fiber lyocell (brand name Tencel) appears in garments.

1992

Hiphop mogul Russell Simmons founds Phat Farm, an urban sportswear line that will grow into a billion-dollar lifestyle company. Entering the same market by the end of the decade, labels like eckō UNLTD, Sean John, and Rocawear will have similar success.

1992

Designers (including Anna Sui) pick up on the grunge style coming out of the alternative music scene centered in Seattle, Washington. At Perry Ellis, Marc Jacobs sends his models down the runway in combat boots and layers of "thrift-store" garments produced in luxury fabrics. Amid the controversy that ensues, Jacobs is fired and the collection abandoned, but the look will continue to resonate with the mood of the new decade.

1993

The Maastricht Treaty goes into effect, creating the European Union. • Canada, Mexico, and the United States sign the North American Free Trade Agreement (NAFTA).

Early to mid-1990s

With clothing at once classical and hyperfeminine, Domenico Dolce and Stefano Gabbana offer a strongly erotic image, often interpreted for the modern woman by their muse Isabella Rossellini.

1994

Alexander McQueen graduates from Central Saint Martins; stylist Isabella Blow purchases his entire degree collection on installment. • Hussein Chalayan debuts in London and Junya Watanabe in Paris. • Tom Ford rises to creative director of Gucci, where his glamorous, at times overtly sexual style turns around the once-faltering company, inaugurating an era of brand revival. When the Gucci Group goes public in 1995 on the strength of Ford's breakout collection, its success will usher in a flurry of IPOs of luxury fashion firms. • China becomes the world's largest manufacturer and exporter of textiles and clothing. • Designer handbags are the rage, a lucrative explosion of interest that carries well into the next century.

Mid- to late 1990s

After the excesses of the 1980s, a minimalist approach to fashion takes hold, from the reductive chic of Calvin Klein and the luxurious restraint of German designer Jil Sander to the edgy sleekness of Austrian designer Helmut Lang.

1995

The World Trade Organization replaces the General Agreement on Tariffs and Trade. • The ILGWU merges with the Amalgamated Clothing and Textile Workers Union (ACTWU) to form the Union of Needletrades, Industrial and Textiles Employees (UNITE), now representing only 250,000 workers. • With the launch of websites such as Amazon.com, e-commerce emerges as the new retail frontier. • Having ridden out sharp criticism of the waifish appearance of Kate Moss and other models in recent advertising campaigns, Calvin Klein pulls TV spots and magazine ads for his jeans line that are seen to imitate 1960s-era pornographic tableau. Sales continue to be brisk.

1995–2000

Dot-com Bubble

Mid-1990s

Gerber Technology introduces its GERBERsuite collection of integrated systems for the design, development, and manufacturing of apparel. • Led by H&M in Sweden and Zara in Spain, fast-fashion retailers push into markets around the globe.

Mid-1990s

Alexander McQueen, whose collections since his debut have included "bumsters," helps to initiate a long-lasting trend for extremely low-rise pants.

1996

While design director of Cerruti, Narciso Rodriguez creates Carolyn Bessette's dress for her marriage to John F. Kennedy Jr: the bias-cut pearl silk column is simple, elegant, and sexy. • Jacques Mouclier, president of the Chambre Syndicale, opens the official list of haute couturiers to ready-to-wear designers; Gaultier and Mugler embrace the challenge. • Bernard Arnault names John Galliano to head Dior and McQueen to take his place at Givenchy, amping up the energy of the couture houses.

1997

Gianni Versace is murdered in front of his Miami home. His sister, Donatella, takes over as head designer for the Versace brand. • Newly appointed artistic director Marc Jacobs produces Louis Vuitton's first ready-to-wear collection, beginning a fruitful partnership with the luxury house. • At Balenciaga, Nicolas Ghesquière is appointed creative director, after designing for one of the house's Japanese licenses. Ghesquière's edgy take on Balenciaga's devotion to silhouette will prove a fortuitous match.

1997

Maison Martin Margiela presents a collection that traces the stages of constructing a garment in which the standard tailor's dress form becomes the foundational garment. In the deconstructivist designs of Margiela and others, whether reclaiming and recycling materials or exposing their inner workings, the whole meaning of clothing and the fashion system is challenged.

1998

The economic crisis in Asia freezes consumer spending. • Whimsical designer Isaac Mizrahi, who has thrilled the fashion press for the past decade, fares less well with retailers; losing his backing from Chanel, he closes his apparel business. • An exemplar of effortless high-low dressing, Sharon Stone reprises a trick from her 1996 Oscar appearance when she walks the red carpet in a long lilac Vera Wang skirt and her husband's white Gap button down.

1999

Miyake introduces A-POC, a line of clothes constructed from a single piece of cloth. • With Helmut Lang and others as a catalyst the previous season, New York Fashion Week moves its position on the global fashion calendar to take place before the European collections.

1999

The House of Dior names Hedi Slimane creative director of menswear, following a successful stint at rival YSL. His Dior Homme collections, with their slender silhouettes and youthfully erotic, almost feminine sensibility, will define a new look for menswear at the beginning of the new millennia.

The System

38
Structure

Since the first formulations of the profession of fashion designer, the underlying structures of the fashion industry have changed, sometimes in slow evolutions, sometimes in swift revolutions. Haute couture, once the dominant model, has been overtaken by ready-to-wear in its many iterations, which itself faces challenges from the model of fast fashion. Innovation based on the ideas of a select group of design professionals whose influence spreads ever-outward to the periphery of fashion gives way to innovation led by consumers who express themselves in a multiplicity of distinct looks. The introduction of new means of production, new spaces of consumption, new methods of reception, and new modes of living all affect the framework for how fashion operates.

72
Specializations

Beyond the divisions of bespoke, haute couture, luxury ready-to-wear, mass production, and fast fashion, with their determinants of price, speed, and volume of distribution, are a myriad of routes to the designed object. Within categories and subcategories (womenswear or menswear, daywear or eveningwear, outerwear or intimate apparel), designers engage with specific activities and communities (outerwear may be intended for casual, work, or formal occasions) as well as seasons and geographies (it may protect against snow or sun while navigating city or suburb). The figure of the imagined customer, her specific body and attitude (a parka thrown over an evening dress), creates further niches by which designers differentiate their work. Beyond the designer, through the cycles of development, production, distribution, and promotion, the industry itself comprises a host of specializations.

Madame Grès at work in her *maison de couture*; drawing by
Eduardo Garcia Benito, 1942. *Private collection.*

Tailoring & Dressmaking

From the early Renaissance until the second half of the nineteenth century, the history of Western fashion is marked by the attempts of a growing middle class to imitate the styles of the nobility and the efforts of the ruling classes to distinguish themselves from those below. During this period, the way in which fashion was made and purchased remained essentially the same. For those with the resources, clothing was hand-made by female dressmakers and male tailors. Fabrics, undergarments, accessories, and trimmings were ordered separately and created by specialized craftsmen. The resulting garments were viewed as a reflection of the wearer's taste and income, not the vision of a designer.

The tailor, whose craft traces back to early medieval linen armorers, specializes in the cutting, construction, fitting, and finishing of men's garments and certain form-fitting women's garments (historically, corsets, outerwear, riding habits, and walking suits). Within a tailoring establishment, cutters are second only to the master tailor, who deals directly with the client. Tailors typically work with woven materials, foremost wool, that give the garment body; they also employ stiffeners, interlining, and interfacing as well as carefully placed seams and darts to sculpt fabric around the imperfect human form.

Bespoke, or custom, tailors create made-to-measure garments, generally suits, for individual clients. By the end of the eighteenth century, the unmarked doors of Savile Row in London's Mayfair district concealed the workshops of bespoke tailors producing some of the finest menswear in the world. Today, despite competition from the Italian tailoring firms that entered the scene in the 1980s, Savile Row remains revered for its flawless craftsmanship, and designers such as Oswald Boateng, whose contemporary approach to tailoring melds refinement with flair, have attracted a new generation of clients.

The counterpart to the tailor is the creator of women's dresses and other draped garments, referred to variously since the seventeenth century as mantua maker, *modiste*, and dressmaker. The dressmaker uses flat patterns or draping techniques to cut, sew, and finish garments and works with more pliant textiles, both knit and woven. Her value has lain in her ability to shape and smooth the female form, to add interest to a garment through fabric manipulations and embellishments, and to translate the latest fashions to suit the tastes of her particular clientele. The custom dressmaker thrived well into the twentieth century, especially in Europe, which sustained a culture of handcraftsmanship far longer than did the British and American markets.

From their earliest days, department stores developed custom salons where dressmakers and tailors could work with private clients. From the 1940s through the 1960s, as the independent dressmaker nearly disappeared from view, Sophie Gimble at Sak's Fifth Avenue, Ethel Frankau at Bergdorf Goodman, and others created copies of couture originals or special one-of-a-kind ensembles for women with the time and money to invest in a personalized experience and a perfect fit.

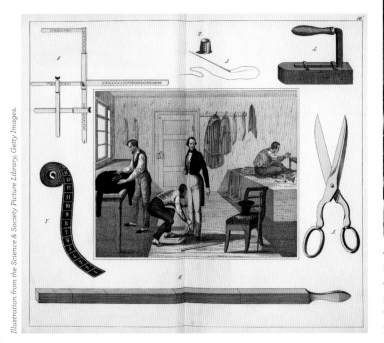

Illustration from the Science & Society Picture Library, Getty Images.

Illustration from the Kean Collection, Getty Images.

Above Dressmakers in the workshop of a department store, late nineteenth century • *Left* Tailor's workshop, the Netherlands, 1849

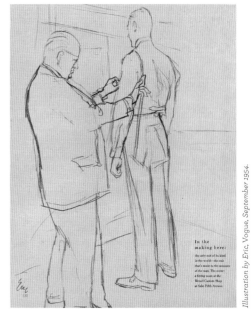

Above Fitting a suit at the Wetzel Custom Shop, Saks Fifth Avenue, 1954 • *Left* Custom dressmaker Fira Benenson of Bonwit Teller, 1940

Below left Bespoke tailor shaping a garment, Gieves & Hawks Tailors, Savile Row, 2008 • *Below right* Bespoke tailor constructing a suit by hand, Henry Poole & Co., Savile Row, 2011

The Couture House

The dynamic between tailor/dressmaker and client would change dramatically with the birth of haute couture in 1858—not coincidentally a time when powerful men adopted the sober suit and women were poised to fulfill a romantic and sensual ideal. At his Paris salon on rue de la Paix, Englishman Charles Frederick Worth elevated high fashion to an art form and established the fashion designer as a profession. His clothing was designed, constructed, embellished, and sold in the same location, his couture house. Breaking with tradition, Worth showed a complete collection, seasonally, on live *mannequins*, or models, for customers who would then make a selection and be measured and fitted in the salon for a custom dress bearing the house's label.

The many couture houses established since Worth's have been organized along similar lines. Despite minor changes to the process (such as showing collections outside of the couture house) and the constant exclamation of its death, French haute couture has operated on much the same model for over 50 years.

At the head of the couture house is the designer. Historically, this was also the name on the outside of the building; however, as couture houses survive the retirement or death of their founder, this is no longer the rule.

In the Parisian couture house, often a *maison particulière*, all activity takes place in close proximity. The design studios and workrooms occupy the upper levels of the building, above the luxurious salons. Typically, the *couturier* creates a design by making a *croquis*, or fashion sketch, though sometimes by draping cloth on a *mannequin*. The fabricated *modèle*, or design, will return to the studio at various stages for the designer to alter or approve.

Photo by Jacques Boyer, Roger Viollet Collection, Getty Images.

Above House of Worth, Paris, 1907

Couturier
Male Designer

Couturière
Female Designer

Modélistes
Assistant designers who work alongside the couturier/couturière to develop each design.

Couture Ateliers

The couturier's intentions are translated into three-dimensional garments in the house's workrooms, customarily divided into the *ateliers flou*, workrooms for dressmaking (dresses, blouses), and the *ateliers tailleur*, workrooms for tailoring (suits, coats). Here, skilled artisans determine volume, proportion, and fit, making first a *toile*, or muslin prototype, then, once perfected, the *modèle* in the specified fabric.

Their profound knowledge of materials and construction techniques and extreme attention to detail and finish, whereby even the invisible is exquisitely crafted, distinguishes haute couture from all other fashion. The prowess of the seamstresses' handwork (only the primary seams may be sewn by machine) allows the couturier to design garments whose ornamentation is inextricable from its structural elements. Creating the consummate garment takes time, of course, and a single couture dress might require 150 hours.

Premiers/premières de atelier
Workroom heads who interpret the *croquis* or draped piece, assign responsibility for each *modèle*, ensure the fittings, and oversee the alterations.

Seconds/secondes de atelier
Workroom managers below the *premières* who coordinate the fabrication of the designs and track materials.

Petites mains
Seamstresses of various levels, traditionally conforming to a rigorous hierarchy of first hands, second hands, and *arpettes* (apprentices).

Above Haute couture ateliers, Chanel, Paris, 2006

Photos by Raphael Gaillarde, Gamma-Rapho, Getty Images.

Above and left Haute
couture ateliers, Valentino,
Rome, 2006

Above Haute couture
atelier, Jean Paul Gaultier,
Paris, 2011

Specialty Ateliers

Artisans working in independent ateliers that specialize in embellishments and accessories create components of most haute couture ensembles. The French government has designated many of these businesses *enterprises du pátrinomie vivant* for their superior technical skills and deep historical archives.

By the mid-1990s, the small ateliers were struggling to survive mass commercialization. Chanel, privately owned by the Wertheimer family, began to purchase a number of the generations-old firms, with the understanding that they could produce work for other couture houses as well: Lesage (beads and embroidery), Lemarié (feathers and camellias), Massaro (shoes), Desrues (buttons and costume jewelry), Michel (hats), Guillet (artificial flowers), and Goossens (gold and silver). By keeping these artisans in business, collected under the company name Paraffection, Chanel has ensured itself a steady supply of artisanal handiwork and helped to preserve their unique knowledge.

Photo by François Guillot, AFP, Getty Images.

Haute Couture Specialists

Bottiers	Bootmakers/shoemakers
Broideurs	Embroiderers
Corsetiers	Corset makers
Crépinières	Braid and fringe makers
Dentellières	Lace makers
Fabricants de boutons	Button makers
Fabricants de paillettes	Sequin makers
Fabricants de rubans	Ribbon makers
Gantiers	Glovers
Joailliers	Jewelers
Modistes/chapeliers	Milliners
Orfèvres	Goldsmiths
Paruriers	Costume jewelers
Parurières floral	Artificial flower makers
Plumassiers	Featherworkers

Photo by Jean-Pierre Muller, AFP, Getty Images.

Above Marcelle Guillet, designer of floral accessories, oversees the *ouvrières fleuristes* in her atelier, 2007 • *Left* An artisan sorts feathers in the atelier Lemarié, Paris, 2004

Photo by Jean-Pierre Muller, AFP, Getty Images.

Left François Lesage, embroiderer extraordinaire, examines a sample from his atelier, 2003 • *Below left* At Lesage, an artisan works her needle through chiffon held taut in an embroidery frame, 2006 • *Below right* Advertisement for Chanel featuring Broderies Lesage, 1985

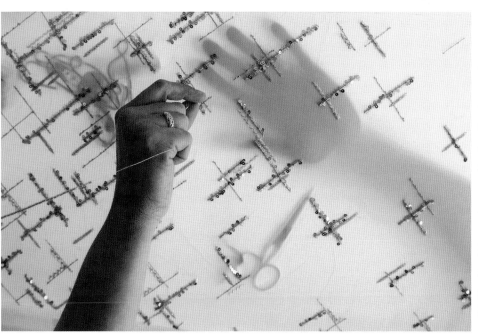

Photo by Raphael Gaillarde, Gamma-Rapho, Getty Images.

Mannequins

Every garment in a collection is fitted and refined on a live model. Historically, each house has had its own models, whose look reflected the taste of the individual couturier. Some also served as muse. (Marie Vernet, the shop girl who displayed shawls and bonnets for Worth at Gagelin et Opigez in 1848, and thus may be seen as the original model, later became his wife.)

By the early 1920s, the trend for presenting new collections on live models was fully embraced. Postwar, the routine was much the same for each *maison de couture*: At the opening show, house models in a *défilé*, or parade, would present the *passage*, or numbered ensembles, to commercial buyers, the press, and special guests. Models might be expected to repeat the presentation throughout the week. After the initial showing, for about a month, the models would gather in their *cabine*, the dressing room–cum-office for both models and dressers, to prepare for afternoon viewings by private clients in the salon.

The house *mannequins volants*, or runway models, were rarely photographed for fear of copying, and until the 1960s only a few, such as Victoire and China Machado, succeeded in joining the great photo models like Suzy Parker and Dovima. Today, the distinction has blurred between models who walk in the haute couture shows and those who appear in the magazines.

Mannequins de cabine
Models, traditionally distinct to each house.

Habilleuses
Fitters and dressers

Photo by Nat Farbman, Time & Life Pictures, Getty Images.

Above Bettina Graziani, chief model and muse to Hubert de Givenchy, with the designer before his first show in 1952, which he named after her.

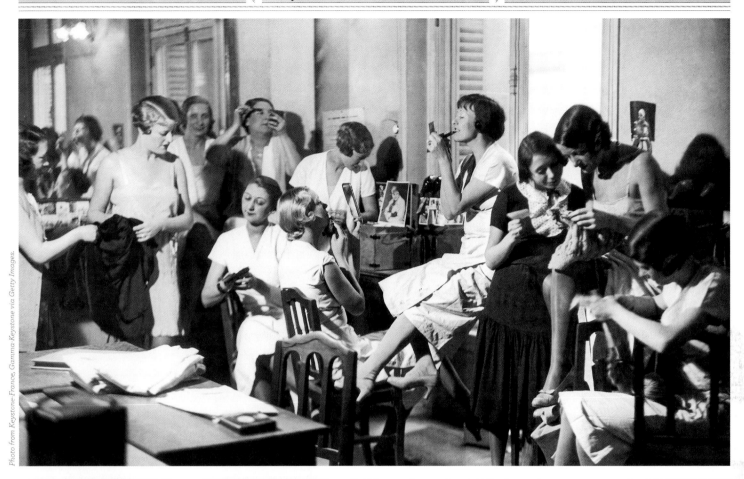

Photo from Keystone-France, Gamma-Keystone via Getty Images.

Photo by Loomis Dean, Time & Life Pictures, Getty Images.

Photo by Gille Bassignac, Gamma-Rapho via Getty Images.

Above Top Mannequins
in the *cabine* of an haute
couture salon, Paris, 1936 •
Above Christian Dior in the
cabine with his *mannequins*
before a showing, 1957

Above Stéphane Rolland and
his design team study a look
on a model in preparation
for the Spring/Summer 2002
haute couture collections.

The Couture Client

At the heart of haute couture is the synergy between the vision of the designer and the body of the client. The singular garment that goes down the runway will be amended to conform perfectly to each client's shape and preferences.

Before the age of celebrity red carpets and Internet coverage, the couture houses formed a discrete realm into which prospective clients entered strictly by referral. Traditionally, after the debut of a collection, a private client would view the designs in the elegant showroom known as the *salon de ventes*, noting her wardrobe preferences on the program. From the moment she arrived, greeted by the *directrice*, she would be pampered. Her *vendeuse*, a kind of saleswoman-confidante, would guide her choices—based on a keen understanding of both her lifestyle and financial means—and would arrange for the desired changes to the original design, the three fittings with the *première* and her assistants, and the final delivery of the garments nestled in layers of tissue in handmade boxes. Today, the clothes, along with key staff, might be flown to the client for fittings.

Since the time when Worth was dressing European aristocracy, the nouveau riche, and the demimondaine, the face of the couture customer has been a record of global shifts in wealth and consumption. During its "golden years," from 1947 to 1957, newly prosperous Americans resuscitated haute couture, as they did again in the 1980s, along with clients from the oil-rich Persian Gulf States. The 2000s have seen an infusion of clients from emergent centers of affluence in Russia and Ukraine, and most recently, China, India, and South America. At the turn of the twentieth century, haute couture clients numbered around 1,500; at present (when a blouse might cost $10,000 and an embroidered gown $200,000, depending on the client's standing within the house), they approximate 200 worldwide.

Directrice
Director of the salon who assigns the *vendeuses*.

Vendeuses
Saleswomen who also negotiate the fabrication and fittings.

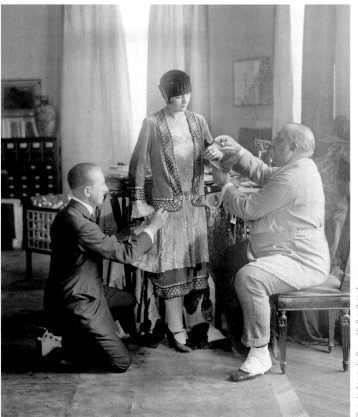

Photo by Lipnitzki, Roger Viollet, Getty Images.

FAITES-MOI CELLE-CI
ROBE DU SOIR. DE DŒUILLET

Nº 7 de la Gazette du Bon Ton.   Année 1921.— Planche 46

Private collection.

Above Paul Poiret and his tailor during a fitting, ca. 1925 • *Left Vendeuses* help their clients select a dress in the *salon de ventes*, House of Georges Doeuillet; drawing by Pierre Brissaud, *Gazette du Bon Ton*, 1921

LUCIEN LELONG

16, RUE MATIGNON   PARIS

(ROND-POINT DES CHAMPS ÉLYSÉES)

NOM DU MODÈLE :

Prelou

MODÈLE DÉPOSÉ
REPRODUCTION INTERDITE

KINDLEY RETURN AS SOON AS POSSIBLE THE
SKETCHES WHICH HAVE NOT BEEN CHOSEN

PRIÈRE DE VOULOIR BIEN RETOURNER LE PLUS
TÔT POSSIBLE LES DESSINS NON CHOISIS

Left Client *croquis* for the
ensemble "Prelou," House
of Lucien Lelong, 1927

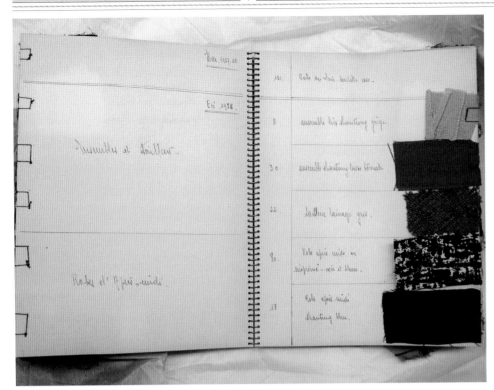

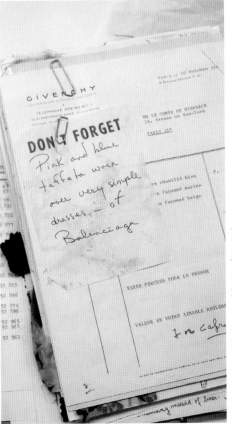

International socialite Countess Mona Bismarck married five times; her third husband, utilities executive Harrison Williams, was the richest man in America. Famous for her silver hair and ice-blue eyes, she was equally known for her carefully chosen fashions. In 1933, Paris's top couturiers voted her "the best-dressed woman in the world." She developed a close friendship with Balenciaga in her thirty years as a patron and reportedly took to her bed for three days when he closed his couture house. Bismarck kept extensive notebooks outlining her selections from each season's haute couture collections. Here, she recorded her back and forth with the designers and *vendeuses* to assure that each garment suited her taste, best accentuated her look, and followed her strict guidelines. In addition to an accounting of the costs, the notebooks include client *croquis*, copies of the hand-drawn sketches of each design, with attached fabric swatches.

Above Couture notebooks kept by Mona Bismarck,
detailing her orders from Balenciaga and Givenchy, 1958–72

Photo by Popperfoto, Getty Images.

Above Directrice Ginette Spanier showing a *modèle* to a fashion editor and a prospective commercial buyer, House of Pierre Balmain, 1952

Private collection. Chanel drawing by Eric.

CHANEL

Hattie Carnegie

Above Evening gowns from the House of Chanel, 1938, and Hattie Carnegie, 1947

The Commercial Buyer

Although predicated on the creation of made-to-measure garments, haute couture long served another client: the buyer for foreign retailers and manufacturers, both small and large. From the start, Worth had disseminated high fashion by selling his designs to other dressmakers and clothing manufacturers, and other couture houses followed his lead. To control the widespread piracy of their collections, haute couturiers in 1947 instituted a system known as patronage, selling reproduction rights according to a fee scale. The *patrons papier* admitted buyers to the shows and gave them the choice of purchasing paper patterns, *toiles* with fabric and trim samples, or finished *modèles*. The *première vision* was a budget-rate sneak peak that allowed buyers to view a collection for "inspiration." Strict rules mandated that all international buyers would receive their samples simultaneously and gave manufacturers thirty days in which to produce their copies in secret. The timing was carefully coordinated with the date by which the press was allowed to release sketches or photographs of a collection.

Legitimate buyers who reproduced a design could advertise it as a "Paris copy" and even name the house from which it originated. American fashion magazines illustrated pieces from Chanel, Dior, or Lanvin Castillo tagged as "Original and copies at Henri Bendel" or "Copied in America at Saks Fifth Avenue." Buyers also modified the originals, sometimes substantially, to appeal to regional tastes and to sell their replicas at an assortment of prices. Even when not announced as an edition of a Paris original, similarities in design among garments reveal the extent of haute couture's influence on fashions made and marketed abroad. By the mid-1960s, reproduction rights still represented over half the sales from haute couture, and the system survived until the 1970s with the ascendency of ready-to-wear.

Chambre Syndicale

A decade after Worth first delineated the haute couture system, he cofounded the forerunner to the Chambre Syndicale de la Couture Parisienne to regulate, protect, and promote French fashion and to ensure proper working conditions. Haute couture, like champagne, is an *appellation contrôlée*, or trademarked term. Now, as in 1868, the Chambre Syndicale establishes the demanding standards that a fashion house must to meet to claim the title. Today's rules date to 1945 but have been revised over time to addresses changes within the industry: An haute couture establishment must create original, hand-finished garments in an atelier in Paris that employs twenty full-time artisans; the couturier must present at least twenty-five ensembles in January and July, which will be made to measure for private clients over several fittings. Newly created houses can, for two years, employ a staff of ten and create a total twenty-five designs.

The number of official haute couture houses changes every year. At the end of World War II, there were over 100; in 2012, only eleven. To address the decline, in 1997 the Chambre Syndicale divided its membership into three categories: full members, correspondent members (foreign designers showing, but not headquartered, in Paris), and guest members (sponsored aspirants). Correspondent members have the same status as official members. Guest members cannot use the label "haute couture," only "couture," but after ten collections, may advance to full membership. More recently, the categories further expanded to embrace accessory and fine jewelry designers.

Haute couture today comprises two different types of practice: the global luxury giants with decades of history and the smaller, more modest, more exclusive operations. On either side, the houses that can reinvent themselves for the current generation will thrive in the coming years, and not surprisingly it is haute couture's newer members that often generate the greatest interest.

Photo from Rue des Archives, AGIP, Getty Images.

Above Couturiers Pierre Cardin and Paco Rabanne receive the Dé d'Or (golden thimble) and Epingle d'Or (golden needle), respectively, January 1977

Haute Couture Members 2012

Official Members

Adeline André
Chanel
Christian Dior
Maurizio Galante
Jean Paul Gaultier
Givenchy
Atelier Gustavolins
Anne Valérie Hash
Christophe Josse
Stéphane Rolland
Frank Sorbier

Guest Members

Julien Fournié
Bouchra Jarrar
Maison Rabih Kayrouz
Alexis Mabille
Maxime Simoens
Giambattista Valli
Iris van Herpen
Alexandre Vauthier
Yiqing Yin

Accessories Members

Massaro
On Aura Tout Vu

Fine Jewelry Members

Boucheron
Chanel Joaillerie
Chaumet
Dior Joaillerie
Mellerio dits Meller
Van Cleef & Arpels

Correspondent Members

Azzedine Alaïa
Giorgio Armani Privé
Maison Martin Margiela
Elie Saab
Valentino
Versace

Photo by Antonio de Moraes Barros Filho, WireImage.

Left Yiqing Yin haute couture, Fall/Winter 2012/13

Emergence of Ready-to-Wear

In the preindustrial period, the most common and often only way to purchase clothes ready-made was via the secondhand market. Throughout medieval and Renaissance Europe, used clothing vendors supplied what few garments the poor could afford. Ready-made apparel produced speculatively did exist, primarily semifitted garments and accessories: shirts, collars, detachable sleeves, petticoats, hats and caps, gloves, stockings, and trims. Clothing might also be commissioned; for instance, for religious orders or armies.

By the nineteenth century, as the intricate rules surrounding dress began to loosen, guild restrictions, too, began to relax, allowing merchant tailors to pursue mass production. Proponents of ready-mades frequently found that experienced tailors refused to work for them. In the 1820s, the French *mercer* Pierre Parissot hired prisoners to make the inexpensive clothing that he sold in his shop innovatively marked with its price.

Mass-produced clothing was more readily accepted in the United States, and a whole industry flourished near the Bowery and along the East River in New York (where sailors could buy their "slops"). The American Civil War helped to identify a need for better-fitting uniforms, which led to the development of systems of standardized sizing for men's garments. In 1866, the Buttericks patented graded paper patterns for women's clothing.

By mid-century, technological innovations like the power loom and the industrial sewing machine began to speed production and, in allowing for unskilled piecework, decreased the overall costs of apparel making. Most ready-made clothing was produced for men and boys, including shirts, collars, suits, and overcoats. But increasingly, women's clothes were becoming available. Outerwear, such as cloaks and mantles, and underwear, such as chemises and hooped petticoats, were among the first items women could easily purchase. By the 1890s, women's fashion embraced a more tailored look based on a separate skirt and shirt, known as a shirtwaist, which rapidly became the star garment of what the Montgomery Ward catalog would dub in 1895 "ready-to-wear."

By the 1910s, American mail-order companies such as Montgomery Ward and Sears Roebuck could bring a full range of ready-to-wear apparel (even bridal dresses) to the remotest of rural communities. As these garments, which often fit better than homemade, became increasingly affordable, class distinctions based on clothing began to blur. And as the focus turned to female customers, the emphasis moved from the durability of the garments to the rapid turnover of fashions. The modern age of mass apparel production and merchandising had begun.

Photo from Liljenquist Family Collection of Civil War Photographs, Library of Congress.

Private collection.

Far Left Unidentified Union soldier, ca. 1861–65 • *Left* Shirtwaists, advertised in *Dress*, January 1912

Left Pages from the Montgomery Ward catalog, 1915

The Department Store

In Europe and North America, the rise of ready-to-wear paralleled the creation of the city department store. Enormous architectural wonders made possible by the newly available steel-frame and plate-glass technologies and the invention of the elevator and escalator, these "cathedrals of commerce" (as Emile Zola termed them) were geared to, and celebratory of, a prosperous urban middle class.

The earliest, and the model for those that followed, was Le Bon Marché in Paris. Founded in 1852 by the dry goods merchant Aristide Boucicault, it gathered under one roof all manner of items that would have otherwise required visits to dozens of shops. Drawing them in through advertisements and store catalogs, Boucicault offered his *petite bourgeois* customers fixed prices, home delivery, discounts, and an exchange policy. Along with tailoring and dressmaking services, he provided a great diversity of tastefully arranged ready-made merchandise. Above all, he established the department store as a place for leisurely browsing and social gathering, with amenities such as restaurants and art galleries.

Other metropolitan department stores soon sprung up—Galeries Lafayette and Le Printemps in Paris; Harrods, Libertys, and Selfridges in London; R. H. Macy's, B. Altman's, Lord & Taylor, and Bloomingdale's in New York, and Wanamaker's in Philadelphia—all devoted to the pleasures of shopping.

Frank Leslie's Illustrated Newspaper, Library of Congress.

Photo by Historic American Buildings Survey, Library of Congress.

Photo by Detroit Publishing Co., Library of Congress.

Above R. H. Macy's, New York, ca. 1908 • *Left* Grand court of Wanamaker's, Philadelphia, early 1930s • *Opposite Page* Le Bon Marché, Paris, 1880, illustrated by Michel Charles Fichot

Utility Clothing

Like the Great War before it, World War II strengthened the ready-to-wear industry. The massive push to provide uniforms for the armed forces drove clothing manufacturers to improve their operations and increase their production capabilities. On the domestic front, as Nazi troops occupied Paris in 1940, North American and British designers were left to define the fashions of the new decade.

The military's diversion to the war effort of rubber, leather, and textiles, both natural and man-made, led to the Civilian Clothing Act of 1941 (CC41) in the United Kingdom and the Limitations Order (L-85) in the United States. These regulations controlled the excessive use of materials, not only in skirt lengths or trouser widths, but also in design elements such as collars, cuffs, and pockets and in embellishments from extra buttons to embroidery. For utility clothing, as such garments were termed in Britain, functionality and affordability trumped other style considerations. Fashions, like uniforms, became standardized. Plain, simply tailored suits and sportswear in durable fabrics were the patriotic mandate. Yet for some designers, wartime restrictions helped to hone their skills.

Taking advantage of Paris's isolation, in 1942 couturiers, including Edward Molyneux, Hardy Aimes, Norman Hartnell, Digby Morton, and Victor Stiebel, formed the Incorporated Society of London Fashion Designers to promote the image of British custom fashion abroad. At the same time, the government charged them with creating a range of attractive garments—each designer was to produce a coat, dress, suit, and blouse—that conformed to CC41 restrictions, suited every season, and could be mass produced. Approved by the Board of Trade, thirty-two of their designs were manufactured as ready-to-wear and were so widely distributed as to account for four-fifths of total wartime apparel production. In the postwar period (clothing rationing remained in effect until 1949 in the U.K.), couturiers like Morton drew on their experience to enter more deeply into the field of ready-to-wear.

Photo from Keystone, Hulton Archive, Getty Images.

Above Right Marking patterns for uniforms, January 1941 • *Right* Utility fashions, London, September 1942, with the original design (left) and its mass-produced counterpart (right)

Photo from Keystone, Hulton Archive, Getty Images.

Private collection.

Above Promotion for the
New York Dress Institute,
March 1947

Photo by Nina Leen, Time & Life Pictures, Getty Images.

Above Dorothy Shaver
reviewing designs for Lord
& Taylor, April 1945

The American Look

By the 1930s, the New York–based garment industry was the fourth largest industry in the United States. Buyers regularly traveled to France to copy the latest couture designs, even if they would be modified for their less trend-conscious, more frugal customers. But on Seventh Avenue, some designers were coming to realize that American women wanted something radically different from what their European counterparts wore. They sought stylish but highly functional clothing that could be adapted for a variety of activities and go from day to night; they also looked for items that were reasonably priced, easily purchased, and could be mixed and matched to expand their wardrobes. Some New York designers, like Valentina Schee, Jessie Franklin Turner, and Elizabeth Hawes, specialized in distinctive custom-made fashions. But it was the creators of ready-to-wear, especially sportswear—coordinated separates that had originated in England but found their strongest expression across the Atlantic—that defined the "American Look."

In 1932 visionary retailer Dorothy Shaver, recognizing that the work of these designers would appeal to the busy lifestyles and tight budgets of her customers, boldly launched the American Designers' Movement program at Lord & Taylor. Over the next seven years, Shaver shifted attention from the name on the label, usually the manufacturer or retailer, to that of the individual designer, by introducing and promoting dozens of American designers by name: Hawes, Muriel King, Annette Simpson, Clare Potter, Adrian, Nettie Rosenstein, Claire McCardell, Tina Lesser, Tom Brigance, Norman Norell, Vera Maxwell, and milliner Lilly Daché.

In the early 1940s, in the absence of Parisian dictates, the American fashion industry came into its own: the New York Dress Institute was formed; publicist Eleanor Lambert put an American spin on the Best-Dressed List and gave birth to New York Press Week; and American designers, especially women such as Lesser, Maxwell, McCardell, Potter, Carolyn Schnurer, and Bonnie Cashin, became increasingly popular. By the time Paris was liberated in 1944, New York had solidified its place as an international fashion capital, with over 8,000 clothing manufacturers on Seventh Avenue. Although the buyers for retailers and manufacturers returned to the French couture shows throughout the 1950s, American designers had forever established their reputation for modern sportswear that combined versatility, ease, comfort, and style.

Opposite Page Coat design by Pauline Trigère, 1949 ▪ *Above* Tennis outfit shot by Toni Frissell for *Harper's Bazaar*, February 1947 ▪ *Left* Separates by Clare Potter and a romper by Tom Brigance, *Vogue*, May 1953

The Rise of the Boutique

Early in the twentieth century, Paul Poiret recognized the importance of the boutique as a marketing tool. He opened one next to his couture house, selling perfume, accessories, and *confection*—ready-made sportswear—to his well-heeled clientele. By the 1920s, other couturiers had followed suit, and soon the *maisons de couture* were offering a variety of merchandise in little shops on the ground floor of their premises.

The French began to use the term *prêt-à-porter* (a direct translation of ready-to-wear) in 1948 to refer to this better-quality but still mass-produced apparel. The first *prêt-à-porter* salon was held in Paris in 1957 when eight couture houses (Carven, De Rauch, Dessès, Griffe, Heim, Lanvin, Ricci, and Rouff) banded together to present their boutique clothing. The Chambre Syndicale, which in 1911 had drawn a clear distinction between couture and *confection*, mandated that all ready-to-wear collections be sold in the couturier's boutique to keep Parisian couture "exclusive and grand." Those who disobeyed would be promptly removed from the exclusive roster, as was Pierre Cardin (at least temporarily) when he showed a ready-to-wear collection at Printemps in 1959.

In 1966, haute couture's tense relationship with *prêt-à-porter* was jolted when the young Yves Saint Laurent stepped down from the couturier's ivory tower on Paris's right bank to open a high-end ready-to-wear boutique on the Seine's more artistic and youthful left bank. The first freestanding boutique from a couture house, the aptly named Rive Gauche sold a new collection from Saint Laurent that took advantage of the prestige of his *maison* but was conceived as an independent line based on the possibilities of mass production and the freer spirit of a new generation of customers. The boutique and the line were quickly embraced. Other haute couture houses saw the benefits of creating new, less expensive lines, and by 1968 couturiers Courrèges, Givenchy, Ungaro, and Philippe Venet had all opened their own *prêt-à-porter* boutiques.

Photo by Lipnitzki, Roger Viollet Collection, Getty Images.

Photo from Keystone-France, Gamma-Keystone via Getty Images.

Above Boutique, House of Paquin, 1939 • *Right* Yves Saint Laurent, Rive Gauche Boutique, 1966

Youthquake and the London Boutique

When *Time* magazine in April 1966 proclaimed London the "swinging city," it was registering a phenomenon well underway. Encapsulating fashion's role in the experimentation and irreverence of the counterculture, boutiques transformed stretches of London like the King's Road and Carnaby Street. Kids coming of age in the late 1950s and early 1960s had more disposable income and a strong desire to break from their parents' generation. At the same time, young designers who were shut out of traditional fashion venues or didn't want to be part of an outmoded system began sewing garments in their homes and selling them in little shops. The boutiques offered a fast-moving array of novel, relatively inexpensive ready-to-wear.

The new attitude toward dressing was reflected in the attention paid to the shopping experience. Quirky interior decorations, innovative displays, and frequently changing shop fronts generated constant buzz. Each boutique had its own identity, but all shared a clublike informality. By the mid-1970s, mainstream fashion had co-opted the boutique movement, but not before it had transformed how fashion was produced and disseminated.

Bazaar

In 1955, self-taught designer Mary Quant, with Alexander Plunkett Green and Archie McNair, opened Bazaar on the King's Road in Chelsea, the boutique that would set the standards for all that followed. Dissatisfied with the available fashion stock, Quant began to produce and sell the clothes she herself wished to wear, notable for their easy, simple shapes and mod leanings. She introduced and popularized the miniskirt, often shown with colored tights, and was the first to incorporate PVC into her garments. By 1963, she went into mass production with her Ginger Group range. She also launched a wildly hued makeup line. Bazaar embodied the Quant lifestyle. Animated, custom-designed mannequins displayed the clothes and witty vignettes rotated in the windows. The shop kept late-evening hours in a partylike atmosphere. When a second Bazaar opened in Knightsbridge in 1957, as the champagne flowed, models danced to jazz or wandered among the assembled carrying books by Marx and Engels.

Photo from Keystone-France, Gamma-Keystone via Getty Images.

Photo by Bob Thomas, Getty Images.

Above Left Mary Quant, ca. 1966 • *Left* Bazaar, King's Road, Chelsea, 1966

His Clothes

A keen observer of how men dressed, John Stephen responded early to the rise of a dandy aesthetic among London youth. In 1956, the Glaswegian clothier, himself in his twenties, opened His Clothes, which he moved the following year to Carnaby, then a quiet backstreet. He stocked denim and flamboyant shirts in a riot of colors, as well as the tight-fitting Italian suits so loved by the Mods. Stephen's approach to retail was revolutionary for menswear: He offered low prices and a fast turnover of styles (nothing remained longer than a few weeks) in a trendy environment. Throughout the 1960s, he expanded his boutique empire, earning the moniker "king of Carnaby Street" by opening a dozen stores there alone. Stephen succeeded by constantly reading his customers to better generate new ideas—shifting to hippie styles and Regency-era fashions and outrageous looks like men's mini-kilts—and by attracting high-profile customers, by 1966 the Beatles, Rolling Stones, and Kinks, among them.

Above John Stephen and models on Carnaby Street, 1966

Mr. Fish

Another important contributor to the Peacock Revolution, as *Esquire* magazine termed the radical change in menswear, was Michael Fish. In the early 1960s, he designed shirts for London clothier Turnbull and Asser, patterned in florals and decorated with embroidery and ruffles. Fish became a leading stylist, dressing rock stars and actors in his unconventional designs. In 1966 with businessman John Barry Sainsbury he opened Mr. Fish on Clifford Street in Mayfair, provocatively close to Savile Row. Catering to a somewhat more affluent crowd, the boutique became known for colorful, vividly printed suits, psychedelic separates, ethnic-derived caftans and tunics, and exuberant wide ties called kippers.

Above John Barry Sainsbury inside Mr. Fish, Clifford Street, 1966

Biba

Opened by Barbara Hulanicki and Stephen Fitz-Simon in a former apothecary's in Kensington in 1964, Biba signaled a change in fashion's direction at a time when postwar optimism was waning. The clothes, which originally came from their mail-order business, looked to the past rather than the future: The historicist styles ranged from sweet little-girl dresses to Hollywood glamour gowns; the colors were all earthy and muted shades. The shop interiors shared this dreamy romanticism, with dark walls and a decadent jumble of Victorian, art nouveau, and art deco furnishings. The communal dressing room was filled with young women, mostly working class, who came for the low prices and stayed to immerse themselves in the Biba ambience. In each of its incarnations—the boutique moved twice, to Kensington Church Street in 1965 and to Kensington High Street in 1969—Biba proposed a way of life. In the third incarnation, a five-story 1930s department store replete with its original deco fittings, Hulanicki even sold housewares and foods packaged with the Biba label.

Granny Takes a Trip

In early 1966, Sheila Cohen, Nigel Waymouth, and Savile Row–trained tailor John Pearse, opened a new boutique on an unfashionable bit of the King's Road known as World's End. Granny Takes a Trip promoted an aura of exclusivity, selling from Cohen's collection of Victoriana, then sourcing other vintage clothes, and as demand grew, adapting the older styles to create new retro-gypsy designs, with prices as varied as the pieces. The interior of the boutique suggested a psychedelic bordello, with lighting kept dim, incense, patchouli, and pot scenting the air, and music blasting from the Wurlitzer. The boutique became known for its series of trippy façades designed by Waymouth and Michael English. Covering over an art nouveau frontage, successive portraits of two Native American chiefs in 1966 gave way to a Pop Art rendition of Jean Harlow's face in 1967. In 1968, the front half of a '47 Dodge appeared to crash out from the shop; initially lemon yellow, it was later repainted black and gold. The mysterious vibe appealed to their stylish hippie customers, who included the entire pantheon of British rock.

Paraphernalia

Although essentially a London phenomenon, the boutique movement registered in New York City when Paraphernalia opened on Madison near 67th in 1965, rocking the fashion scene. British entrepreneur Paul Young hired a team of designers, including Betsey Johnson (whose fit model was Edie Sedgwick and future husband John Cale) to create fun, youth-oriented clothing that could hit the shop floor within days of its conception. The designs were cheap (nothing cost more than $99), disposable (they often fell apart after a few wears), and unexpected: dresses were made of paper and plastic, one dress grew when it was watered, another glowed in the dark. Architect Ulrich Franzen designed an interior as modern and slick as a spaceship, in which the clothing hung on steel and chrome fixtures against white walls. Rock 'n' roll rang from the speakers and go-go dancers grooved in the windows. The shop girls, with slim, boyish figures and a hip demeanor, embodied the Paraphernalia ideal.

Photo by George Freston, Fox Photos, Getty Images.

Photo by Brain Shuel, Redferns, Getty Images.

Photo by Susan Wood, Getty Images.

Above Biba, Kensington Church Street, 1965 • *Right* Granny Takes a Trip, World's End, 1967 • *Far Right* Studio of Paraphernalia designer, Betsey Johnson, 1966

Redefining Ready-to-Wear

The fashion industry experienced enormous structural changes in the decade from 1965 to 1975. A new breed of ready-to-wear designer emerged to fill the gap between the expensive luxury ready-mades of the couture salons and the unsophisticated mass productions of the apparel companies. In 1964, Emmanuelle Khanh, who with Christiane Bailly had founded the French brand EmmaChristie, could declare, "Haute couture is dead. I want to design for the street . . . a socialist kind of fashion for the grand mass." In Paris, ready-to-wear designers, increasingly known as *créateurs*, began to create affordable garments that were also innovative and unconventional.

In 1971, Didier Grumbach, whose manufacturing company contracted with a number of couture houses, including Saint Laurent's, founded Créateurs et Industriels, a fee-based alliance between designers and manufacturers that served to promote this forward-looking *prêt-à-porter*. The organization opened a multibrand clothing and design emporium and held professional runway shows for its young members. Didier's goal was to improve the image of ready-to-wear, making it distinct from, but equally as valued as, haute couture—and not incidentally bathe the whole enterprise in a clearly Parisian light, no matter that some of the designers were not French. Khanh and Ossie Clark were the first of the group, joined in the course of its five years by Jean Muir, Issey Miyake, Jean-Charles de Castelbajac, Roland Chakkal, Thierry Mugler, Claude Montana, and Jean Paul Gaultier, among others. The creative output of these designers was phenomenal. Recognizing that this level of ready-to-wear also now commanded a far larger market, with greater profits, than haute couture, in 1973 the Chambre Syndicale essentially folded Créateurs et Industriels into its organization, by establishing a broader governing entity known as the Fédération Française de la Couture, du Prêt-à-Porter des Couturiers et des Créateurs de Mode. Under Grumbach's guidance, the Fédération continues to oversee the French fashion industry.

The elevated status of *prêt-à-porter* was felt around the globe. In Milan, where the ready-to-wear industry began to congregate in the early 1970s, one of the *stilisti* changing people's perceptions was Giorgio Armani. The easy elegance of his first eponymous collections for men and women in 1975 satisfied the hunger of those for whom haute couture was no longer an option but who still sought an image of luxury. His genius lay in creating a close, tightly supervised partnership between designer and textile manufacturer that carried through every phase of production and distribution—solidified in 1978 by his agreement with Gruppo Finanzario Tessile—and in establishing a diffusion of lines and licenses that shared the same stylistic quality. Armani's business model would define Italian ready-to-wear through the 1980s.

Above Top Ossie Clark with a model, 1972 • *Above* Giorgio Armani with a model, 1979

Photo from Hulton Archive, Getty Images.

Photo by David Lees, Time & Life Pictures, Getty Images.

Mass Appeal

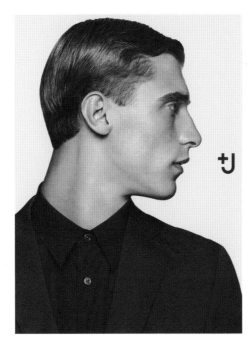

Above Top Uniqlo flagship store in Tokyo • *Above* Designs from +J, Uniqlo's collaboration with Jil Sander

For most of its history, ready-to-wear that lacked direct association with a designer's name was not considered fashion, if it was considered at all. But by focusing on mass-producible basics such as jeans and T-shirts, retail companies like Uniqlo have transformed core wardrobe components into relevant factors in the fashion equation. Initially, in 1969, the Gap stores carried only Levi's and LPs, but by 1974 they were selling their own merchandise. The Gap is now considered a pioneer in the world of specialty retailers of private label apparel (SPA), a business strategy by which a company produces clothing and distributes it exclusively through their own retail operations. It is the model that Japanese-owned Uniqlo has followed to astonishing success.

Founded in 1984 by Tadashi Yanai, Uniqlo defines its brand as basics, "simple and essential yet universal." It produces large quantities of a limited range of designs in an abundance of colors; the polo shirt, for example, might come in eighty hues. Unlike most fast fashion retailers, Uniqlo uses high-quality materials because it expects its garments to be worn much longer. After a backlash to its oversaturation of the Japanese market, in 2001 the company looked overseas; in early 2012 it had 849 stores in Japan and 234 in major cities worldwide.

In 2009, Uniqlo established what turned out to be a three-year collaboration with designer Jil Sander to design "uniforms for the future." The +J collection was a way to elevate the brand's fashion status within the industry and in the eyes of the public, while keeping its commitment to plain, well-made, inexpensive clothing. Now the company has switched gears in a new partnership with Jun Takahashi, the designer behind the cult brand Undercover, who like Uniqlo has experimented with high-tech fabrics.

The Speed of Fashion

In today's fashion arena—transformed by digital technologies and high/low mixing—luxury ready-to-wear brands face competition from low-cost specialty chains such as Topshop, H&M, and Zara. These mass-market retailers can identify trends as they develop, and relaying this knowledge through the supply chain, deliver a constant stream of new products at previously unheard of speeds. Hedging against uncertain consumer demand, the companies produce short-cycle fashion apparel in relatively small quantities. Their styles are typically aimed at a younger market, although this demographic seems in flux.

British Topshop opened its first stand-alone store in 1974. Now under the ownership of Sir Philip Green's Arcadia Group, its U.K. stores and international franchises (together with those of menswear brand Topman) offer a profusion of stylish, affordable garments. To lure in shoppers, no items remain on the shelves for long and hundreds of new designs are introduced each week.

Swedish H&M (Hennes & Mauritz), whose retail history reaches back to 1947, has established itself as a leader in providing fashion in real time. Its commitment to low-investment, on-trend dressing translates into accessible fashion for men, women, and children. Its strategy of partnering with marquee designers to create limited-edition capsule collections has helped position the company as a relevant fashion brand.

Spanish Zara was founded in 1975 by Amancio Ortega Gaona. With 1,631 stores across the globe, it is the key brand of Inditex, the world's largest clothing retailer. Unlike H&M, which manufactures large quantities of basics in Asia and smaller quantities of limited designs in Europe, Zara has built its success on an efficient vertical integration of design, production, and distribution at their campus in Galacia. Store managers convey customer feedback to the design teams, who can take a trend from concept to the sales floor in as few as two weeks.

With a business model that focuses on distribution more than production, these companies can immediately gratify their customers' yearning for the latest styles, and at prices that make disposing of them equally satisfying. Of course, the pace is intensified for all designers, contributing to the pressure on traditional fashion houses to produce mid-season collections. And a system that can turn around a look from the runway in a matter of weeks throws into question the very viability of the seasonal fashion calendar.

Above Topshop lookbook, Summer 2012

Photo by Markel Redondo, Getty Images.

Courtesy of Inditex.

Above Top Zara store,
Madrid, 2009 • *Above* Zara
lookbook, Fall 2011

Above H&M lookbook,
Fall 2012

Top to bottom H&M stores in
Las Vegas, Milan, and Beijing

Photos courtesy of H&M; Beijing by Peter Chen.

Copy Rights

"Society may give an exclusive right to the profits arising from them, as an encouragement to men to pursue ideas which may produce utility."
Thomas Jefferson, 13 August 1813

Copyright refers to the exclusive right to make copies, license, and otherwise exploit an artistic work. In fashion, courts have generally ruled that articles of clothing are too utilitarian to qualify for such wide protection. France, the birthplace of fashion, has had some form of protection in place since 1793, and couturiers early on organized against piracy. Today, the European Union gives designers a three-year copyright, with the option to apply for a twenty-five-year extension, but the Community Design System's low novelty standard discourages interest in registering garments or pursuing court cases. Japan, like India, grants designers an automatic ten years of protection, but Japanese design law has such a high novelty standard that few designs are eligible.

U.S. trademark law safeguards labels and logos. Precise copies on the black market can be prosecuted as theft; in essence, they dilute, if not divert, the stream of profit derived from a designer's ideas. Such piracy is also pursued as fraud; passing off a forgery as an original profits from the reputation of an established brand. But as the suit shows that footwear designer Christian Louboutin brought against Yves Saint Laurent for infringement of their red lacquered sole—a company signature since 1992 and a registered trademark since 2008—elements like color remain a contested area.

The United States also protects exclusive fabric patterns; not, however, the form, components, or tailoring of the design they may be developed into. Since 2007, industry professionals, among them the Council of Fashion Designers of America, have been championing Congress to pass the Design Piracy Prohibition Act. The DPPA has faced strong opposition from both manufacturers and retailers worried that strict legislation that would encourage frivolous litigation, potentially create monopolies, and be expensive to enforce.

Under the current bill, which would ensure a minimum three years of protection for unique and original designs, designers would have to prove that their designs are truly original, that the defendant's copy is "substantially identical," and that the defendant had knowledge of their work.

Supporters of fashion design copyright argue that garment designs are creative expressions with the same qualities as other protected works of intellectual property. "Our unique items are what have established Proenza Schouler's identity," points out Lazaro Hernandez. "To have our creativity stolen dilutes the value of what we have worked so hard to build." Or as Maria Cornejo has said of the copyists, "They're basically putting their hand in my head, which is my bank, and stealing ideas." Many argue copyright is an incentive to innovation, allowing individual designers as well as corporations to benefit from the production and distribution of their creations. This becomes especially important when defending the economic interests of new designers, who rely less on the draw of their label and more on the originality of their work. Companies that are in a position to grab an idea, produce it cheaply, and distribute it quickly often beat a designer to market. Fashion businesses without the financial resources to take legal action, or the brand cache to compete, have little recourse and may falter as a result.

Private collection.

Top Label marked with Madeleine Vionnet's thumbprint to combat piracy • *Middle* Labels in a Maison Martin Margiela original and in a Korean knock off • *Right Harper's Bazaar* anticounterfeiting campaign, 2010–11

Sportswear Separates

Photo by Sandra Flores, www.sandra-flores.com; T-shirt by Sudaca.

Photo by Joel Benjamin.

Photo by Andrew H. Walker, Getty Images.

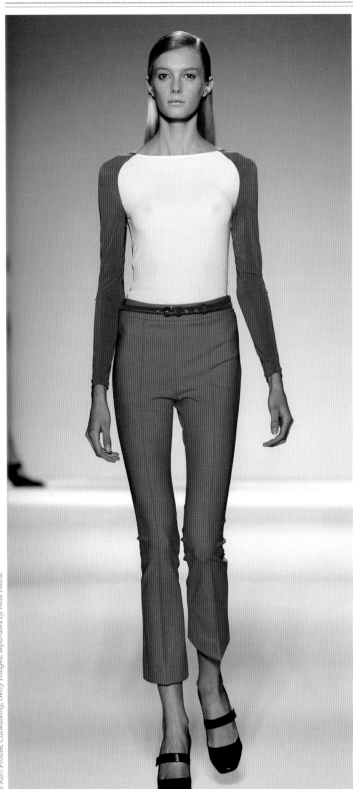

Photo by Karl Prouse, Catwalking, Getty Images; separates by Max Mara.

Photo by Tullio M. Puglia, Getty Images; separates by Costume National.

Photo courtesy of H&M.

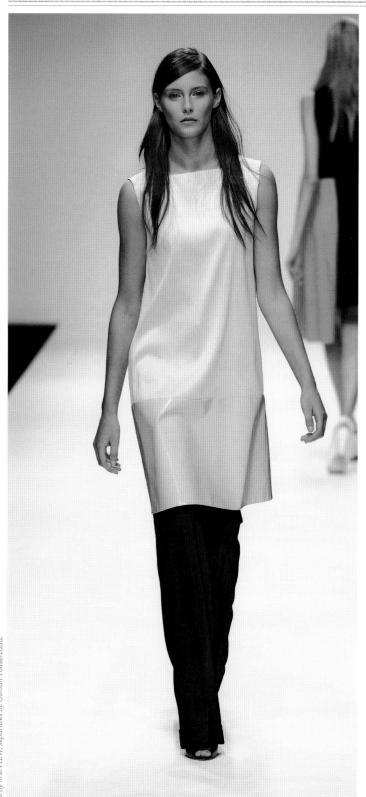

Photo by firstVIEW; separates by Osman Yousefzada.

Photo by Patrick Kovarik, AFP, Getty Images; separates by Dries Van Noten.

Dresses

Photo by Chris Moore, Catwalking, Getty Images; dress by Thakoon.

Photo by Richard Bord, Getty Images; dress by Roland Mouret.

Photo by firstVIEW; dress by Costello Tagliapietra.

Suits

Photo by Thomas Concordia, WireImage; suit by Rag & Bone.

Photo by Joel Benjamin.

Photo by originalpunkt, Fotolia.

Eveningwear

Photo by firstVIEW; dress by Vera Wang.

Photo by Victor Boyoko, Getty Images; dress by Giambattista Valli.

Photo by Jerral Countess, Getty Images; ensemble by Jason Wu.

Photo by Joel Benjamin.

Photo by Andrew Swaine; dress by Nara Paz.

Outerwear

Photo by Karl Prouse, Catwalking, Getty Images; parka by Joseph Altuzarra.

Photo by J. P. Yim, WireImage; trenchcoat by Tommy Hilfiger.

Photo courtesy of Wallis.

Photo by FirstVIEW; bomber by Burberry Prorsum.

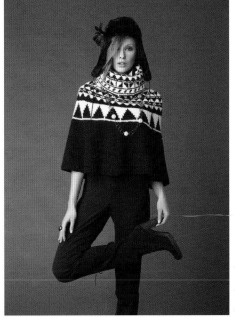

Photos by Joel Benjamin.

Accessories

Accessories have traditionally been seen as embellishment, always secondary to the ensemble, but today, style strategies are often built upon a key accessory. The accessories umbrella covers many different categories, each with a full industry behind it: footwear, handbags, hats, eyewear, jewelry, scarves, ties, belts, gloves, hosiery, umbrellas, even fans and walking sticks. Although designer accessory lines are seamlessly woven into collections on the runway or in print, the distinction must be made that each represents considerable specialized training. These makers must ultimately develop a mastery of the craft unique to their product, skills that often go above and beyond those of the clothing designer.

Accessories have grown in importance to the industry as designer brands have relied on them so heavily to influence the bottom line. Accessories play many roles in improving sales. Timeless pieces symbolic of the label become worthy of an investment and collectible. Some designers create a powerful draw by manipulating supply and demand to elevate special items to "it" status. And while price points may vary, accessories often serve as gateway purchases for customers aspiring to brand loyalty.

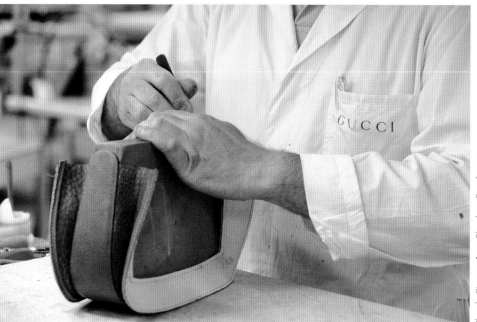

Photo by Giuseppe Aresu, Bloomberg, Getty Images.

Private collection.

Above Top Fabricating a handbag, Gucci factory, Casellina, 2009 • *Above* Classic Hermès handbags

Photo by firstVIEW.

Left Prada, Spring/
Summer 2011

Above Top "Misplaced heel"
shoe, Marc Jacobs, 2007
• *Above* Creating a new
model, Christian Louboutin
studio, Paris, 2011 • *Above
Right* Mary Janes, Manolo
Blahnik, 2007

MANOLO BLAHNIK

31 WEST 54TH ST NEW YORK • 49-51 OLD CHURCH ST LONDON • BERGDORF GOODMAN NEW YORK • NEIMAN MARCUS STORES

Above Manolo Blahnik
advertisement, 2004

Left Milliner Marie Galvin
in her studio, Boston, 2011

● *Below* Galvin-ized
Headwear, 2011

The Players

Depending on the scale of a company, many of the jobs involved in the development and distribution of a fashion collection may be integrated into positions that are responsible for more than one set of duties as described here.

Concept

Forecaster: A forecaster makes predictions about future trends by analyzing a range of cultural, social, and economic indicators, filtered through a command of fashion history and practice. Forecasting may be approached from the broad perspective of overall trends or focus more narrowly on color, textiles, accessories, or other targeted design categories.

Product Researcher and Developer: Research and development teams ascertain how well a product aligns with a brand and whether it is viable. They create and fabricate a prototype, testing it for quality and performance, then evaluate the product's marketability, gauging affordability and probability of reception.

Textile Designer/Buyer: Working independently or as part of a design house or mill, a textile designer may be involved in both the artistic and scientific development of fibers and fabrics. Some design houses employ a textile buyer to purchase and manage the fabric stock each season. Textile designers and buyers create fabric collections with a cohesive mix of color, texture, and pattern.

Designer: Pulling from a broad menu of design elements, designers shape their creative vision into a fashion product that responds to the needs and desires of their clients. By mastering sets of technical skills, designers can solve design challenges in any apparel category and transcend the borders between bespoke and mass production. Most designers work on seasonal collections and adhere to brand guidelines.

Analyst: An analyst evaluates any step in the design process, from current business operations to the integration of a trend or product into a brand, and suggests a course of action for improvements.

Workroom

Patternmaker: Using measurements, a draped *toile*, and/or a designer's sketch, the patternmaker drafts a flat pattern by hand or computer. The job requires exceptional accuracy, comprehension of the transition from two to three dimensions, and a good understanding of construction and fit.

Draper: Using a dress form, a draper manipulates muslin to create the basis for a pattern that requires a more organic silhouette than can usually be achieved by flat patternmaking techniques. The draper must transfer the resulting fabric pattern to paper and correct it to provide a finished pattern.

Cutter: A cutter uses flat patterns to cut fabric pieces that will be assembled into a finished garment. Traditionally an entry-level job, it requires an understanding of patterns, fabric grain, grading, markers, and construction.

Illustrator/Sketcher: A fashion illustrator produces art-driven renderings for commercial or editorial use. A sketcher develops clear drawings that communicate more technical information for spec/line sheets. Both may use traditional art media or computer-aided design programs.

Seamstress: Also known as a stitcher, the seamstress assembles a garment, using both hand and machine techniques. The seamstress may complete an entire garment from beginning to end in a design workroom or do piecework in a factory. Outside these settings, she may also be referred to as a dressmaker.

Tailor: Skilled in cutting, fitting, pressing, and finishing techniques unique to the craft, a tailor specializes in suiting, coats, and trousers. The bespoke tailor creates made-to-measure garments from scratch. In addition to making original garments, a tailor may also repair or alter clothing.

Sample maker: The sample maker follows patterns, sketches, and design specifications to produce sample garments. Sample-making companies provide services at any step in the process—cutting, stitching, or finishing—for smaller fashion houses.

Fit model: A fit model reflects the ideal proportions of a designer's intended customer. A live model provides direct feedback about fit before a sample goes into production.

Apparel Sourcing Specialist: This liaison bridges the gaps between design, planning, purchasing, and any overseas operations involved in development, production, and shipping. The specialist must report on materials/services costs, agency fees, and payment terms. The job usually requires international travel.

Intern: Interns provide much-needed support to design teams. Interns are usually placed in entry-level positions and groomed to become the next generation of fashion design talent.

Production

Production Manager: This operations manager coordinates and controls human and material resources throughout the manufacturing process so that the work remains on schedule and on budget and meets the established standards of quality.

Technical Designer: Drawing on both computer and patternmaking skills, technical designers oversee fittings, establish specs for each garment, develop tech packs, and manage the construction process to maintain quality control. They liaise with the designer, vendors, and production managers at the factories.

Pattern Grader: Graders reduce or enlarge each sample-size pattern to create a complete set of standardized sizes for each design. Grading can be accomplished by hand or with a computerized grading system.

Marker Maker: The marker maker places the pattern pieces in a configuration that conforms to the constraints of grain line, fabric type, width, nap, and pattern. The process optimizes the consumption of fabric during the cutting process.

Shipping Manager: Distribution professionals prepare goods and manage the logistics of their transport from the supplier to the client or other destination points.

Sales

Showroom Salesperson: Account representatives introduce new designer collections to buyers from boutiques, department stores, and other retail outlets. They may be based in a showroom or travel to stores and trade shows.

Fashion Buyer: A buyer selects and purchases wholesale merchandise seasonally from vendors. Many buyers work from an "open-to-buy" plan that helps control the flow of inventory. They also develop category-specific assortments plans tailored to the needs of individual stores or retailers. Buyers analyze sales and monitor turnover, markdowns, and sales ratios.

Retail Sales Team: Regional, store, and assistant managers oversee specific retail locations, training and motivating staff to reach sales goals. Together, with sales associates, stock managers, and display personnel, they also maintain the interior of the store and provide customer service. Retail teams might include personal shoppers.

eCommerce/Catalog Salesperson: As part of handling the sales from non-brick-and-mortar concerns, this salesperson oversees inventory control, distribution, and sales analysis.

Merchandise Planner: A planner develops store plans, inventory mixes, and product distribution among retail locations, working with buyers on price points, trends, sizes, and styles.

Visual Merchandiser: Merchandisers configure store interiors and style mannequins and window displays to increase traffic and sales. At the corporate level, they establish the visual standards for a company.

Brand

Creative/Artistic Director: In a job sometimes aligned with the responsibilities of a head designer, the artistic director guides the creative course for a brand's fashion and accessory collections as well as extensions of the brand, like fragrance and beauty products. The creative director may also be involved in advertising and marketing campaigns.

Merchandise Coordinator: Coordinators ensure that retail stores are meeting brand standards for merchandising. In department stores, they negotiate floor space for their brand.

Public Relations Representative: PR professionals maintain press relationships, act as spin doctors to control messages, and help build social network platforms for a brand. They may also be involved with event planning and list management at fashion shows.

Marketer/Promoter/Publicist: Marketers are charged with identifying, satisfying, and retaining customers, using a variety of strategies: advertising, direct mail, product placement, loyalty rewards, demonstrations, visual merchandising, and word of mouth. Promoters combine product, price, and place to present information, increase demand, and differentiate a brand from its competitors. Publicists help to manage public perception of a brand via event sponsorship, public speaking, testimonials, and involvement in public debates.

Fashion Editor: Editors create the narratives for magazines based on an expert knowledge of fashion and an ability to forecast trends. They cultivate relationships with designers and showrooms, selecting and styling work for publication that is consistent with the interests of their readership. Freelance fashion editors often work as stylists.

Journalist: Reporters are concerned with fashion news, especially relating to trends, markets, designers, and runways. They report across a variety of platforms, including newspapers, magazines, websites, and blogs.

Blogger: Online citizen journalists now rival professional editors and journalists in influencing consumers. Fashion blogs can take the form of personal reflections, pictorial documentations, editorial concepts, news flashes, and storytelling.

Copywriter: A copywriter creates the headlines and texts for websites, catalogs, and other promotional or sales literature, giving a brand a voice that enhances its image.

Photographer/Videographer: Photographers use digital and film formats to capture images for catalog, editorial, and advertising work, sometimes operating at a high artistic level. They also document runway and street fashion for newspapers, magazines, and websites. Videographers extend the recording of fashion to the moving image.

Model: Models may do catalog, editorial, advertising, or runway work, each of which requires specific skills. The standards of beauty for a model in any category change with the cycles of the fashion industry. Subcategories of modeling include plus-size, petite, and a variety of age-related divisions.

Stylist: A stylist coordinates every element of a presentation to create an overall impression. Stylists work with designers to define the message behind a collection. Photo stylists help to realize the vision of an art director or photographer for photo shoots, commercials, or films. In retail, stylists function as visual merchandisers. Personal stylists select ensembles and develop coordinated wardrobes for private clients.

Beauty Professional: Hair stylists and makeup artists are integral to packaging a designer's concept for promotional materials, advertising, and the runway.

Licensor: Licensing companies secure permission from designers to manufacture a product under their name for a specified payment.

Event Manager: An event manager produces theatrical presentations for a designer, including runway shows, special exhibitions, designer visits, trunk shows, and other events designed to generate press, sales, and in-store traffic.

Communications Designer: Communications designers develop the visual language for a brand, creating logos, websites, publication graphics, advertisements, and product packaging.

Archivist: An archivist collects and preserves materials that document the history and evolution of a company or brand. These archives serve internally for inspiration and sometimes for publication or exhibition.

Curator: A gallery or museum curator collects historic and contemporary fashions and textiles for exhibition, scholarly research, and publication purposes.

Label, Line, and Collection

A label encompasses what an overall brand stands for. A company like Ralph Lauren provides a good example of a designer label that produces collections each season for various lines within the brand: Purple Label, Black Label, Polo Ralph Lauren, Rugby, RLX, (tech/performance), Double RL (heritage), Denim & Supply, and Golf.

In a small fashion house, the differences between a line and a collection are negligible. In the context of a large corporate brand, a clearer distinction can be made because the company may serve as an umbrella for a variety of brand extensions in different classifications, such as outerwear, jeans, or fragrance. A line may refer to one of these extensions. Lines may also be separated by price point.

Collections are usually season-specific groups of designs created for a line of the brand, which are produced, presented, and delivered conforming to an established fashion calendar. Capsule collections are small selections of pieces that represent the brand.

Photo by Dmitri Beliakov, Bloomberg via Getty.

Photos by Chris Ratcliffe, Bloomberg via Getty.

Above Ralph Lauren and family at the opening of the company's Moscow store, 2007 • *Far Left* Ralph Lauren Purple Label • *Left* Ralph Lauren Polo

Calendar of Fashion Weeks

January
Milan Fashion Week, Menswear, Fall/Winter
Berlin Fashion Week, Fall/Winter
São Paulo Fashion Week, Fall/Winter
Paris Fashion Week, Menswear, Fall/Winter
Paris Fashion Week, Haute Couture, Spring/Summer

February
New York Fashion Week, Fall/Winter
London Fashion Week, Fall/Winter
Milan Fashion Week, Fall/Winter

March
Paris Fashion Week, Ready-to-Wear, Fall/Winter
Lakmé Fashion Week, Mumbai, Summer/Resort
Los Angeles Fashion Week, Fall/Winter
Tokyo Fashion Week, Fall/Winter
China Fashion Week, Beijing, Fall/Winter

April

May
Australian Fashion Week, Sydney, trans-seasonal
Milan Resort/Cruise (May–June)
New York Resort/Cruise (May–June)
London Resort/Cruise (May–June)

June
Rio Summer Fashion Week, Swimwear
São Paulo Fashion Week, Spring/Summer
Milan Fashion Week, Menswear, Spring/Summer
Paris Fashion Week, Menswear, Spring/Summer
Paris Resort/Cruise (June–July)

July
Paris Fashion Week, Haute Couture, Fall/Winter
Berlin Fashion Week, Spring/Summer
Miami Fashion Week, Swimwear

August
Lakmé Fashion Week, Mumbai, Winter/Festive

September
New York Fashion Week, Spring/Summer
London Fashion Week, Spring/Summer
Milan Fashion Week, Spring/Summer
Paris Fashion Week, Ready-to-Wear, Spring/Summer
(September–October)

October
Los Angeles Fashion Week, Spring/Summer
Tokyo Fashion Week, Spring/Summer
China Fashion Week, Beijing, Spring/Summer

November
Milan, Pre-Fall (November–December)

December
London, Pre-Fall
New York, Pre-Fall (December–January)
Paris, Pre-Fall (December–January)

Centers

92
Cities

Fashion today has no frontiers. In how it is conceptualized, produced, and received, fashion is truly global. And yet as designers from different regions gravitate to various style hubs they bring with them their traditions and languages, which mix with the culture of the city where they've landed. The major fashion centers each have an identity: Paris is steeped in history and haute couture. London is the home of bespoke menswear and idiosyncratic, experimental design. New York embodies the essence of American sportswear. Milan draws on a thriving textile industry for luxurious ready-to-wear. Tokyo challenges expectations in its conceptual designs and in its streetwear. As new fashion cities emerge, their flavor is added to the blend.

104
Schools

Fashion centers depend on a steady influx of skilled professionals to preserve and develop the industry in their region. Schools are a conduit through which the stream of new talent is nurtured by curriculums designed to produce the next generation of fashion designers, craftspeople, artists, scholars, and technicians. Models of fashion education may run the gamut between small vocational training programs and large educational institutions; programs may focus on the business of fashion or the theory of design, their slant may be industrial or artisanal. Supplementing coursework is a vital tradition of mentorships, often from professionals returning to their alma maters, which connect students to the working design community.

Miss Finland in Marimekko, Miss France in Emmanuelle Kahn, Miss Italy in Emilio Pucci, Miss England in Mary Quant, and Miss Switzerland in Geneva, 1966.
Photo by Keystone-France, Gamma-Keystone, Getty Images.

Paris

As early as the Renaissance, France was at the center of fashion. Louis XIV, a young king with a sense of style, turned his attention to the decorative arts, and with the help of his finance minister, Jean-Baptiste Colbert, he secured Paris as the capital of the fashion world. They recruited master weavers and lace makers from all over Europe, turned the city of Lyon into an extensive silk-weaving center, and simultaneously enacted laws prohibiting the purchase of these goods from other countries. The king's extravagance prompted trends to pass rapidly and members of the royal court to follow suit, with Versailles becoming a stage upon which the fashionable could strut and fret. The introduction of fashion publications allowed style aspirants to keep in step with the aristocracy and the *modes* of the day.

In the mid-nineteenth century, haute couturier Charles Frederick Worth built a legacy that eliminated any doubt that all high fashion originated in Paris. In 1929, the Ecoles de la Chambre Syndicale de la Couture were founded not to instruct designers, but to train craftsmen for the various couture ateliers and subsidiaries. In France, the state, the public, and the industry support fashion as an integral part of the culture and the economy. Although society has become more democratic regarding the dictates of fashion, Paris retains a cachet with which few centers can compete, thanks to a cultivated sensibility that elevates fashion to an art form. And although this laboratory of luxury is not necessarily where designers will profit, the investment in fine workmanship makes it fertile ground for creativity and a source of inspiration for designers around the world.

Photo by Nora Feller, Time & Life Pictures, Getty Images.

Photo by Nathalie Lagneau, Catwalking, Getty Images.

Above Karl Lagerfeld for Chanel, 1990 • *Left* Isabel Marant, Fall/Winter 2010/11

Photo by Karl Prouse, Catwalking, Getty Images.

Above Céline, Fall/Winter 2010/11

Photo by firstVIEW.

Above Stéphane Rolland, Fall/Winter 2011/12

London

Savile Row in Mayfair was long the epicenter of men's fashion, based on a legacy of fine tailoring going back to the late 1790s. While social conduct and dress codes still revolved around the monarchy, the nineteenth century in Britain was a period of industrial modernization. At the same time, British imperial dominance allowed London to claim a kind of fashion authority, upheld by the establishment of world-class department stores. Couturiers followed Paris fashions but adapted the designs to suit the customs of London society.

World War II allowed the couturiers of the Incorporated Society of London Fashion Designers to enter the international spotlight. But in addition to custom design, Londoners who dressed through CC41 restrictions came to embrace ready-to-wear clothing. By the 1950s, British designers were known for producing small saleable collections. In the postwar period, the Royal College of Art added a fashion department; from the start, the London schools encouraged innovation as well as technique.

London emerged in the mid-fifties as a center for countercultural style that originated on the street. Tastemakers frequented boutiques in Camden and on Portobello Road, where they could self-style vintage or ethnic clothing. From Teddy Boys to Mods, punks to anarchists, the city inspired a host of subcultural movements with a rebellious sensibility. Exquisite tailoring, eclectic experimentation, and a sense of theatricality often combine in British fashion (and may be why so many of its young designers have headed up Parisian houses). Whether subtle or overt, there's an edginess that continues to underlie both London fashion design and the publications that promote it.

Above Fashion shoot in Piccadilly Circus, London, ca. 1965

Photo by David Redfern, Getty Images.

Above Clements Ribeiro,
Spring/Summer 2011

Above Stella McCartney,
Spring/Summer 2011

New York

Americans embraced ready-to-wear fashion early and while they may not have invented it, they certainly perfected it. American menswear manufacturers had set up in New York in the nineteenth century, and by the 1930s, the core ideas of American apparel were already established. Promoted by Dorothy Shaver of Lord & Taylor and showcased to the world by photographers like Martin Munkácsi, Louise Dahl-Wolfe, and Toni Frissell, the look was modern, simple, and comfortable, made for women who were eternally youthful, active, and chic. These were "placeless" garments that could be worn all day, any day, not prescribed by an occasion. And a nimble manufacturing sector on Seventh Avenue could produce them quickly and in quantity.

In 1943, publicist Eleanor Lambert established press coverage for the New York collections. Though manufacturers and retailers alike continued to look to Paris until the 1960s, no place surpassed New York for the ingenuity of its sportswear. Borrowing elements from menswear, designers combined economy and invention to create easy, functional garments that continued to resonate throughout the century. Many styles, from jeans and a white shirt to an Ultrasuede shirtdress, have become classics. American sportswear, too, is intertwined with the ideals of democracy and self-expression, an image that advertising and merchandising have spread worldwide. Today, fashion emanating from the New York workrooms evokes an uncomplicated, pragmatic approach to dressing, whether in urban or luxury mode.

Photo by Brian Ach, Getty Images.

Above The Tents at Bryant Park, New York, February 2010

Photo by Andie Guran.

Left Mercedes-Benz Fashion Week's new quarters at Lincoln Center, January 2011

Photo by J. P. Yim, WireImage, Getty Images.

Photo by Pascal Le Segretain, Getty Images.

Far Left Michael Kors, Fall/Winter 2011/12 • *Left* Proenza Schouler, Spring/Summer 2011

Milan

The Ente Nazionale della Moda was founded in 1928 to strengthen the Italian apparel industry by bringing together its tailors, leather workers, dyers, textile workers, and other fine trades. But not until after World War II, with the reconstruction of the textile industry (aided in part by U.S. funding), did Italy capture the attention of the fashion community outside the country. The *alta mode* houses settled in Rome. But it was the ready-to-wear designs shown in Florence in 1951 that received most of the headlines for their breathtaking fabrics and creative construction. American buyers responded particularly well to the chic resort wear and to the general affordability and ease of Italian fashions compared to Paris couture.

Throughout the 1950s and 1960s, Italian cities vied for industry dominance, with an especially strong rivalry between Rome and Florence. In the early 1970s, modern, creative Milan, already home to the northern textile firms and to the Italian fashion press, emerged as the new leader. In 1975, the city held its first organized fashion shows for both men and women. Marrying design with industry, Milan developed a vertically integrated model for the production of high-end *prêt-à-porter* in a variety of aesthetics: understated, flamboyant, or irreverent. "Made in Italy" became a mark of quality.

Fashion in Italy has always been dispersed across its different regions. Since the 1990s, Milan has seen renewed competition from Florence with its Pitti Immagine trade shows and, more recently, has been pressured to reduce the length of its fashion weeks on the international calendar. The newest voices in the city represent a departure from the industrial model, mixing the artisanal, technological, and conceptual to create an extreme sartorialism.

Photo by Iceppzro, iStock Photo.

Photo by Jacopo Raule, Getty Images.

Photo by Victor Vergile, Gamma-Rapho via Getty Images.

Above Left Galleria Vittorio Emanuele, Milan, 2007 • *Above Right* Canali, Fall/Winter 2011/12 • *Right* Bottega Veneta, Fall/Winter 2011/12

Left Gucci, Fall/Winter
2011/12

Tokyo

In Meiji-era Japan, newly open to the West, European clothing represented modernization and by 1886 was mandated for both sexes even at the emperor's court. Simultaneously, the kimono form and Japanese aesthetics made their way into designs coming out of London and Paris. Not until 1970, however, with the opening of Jungle Jap in the Galerie Vivienne, did the work of Japanese designers register within the fashion system. Gradually throughout the 1970s and with a jolt in 1981, Japanese designers brought to the catwalk unfamiliar ideas about the relationship between clothing and body, deconstructing the accepted forms of fashion to present a radically new interpretation of its possibilities.

Tokyo organized its first fashion week in 1999, though most of Japan's top designers continue to view Paris as vital to their international success. Tokyo, however, is home to their studios and to those of many others who, at least domestically, have an almost cultlike following. Drawing on a rich textile tradition while embracing technological advances, Japanese designers often produce their own fabrics. They also innovate in silhouette and pattern construction. From the 1990s, as the country went into recession, till today, Tokyo has generated large clusters of style tribes. The norm-breaking, fanciful dress of these tweens and teens derives from a range of Western trends and Japanese pop culture, especially *kawaii*, or cuteness. The city's streetwear designers tend to blend these subcultural styles with their own avant-garde takes on clothing. What seems to unite Japanese designers at every creative level is how their garments contain opposing ideas, be it beauty and ugliness or rawness and refinement.

Photo by Nikada, iStock Photo.

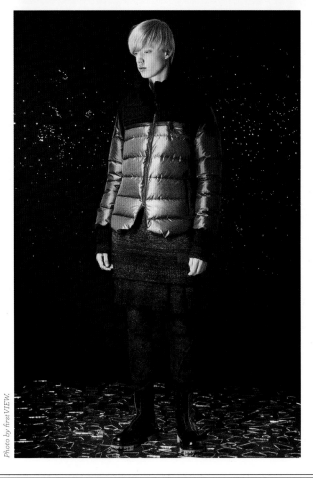

Photo by firstVIEW.

Above Shibuya Crossing, Tokyo, 2006 • *Left* Undercover, Fall/Winter 2009/10

Left Tokyo street fashion, December 2009 • *Below Left* Hiroko Koshino, Spring/Summer 2011 • *Below Right* Tamae Hiro-kawa for Somarta, Spring/Summer 2010

Berlin

While Düsseldorf remains Germany's center of high-end fashion production, since 2007 it is to the more design-energized city of Berlin that European designers, from Antwerp to Hungary, come to show a mix of classic and avant-garde styles in the biannual fashion weeks. Internationally recognized German luxury labels make an appearance, with stylish collections of wearable and saleable garments. But the city's focus is on emerging talent. Berlin thrives on its intense art scene, and many homegrown fashion labels express their vision with an art-practice sensibility. Pure, playful, edgy, out-of-the-box: The designers reflect the versatile expressions of a happening city.

São Paulo

An emerging economic power that has ridden out the world financial crisis, Brazil has become fertile ground for global luxury brands, attracting them despite high import duties. The country also has abundant natural resources for a thriving textile and apparel industry. This former colony exhibits a new self-confidence, and since 1996 São Paulo, the base for many designers, has hosted Latin America's most important fashion weeks. Renowned for its glamorous swimwear, Brazilian fashion is discovering itself. São Paolo showcases a wide variety of colorful, relaxed, body-conscious designs for men and women. But its designers, some of whom show regularly in New York, develop and mix materials in new ways that may be coolly minimal as well as hotly tropical.

Photo by firstVEW.

Above Vladimir Karaleev, Fall/Winter 2011/12

Photo by Victor Virgile, Gamma-Rapho, Getty Images.

Above Priscila Daroit, Spring/Summer 2012

Sydney

Since 1995, fashion buyers and press have gathered once a year in Sydney for Australian Fashion Week (now part of the Mercedes-Benz–sponsored family and not to be confused with the retail-led event in Melbourne). Established and upcoming brands from across the Asia-Pacific region introduce designs that are easy, breezy, and rich in color. Most Australian designers create trans-seasonal collections suited to the country's climate and to lifestyles that might play out in the bush, on the beach, or in the city. Many designers who find success on the runways in Sydney can translate their work for other markets and, like the quintet of bright talents who showed in New York for the Fall/Winter 2012 presentations, bring a taste of Down Under to the rest of the world.

Beijing & Mumbai

China is the world's largest apparel manufacturing country and India is among the top ten. Since the late 1990s, backed by the central government, Beijing's fashion weeks have targeted the domestic industry. The events showcase a still somewhat random array of established and new designers. French luxury brands are also making the trip to Beijing, to present their latest collections to a Chinese audience that is definitely buying. At Lakmé Fashion Week in Mumbai, now entering its second decade, Indian designers, traditionally known for their bold color palettes and exotic embellishments, are redefining the balance between Eastern and Western design elements to find a harmonious point between culture and commerce. Time will tell how these centers compete on the global fashion stage.

Photo by firstVIEW.

Above Josh Goot, Spring/Summer 2012

Photo by ChinaFotoPress via Getty Images.

Above Cabeen Chic, Fall/Winter 2012/13

United Kingdom

Central Saint Martins College of Art and Design, London

Considered by many as the top fashion school in the world, Central Saint Martins is famous for graduating designers who are creative, experimental, innovative, and risk taking. Some of the biggest names in the fashion world got their start here: Alexander McQueen, John Galliano, Stella McCartney, Hussein Chalayan, Phoebe Philo, Riccardo Tisci, Giles Deacon, Alice Temperley, Jonathan Saunders, and Matthew Williamson. Founded relatively recently, in 1989, with the merger of the Central School of Arts and Crafts (1896) with the Saint Martins School of Art (1854), the college is partially subsidized by the government, which allows for students from a broader economic and social background. The School of Fashion offers degrees in fashion, textile, and jewelry design as well as postgraduate work in fashion and "textile futures." The school is a driving force in the industry, pushing concepts of design and training designers who are often hired to work in haute couture.

Royal College of Art, London

Founded in 1837, the Royal College of Art is exclusively postgraduate. With programs in textile design and men's and women's fashion design, alongside programs in contemporary art curation and the history of design, the college is a pioneer in art and design scholarship. Its fashion design department is the only postsecondary program in the world to offer a degree that focuses wholly on menswear. The alumni list includes Ossie Clark, Zandra Rhodes, Philip Treacy, Christopher Bailey, Erdem Moralioğlu, and Julien Macdonald.

London College of Fashion

The London College of Fashion, established in 1906 as a trade school, is, like Central Saint Martins, now part of the six-college University of the Arts. Located in the heart of the city's garment district, the college is known less as a design school than for its portfolio of specialist courses including bespoke tailoring and beauty therapy. Its degree programs in fashion journalism are held in high regard. In 2000, the school merged with Cordwainers College, famous for its expertise in footwear and accessory design and its graduate Jimmy Choo.

University of Westminster, London

Often overlooked, the small but competitive fashion program in the School of Media, Arts and Design at the University of Westminster prizes individuality and creativity. The school offers both a three- and a four-year undergraduate degree in fashion design as well as degrees in fashion buying, merchandise, and business management. Joining Vivienne Westwood in calling Westminster their alma mater are Christopher Bailey, Michael Herz, Stuart Vevers, Carrie Mundane, Katie Hillier, and fashion editor Sophie Dean.

Glasgow School of Art

Best known for its connection to the artist and architect Charles Rennie Macintosh, the Glasgow School of Art was founded in 1845 to teach creativity and innovative thinking in the fields of art and design. Today, the school offers degrees in textiles and fashion as well as an innovative M.A. degree "textiles as fashion." The Centre of Advanced Textiles specializes in researching new methods of computerized textile design and digital printing. The school's fashion and textile graduates work for a range of fashion companies, from Topshop and the Gap to Phillip Treacy and Alberta Feretti.

Above Wun Wun Nova Chiu, London College of Fashion, 2011

Photo by Alex Lentati, Evening Standard, ZUMA Press.

Photo by Ian Gavan, Getty Images.

Photo by Dan Kirkwood, Getty Images.

Above Phoebe English, Central Saint Martins, MA show, 2011 • *Left* Rebecca Thomson (left) and Lorren Johnson (right), Royal College of Art, MA show, 2012

Europe

Royal Academy of Fine Arts, Antwerp

While the Royal Academy of Fine Arts has been around since the seventeenth century, not until the 1960s was a fashion department formed under the leadership of Mary Prijot and Marthe Van Leemput. By the early 1980s, the department had emerged as an incubator of creativity and rigor in fashion design, and "The Antwerp Six"—Dirk Bikkembergs, Ann Demeulemeester, Walter Van Beirendonck, Dries Van Noten, Dirk Van Saene, and Marina Yee—firmly put the institution and city on the fashion map when they took their designs to Paris and London. The school, which is substantially subsidized by the Belgian government, embraces a broad and critical understanding of fashion that helps to foster experimental and innovative designs. Other notable alumni include Martin Margiela, A. F. Vandevorst, Haider Ackermann, Peter Pilotto, and Veronique Branquinho

École de la Chambre Syndicale de la Couture Parisienne, Paris

Founded in 1927 to continue the French tradition of haute couture craftsmanship, the prestigious École de la Chambre Syndicale has trained some of the twentieth century's best-known talents, from Yves Saint Laurent and André Courrèges, to Valentino and Issey Miyake. More recent graduates include Adeline André, Anne Valérie Hash, Dominique Sirop, Stéphane Rolland, Gustavo Lins, Mario Lefranc, and Béatrice Ferrant. The school's four-year program is renowned for its classes in couture techniques and for its ties to federation member companies. Training emphasizes the artistic and technical skills needed to design and produce high-quality, structurally complex garments for both the haute couture and ready-to-wear markets. In 2010, the school moved to a new 27,000-square foot (2,430 sq. m) building on the rue Réamur.

Studio Berçot, Paris

Created by fashion illustrator Suzanne Berçot in 1955 and now headed by Marie Rucki, the highly regarded Studio Berçot offers a three-year program in fashion design. A year apprenticeship follows two of intensive courses in drawing, draping, patternmaking, construction, and history. Studio Berçot has many close connections with fashion houses, including Balenciaga, Cacharel, Chloe, Eres, Kenzo, Kookai, Nina Ricci, Sonia Rykiel, and Yves Saint Laurent. Among the graduates of this small but prestigious school are Martine Sitbon, Nicole Farhi, Lolita Lempicka, Isabel Marant, and Sophie Theallet.

Istituto Marangoni, Milan

Founded in 1935 as the Italian apparel industry was finding its voice, the school developed along with the tailoring and ready-to-wear industries. Today, with campuses in Paris and London as well, Marangoni has a presence in three major fashion capitals, and the institute claims a ninety percent placement rate. It counts among its graduates heavy hitters Domenico Dolce and Franco Moschino, but also a range of younger players from Alessandra Facchinetti to illustrator Alexandro Palombo.

Polimoda International Institute of Fashion Design and Marketing, Florence

Polimoda opened in 1986 as a collaboration between the cities of Florence and Prato and FIT in New York. Currently, forty percent of the student body is international. Better known for its ancillary fashion degrees than for its design program, the institute has a high rate of placing its graduates within the industry. Its location provides easy access to many of Italy's luxury mills and trade shows while its programming offers a technological and global fashion perspective.

Photo by Didier Messens, Getty Images.

Photo by Emma Peios, WireImage, Getty Images.

Above Christina Economu,
Istituto Marangoni, Paris
division, 2011

Photo by Yorick Jansens, AFP, Getty Images.

Above Terumasa Nakajima,
Royal Academy of Fine
Arts, Antwerp, 2010

Opposite Page Paula Selby
Avellanda, Royal Academy
of Fine Arts, Antwerp, 2009

United States

Parsons, The New School for Design, New York

The New York School of Fine and Applied Art was founded in 1896 and in 1904 established a department dedicated to costume and, later, fashion design. Frank Alvah Parsons became its director in 1910; his work to define an American concept of design, and its intersection with industry, was recognized in 1941 when the school took his name. In 1970, Parsons joined with the progressive New School, strengthening its engagement with social issues. Today, a commitment to sustainable design is central to its fashion program. Parsons is alma mater to a long list of important designers, including Claire McCardell, Norman Norell, Donna Karan, Marc Jacobs, Tom Ford, Narciso Rodriguez, Jack McCollough, Lazaro Hernandez, Doo-Ri Chung, Prabal Gurung, and Thakoon Panichgul, many of whom return to teach classes or workshops. Widely known for its association with the television show *Project Runway*, the school has partnered with many retailers and corporations globally.

Fashion Institute of Technology (FIT), New York

The Fashion Institute of Technology opened its doors in 1944. The apparel industry had recognized the need to train the next generation of professionals for New York to survive and grow as a fashion center, and a small school of 100 students was organized on the upper floors of the High School for the Needle Arts on West Twenty-fourth Street. In 1951, the institute became part of the State University of New York (SUNY) system and in 1959 it moved to Seventh Avenue in the heart of the garment district. Today, FIT takes up an entire city block and accommodates over 1,000 students studying forty-three different subjects. The campus is also home to the vast Gladys Marcus Library and the renowned Museum at FIT. Fashionable alumni include Carolina Herrera, Michael Kors, Norma Kamali, Calvin Klein, Nina Garcia, Ralph Rucci, Francisco Costa, and Nanette Lapore.

Rhode Island School of Design (RISD), Providence

In 1877, members of the Rhode Island Women's Centennial Commission voted to invest the group's $1,675 surplus in founding a school dedicated to the cultivation of art and design. Now considered one of the top design schools in the world, RISD values individuality in its students and encourages experimentation. Recently reorganized into five overarching divisions, the school offers degrees in textiles and jewelry design in addition to apparel design. The RISD Museum of Art, established simultaneously with the school, provides an additional resource for hands-on study. Graduates—from Nicole Miller to Marcia Patmos, Sari Gueron, Philip Crangi, Robert Geller, Katie Gallagher, and Diana Eng—follow widely divergent fashion paths.

The School of the Art Institute of Chicago (SAIC)

The largest museum and college program in the United States, SAIC was founded in 1866 as the Chicago Academy of Design and renamed in 1882 to incorporate the museum. The Department of Fashion Design offers a traditional design curriculum geared toward entering the fashion industry, but also a course of study that examines clothing from a more experimental and conceptual perspective. The school offers a unique interdisciplinary Master of Design in Fashion, Body, and Garment. Joining Halston among the alumni are Cynthia Rowley, Matthew Ames, Gary Graham, Maria Pinto, and Shane Gabier and Christopher Peters (of Creatures of the Wind).

Photo by Ilya S. Savenok, Getty Images.

Above Jin Kay, Parsons, The New School for Design, 2012

Above Katherine Kim, Parsons, 2011 • *Left* Amanda Henderson, FIT, 2010

Asia, Oceania, and the Middle East

Bunka Fashion College, Tokyo

Bunka was founded in 1919 as the Namiki Dressmaking School. It was an early proponent of Western dress in Japan and not only trained students in these techniques but also published books on Western design. In 1936, the school launched the country's first fashion magazine, *So-en*. In the postwar years, the curriculum began to focus on more commercial practices in response to the success of the ready-to-wear market. The college gained worldwide recognition when its graduates Kenzo Takada and Yohji Yamamoto began to show their collections in Paris. Other graduates have included Junya Watanabe, Hiroko Koshino, Chisato Tsumori, and Jun Takahashi. Today, synonymous with cutting-edge design, Bunka offers four departments: fashion creation; fashion technology; fashion marketing and distribution, and fashion accessories and textiles. The Bunka Body Structure and Function Lab, in conjunction with the Digital Human Body Lab, has recently developed a female body-form to reflect accurately the shape and proportions of the modern Japanese woman.

TAFE Institute of Technology, Sydney

This large university system began life as a small vocational college in 1891. Today, two of its colleges, Ultimo and St. George, offer fashion programs, including textile design, millinery, footwear design, and fashion technology. The Fashion Design Studio at Ultimo especially is known for its innovation and creativity and has established partnerships with design institutes throughout the globe. The school has produced many well-known Australian designers, among them Dion Lee, Lisa Ho, Nicky Zimmermann, and Akira Isogawa.

National Institute of Fashion Technology (NIFT), New Delhi

Founded in 1986 and run by the government under the Ministry of Textiles, NIFT is the largest design school in India with a network of twelve campuses in New Delhi, Bangalore, Chennai, Gandhinagar, Hyderabad, Kolkata, Mumbai, Raebareli, Bhopal, Kannur, Patna, and Shillong. It offers degrees in fashion, textile, knitwear, leather, and accessory design, as well as fashion communication, management, and technology; it has also partnered with a long list of design schools worldwide. Notable alumni include Manish Arora and Prabal Gurung.

Shenkar College of Engineering and Design, Ramat Gan

Founded in 1970, this college on the outskirts of Tel Aviv offers undergraduate programs in fashion, textile, and jewelry design. Far from the centers of fashion and with limited access to materials, the fashion department encourages inventiveness and collaborations with the school's other departments in the areas of new materials and technologies. In 2010, it formed an Internet-based cultural exchange program with Bunka College in Japan. Of great advantage to students, Shenkar houses the Middle East's only archive devoted to fashion and textiles. Graduates include Kobi Halperin, head of design at Elie Tahari, Avshalom Gur, Nili Lotan, and, most famously, Alber Elbaz.

Below Ayumi Mitsukane and Rie Hosokai, Bunka Fashion College, Tokyo, 2010

Photo by Toru Yamanaka, AFP, Getty Images.

Photo by Stefan Gosatti, Getty Images.

Photo by Yoshikazu Tsuno, AFP, Getty Images.

Above Shinji Kajinaga, Bunka, 2010 • *Above Right* Kaylene Milner, TAFE, Sydney, 2012 • *Left* Madoka Asano, Bunka, 2009

Styles

114
Subcultures

One of the most profound changes in the innovation and consumption of fashion in the twentieth century was the powerful force exerted by styles that came up from the street instead of filtering down from on high. Street cultures adopt apparel outside of the "proper" sphere of fashion (costume, workers' uniforms, sports gear) to create an authentic identity in times of social upheaval or disaffection. Even the dandy, whose dress draws from upper-class sartorial traditions, uses style as a tool to stake his place within shifting social mores. Distinguishing themselves from the conventions, and sometimes realities, of the day, these style tribes form communities of shared values that are expressed in what they wear. Although subcultural styles are by nature separate and alternative, in the twenty-first century they have become central to fashion, not only cycling through the mainstream as trends *du jour* but also forming part of the high/low sampling that increasingly defines how consumers dress.

122
Aesthetics

Successful fashion brands build audiences based on the underlying consistency of a design sensibility, regardless of where a collection goes in a particular season. This aesthetic layer captures the essence of a design practice and speaks in a clear, consistent voice to the consumer. Each descriptor (minimal, classic, romantic, sporty, urban, postmodern, deconstructivist, antifashion) sets certain creative boundaries for designers to help ensure that elements do not cloud the purity of their core message—unless, of course, the blur is intended.

Anglomania by Vivienne Westwood, Spring/Summer 2009
Photo by firstVIEW.

The Dandy

The world of the dandy privileges good taste. The dandy constructs a consciously studied aesthetic where physical appearance and perfection of dress are not just a priority, but an entire way of life. The original dandy, George Bryan "Beau" Brummell, promoted an immaculately clean, well-tailored form of dress: pants (not breeches) and shirt, soberly colored waistcoat and jacket, white stock tie, sturdy riding boots, and face free of paint. A repudiation of the French-style fripperies worn by the upper-crust English male in the early 1800s, Brummell's understated look suggested a democratic uniform while earning him a place, at least for a time, beside the Prince Regent. Later in the century, another dandy, the writer Oscar Wilde, cultivated an extreme aestheticism in opposition to all things vulgar. He used his flamboyant but carefully considered dress and decadent pose as a means to enter the highest echelons of British society. The hallmark of Wilde's style was to make the performance of the self into an art form. An important instance of the reemergence of the dandy in the twentieth century was the Teddy Boy. In the 1950s, working-class youth in England took control over their public image by adopting the refined styling of an Edwardian gentleman and mixing it with an American cut and rock 'n' roll accent. The signature elements of the Teddy Boy wardrobe were tailored suits with long boxy jackets, narrow trousers, high-collared white shirts, Slim Jim ties, waistcoats, socks in bright colors, and suede brothel creepers.

Two embodiments of the twenty-first-century dandy are Thom Browne and André Benjamin. Browne captured the essence of his grandfather's 1950s Brooks Brothers suits by tailoring his own vintage pieces before launching a menswear company based on this retro aesthetic. His own best model, he sports classic, slim-fitting suits with exaggeratedly shortened sleeves and pants. The designer, who now creates Brooks Brothers' Black Fleece line, connects with the man looking for a neatly conservative yet idiosyncratic style. Dress and celebrity are strongly tied. Musician and actor Benjamin (better known as André 3000) impresses fans with his flair for fashion. He masterfully dips into dapper, pulling from the classics of men's haberdashery—hats, bow ties, waistcoats, jodhpurs, and pocket squares—that he updates with bold patterns, bright colors, and unusual fabrics. It is a polished look that is inventive, but as Benjamin clarifies, "not so inventive that it's a turnoff."

Illustration from Hulton Archive, Getty Images.

Photo by Napoleon Sarony, Library of Congress.

Photo by Scotsman, ZUMA Press.

Above Thom Browne, 2010
• *Rigth* André 3000 of
Outkast, 2004

Opposite Page Far Left
Beau Brummell, 1810 •
Middle Left Oscar Wilde,
1882 • *Left* Teddy Boy,
London, ca. 1954

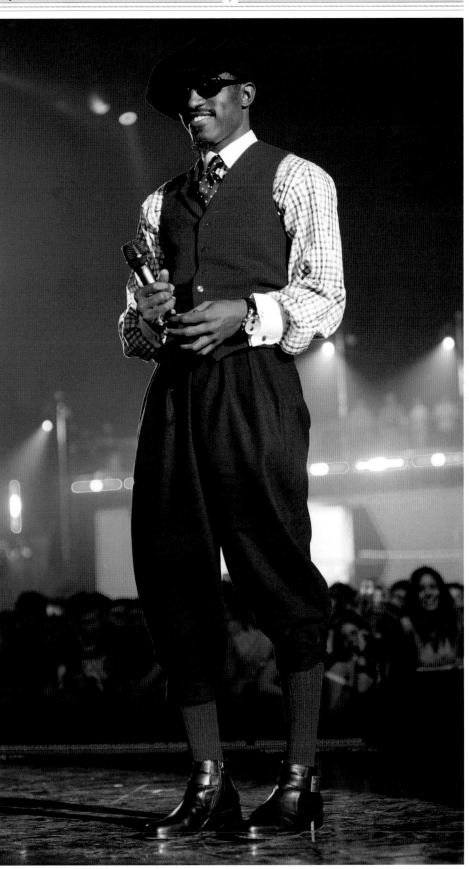

Hiphop

Hiphop traces back to African American youth in the Bronx basement parties of the 1970s and reached the mainstream in the 1980s. It is both the voice of alienation and the story of success. Stylistically, the first looks celebrated the vibrancy of the music and dance culture: brightly colored tracksuits, appliqué leather jackets, fat-laced sneakers (Pumas, Adidas), Kangol hats. Prison life influenced gangsta style, identified by tattoos, bandanas, and oversize T-shirts worn outside low-slung baggy jeans. By the late 1980s, hiphop acquired a much flashier personality, with big gold jewelry, or bling, and designer logos added to the mix. In the 1990s, streetwear brands by hiphop entrepreneurs such as Phat Farm, FUBU (For Us By Us), Mecca, and Enyce proliferated. Hiphop style sampled new elements: overscale ornamental belt buckles, trucker caps, vintage sports jerseys, loud patterned hoodies, camouflage, and snow gear. Timberland boots and Nike's Air Force One each had their moment as the shoe of choice. By the mid-2000s, hiphop had embraced an upscale image. Jay-Z's Rocawear offered a preppy aesthetic, while Sean Combs's Sean John label promoted a more sophisticated tailored look.

Photo by Ebet Roberts, Redferns, Getty Images.

Photo by Neil Mockford, FilmMagic, Getty Images.

Above Left Run-DMC, 1986

● *Left* Diddy (Sean John Combs), 2011

Skater

Photo by Doug Pensinger, Getty Images.

Skateboarding has been around since the 1950s, but in 1975 the Z-boys—the Zephyr Competition Team—launched it into a high-flying sport and created a cultural phenomenon. Just as skateboarding itself has evolved (vert, street, downhill) so, too, has the dress. Initially, skateboarder style was associated with the kids' outsider status; this changed as the sport was introduced to a broader urban audience. Sneakers, baggy pants, hoodies, and loose T-shirts make up the basics. Music has influenced skater culture. The punk skater wears jeans and old rock T-shirts, skull jewelry, and classic Vans or Chuck Taylors. The fresh, or hiphop, skater adopts more athletic apparel, incorporating gel or air sneakers and baseball caps. The artsy or jazzy skater sports a skinnier silhouette in thrift-store chic and black Vans sneakers. The Rasta skater interprets the look with a predominance of red, yellow, and green.

Right Mark Gonzalez, 1985

• *Below* Kurt Cobain, 1993

Photo by Ebet Roberts, Redferns, Getty Images.

Grunge

Grunge is an antifashion aesthetic founded in an unapologetically unkempt look. It emerged among alternative rock musicians centered in Seattle, Washington, with bands like Pearl Jam, Nirvana, and Hole singing about the disenfranchised and apathetic. Discomfort with celebrity, commerce, and the excesses of the 1980s inspired a way of dressing that was primarily brandless, often coming out of thrift shops, or from small indie designers. The impoverished style layered band T-shirts, worn jeans, short floaty dresses, sneakers or combat boots, with stocking caps, thermal underwear, and logger shirts to keep warm in the chilly Pacific Northwest.

Punk

Born in the mid-1970s on the streets of an economically depressed Britain with bands like the Sex Pistols and the Clash, punk culture immediately aligned music with fashion. Like the music, punk styles were meant to confront and offend. Whether from the London boutique SEX or a thrift store, the look was defiantly antifashion. Influenced by an amalgam of earlier subcultures (and in direct opposition to disco culture), punks wore clothing that was ripped and frayed, safety pinned or duct taped, and scrawled with anarchistic slogans. The vocabulary of B&D and S&M—leather, rubber, vinyl, straps, chains, spikes—was strong. Shaved or mohawked hair, tattoos, piercings, and other forms of body modification were the norm. The modern punk has taken numerous directions, with new sartorial interpretations by the anarchopunk, the crust punk, the deathrock punk, the hardcore punk, the pop, or emo, punk, and the punk-cholo, among them.

Photo by Chris Moorhouse, Evening Standard, Getty Images.

Above Punk rockers outside the Rainbow Club, London, 1977

Fetish

Fetish wear, long kept behind the doors of private homes and sex clubs, appeared in public in the 1970s, both on the streets as appropriated by the punks and in the magazines as shot by photographers like Helmut Newton. Erotic stand-ins, the garments are about extreme provocation. Second-skin materials such leather, latex, PVC, Spandex, and fishnet are worked into body-conscious and restrictive clothing. Body stockings and lingerie reveal and titillate, collars and straps restrain. Hobble skirts and bondage pants redirect the body's movements; stiletto shoes, "ballet" or "kinky" boots, and corseting reshape its natural form. Fetishwear implies control, and the image of the dominatrix is that of a woman in power.

Photo by James Coldrey, Getty Images.

Above Schwarzer Reiter–clad fetishists at the Asphalt Club, Berlin, 2011

Above Left Lolitas strolling Takeshita-dori, Harajuku, Tokyo, 2005 • *Above* Cosplay character, Tokyo, 2009 • *Left Gyaru* girls on Takeshita-dori, 2011

Minimalist

Bare and often bold, minimalist fashion simplifies the silhouette and offers a palette of neutral tones. Striking sculptural lines paired with quality fabrics and nominal details serve a modern urban customer who prefers clothes that stand outside of time. The overall effect is understated and subdued, with an undeniable respect for form. The aesthetic rose to prominence in the 1990s with the rigorous work of Jil Sander, Helmut Lang, and Calvin Klein; the minimalist DNA has thrived in the designs of Narciso Rodriguez, Raf Simons for Jil Sander, Francisco Costa for Calvin Klein, and Phoebe Philo for Céline.

Photo by Fernanda Calfat, Getty Images for IMG.

Left Calvin Klein, Spring/Summer 2011

Classic

Classic garments constitute those pieces of a wardrobe that have come to be deemed essential: trench coat, little black dress, white shirt, blazer, tailored suit, pair of jeans. The classic aesthetic appeals to those who are at ease sticking to certain staples throughout their life, whatever the dictates of fashion; it also appeals to those who find assurance in following a long line of tastemakers. Above all, the style is timeless. Ralph Lauren has made a career of presenting variations on many a classic filtered through a thoroughly imagined lifestyle.

Photo from the Everett Collection, Alamy.

Left Nacho Figueras in Ralph Lauren, May 2009

Photo by firstVIEW.

Right Alberta Ferretti,
Spring/Summer, 2010

Romantic

In opposition to a more tailored silhouette, romantic fashion evokes images of soft feminine dresses, skirts, and blouses in pastel colors and weightless fabrics, often with fairytale florals, cascading ruffles, and other feminine details. The romantic aesthetic has been associated with styles as diverse as the nostalgia of Laura Ashley's neo-Edwardian country girl in the 1970s and the theatricality of Vivienne Westwood's "New Romantic" rebel in the 1980s. Today, designs can range from Alberta Ferretti's subtle fluttering chiffons to Alice Temperley's bolder confections.

Photo by Karl Prouse, Catwalking, Getty Images.

Right Y-3, Fall/Winter
2008/09

Sporty

From activewear to dressier sportswear, the sporty aesthetic relies on versatility, comfort, and mobility. Its details come from the athleticwear that serves as its direct inspiration: zippers, drawstrings, racer backs, mesh inserts, stripes, and a variety of high-tech fabrics. Some designers have formed fruitful partnerships with athletic companies—Yohji Yamamoto and Stella McCartney with Adidas, Hussein Chalayan with Puma—to create high-performance but stylish clothing for active consumers.

Urban

The urban aesthetic favors dark-colored tailored garments with a hard edge that identifies the city dweller. Some designers like Rick Owens, who has a softer take, add interest to their otherwise monochromatic ensembles by combining textured materials like fur or leather with wool, silk, or cotton. Above all, these garments camouflage and protect. In the hands of someone like Gareth Pugh, they become beautiful armor for fashion warriors.

It should be noted that urban is also used in the context of streetwear as a racially coded term for black or Latino culture, with particular socioeconomic connotations.

Photo by firstVIEW.

Left Gareth Pugh, Fall/
Winter 2011/12

Postmodern

The postmodern sensibility, felt as early as the 1970s, in large part defines the fashions of the 2000s. It looks to pair high and low, designer labels with thrift-store finds. Postmodern designers play with norms; they appropriate and recombine silhouettes and elements from all of fashion history. The approach has informed designs as diverse as Vivienne Westwood's minicrini of 1985, Rei Kawakubo's Lumps and Bumps collection of 1997, and most every collection by Karl Lagerfeld for the House of Chanel.

Photo by Charly Hel, Prestige, Getty Images.

Left Chanel, Spring/
Summer 2002

Right Maison Martin
Margiela haute couture,
Fall/Winter 2011/12

Deconstructivist

The deconstructivist approach challenges
the traditional rules of garment making by
exposing the very process of constructing a
garment. What is usually finished is left raw
and fraying. What is usually eliminated, like
basting, or hidden, like pinked edges, seams,
linings, or shoulder pads, is brought to the surface. It is an aesthetic of reverses and reassem-
blings. Martin Margiela, the deconstructivist
par excellence, deconstructed not only his
clothing, but also the workings of the fashion
system itself.

Right Bless,
Spring/Summer 2011

Antifashion

The antifashion label has repeatedly been
applied to styles that go against the grain of
current understandings of what constitutes
fashion. These counterexpressions may be in
protest of the societal status quo (subcultural
dress) or in opposition to fashion's prevailing
direction (dress reform movements). They may
propose to undermine fashion with garments
that are dysfunctional or unraveling or to step
outside of it with reductive, label-less clothing.
Although inevitably these styles will be shown
on the catwalk or absorbed by the canon, they
serve to trouble fashion's dominant image.

Forecasting

Fashion forecasters make predictions about future style trends—and in many ways also determine those trends. The forecasting process relies on multiple information streams to successfully predict the direction in which a market is moving. Forecasters study the haute couture collections, emerging designers, artistic and cultural events, popular websites and blogs, political and social shifts, scientific and technological innovations, and global business strategies. Today, most designers, retailers, buyers, product developers, and manufacturers subscribe to forecasting services, which may narrow their focus to color, fabric, notions, design concepts, or developments on the street or in specific regions.

The cycle of fashion forecasting usually starts with color. Companies like Pantone establish well in advance the prevalent color schemes for any given season and work closely with designers to incorporate these color trends within their collections. Textiles are the next step in the forecasting supply chain. To bridge the gap between color research and designers' inclinations, manufacturers must pursue their own specialized research. Textile trade show such as Première Vision cooperate with weavers and raw materials experts to present not only fabrications of color and texture for designers to see and touch, but also an expert forecast of their own.

Right Pantone Fashion Color Reports for Spring and Fall 2011

Honeysuckle
PANTONE 18-2120

NEW YORK FASHION WEEK | FEBRUARY 10 - 17, 2011

PANTONE fashion color report
fall 2011

Photos by Timothy A. Clary, AFP, Getty Images.

Above Left Indigo New York, part of the Première Vision family and the leading American show for patterns and textile design, 2010 • *Left* Première Vision Preview New York, January 2010, an offshoot of the French trade show

Principles

The principles of creating a collection follow a cycle of design, construction, and production, leading from concept to finished garment. Informed by the broader choices for their practice (which specific audience to target, whether to adopt a slow- or fast-paced business model), designers chart a course through myriad decisions and refinements, both practical and intuitive. The careful selection of colors and materials, combined with ideas for overall shapes and proportions, will set a strategy in motion for the development of a prototype that manifests what has only been envisioned. Drafted or draped, a pattern emerges, and a sample is stitched, fitted, and finished. If judged production-worthy, the pattern is adjusted for replication in different sizes and at scale. As the collection moves into the factory setting, new samples test the quality and consistency of the work before commencing on production and distribution. The systems currently in place are constantly being questioned and refashioned to meet the needs of the industry, the public, and the planet. While the industry as a whole has begun to address issues of sustainability, designers today actively engage in practices that are altering preconceptions about the designed object. Meanwhile, the accelerated pace of technological change allows designers to rethink the possibilities for fashion with garments that are evermore innovative and extraordinary.

Design

132
Approach

When designers begin to conceive a new collection, they face the task of filling a blank canvas. Inspiration comes from everywhere: literature and the arts, home and other cultures, nature and the city, memory and current events, a taste, a scent, or fashion's own lineage. Designers organize the visual documentation of these sources so that they reside together. Their arrangement creates unique connections from which emerge colors, patterns, textures, and silhouettes, allowing designers to paint, in broad strokes, a cohesive picture. Into this mix designers add their sketches, by which they refine a collection's theme, ensemble by ensemble.

134
Color

Color, whether intensified or tempered, has a profound impact on fashion. Designers must analyze how colors, alone or in combination, will affect a design when integrated into the mix of silhouette, pattern, and detail. They must also anticipate how colors will answer the demands of the season, hour, place, and activity associated with each garment. Colors elicit a physiological and a psychological response. Colors are cultural constructs, whose meanings differ from region to region and change over time, yet always leave their trace. These complex dynamics are embedded in the color story of every collection.

144
Textile

Most garments comprise textiles, formed from natural or man-made fibers, whether weaves, knits, crochets, laces, or felts. Regardless of the type, designers have three distinct choices when it comes to working with fabric. They can follow, force, or invent. Designers interested in a harmonious process will take their cues from the natural properties of a textile. The opposite approach involves manipulating a fabric so that it performs in a way contrary to its innate characteristics. Alternatively, designers can discard conventional fabrics altogether and innovate an entirely new kind of cloth that offers a novel menu of textile traits.

158
Silhouette

The fashion silhouette reflects the physical relationship between the garment and the body of the wearer. Designers might decide to conform to the natural angles, curves, and movements of the human form. They might reshape the body by distorting it into predetermined shapes. Or they might build outward, using the figure as a foundation for shapes that stand alone and apart from it. Unique combinations of garment components—collar, bodice, sleeve, skirt, pant leg—also factor into the final silhouette. When garments are brought together in an ensemble, a new overall shape may emerge that resonates with the collection's individual pieces.

Mary Katrantzou, Spring/Summer 2010.
Photo by Ian Gavan, Getty Images.

Mood Boards

Mood boards provide a physical representation of an otherwise abstract survey of ideas and inspirations. A repository for every photograph, sketch, swatch, and notion, they help to coalesce all information into one central theme. Whether assembled in the form of a collage, a notebook, a file folder, a bulletin board, or an entire wall, the proximity of one image to another, one color to the next, yields many unexpected visual associations. A successful mood board is a living, breathing visual document that continues to evolve throughout the design process.

Photo by Mode Images Limited, Alamy.

Left A mood board overruns the walls of a designer's workspace, 2011
● *Below* Mood boards, design center, Zara, A Coruña, Spain, 2005

Photo by Xurxo Lobato, Cover, Getty Images.

Sketches

The sketch, or *croquis*, is the first schematic for a design. It may be rendered by hand using pencil, marker, ink, or paint; it may also be executed with the assistance of computer-aided design software. The mark of a good fashion sketch, whether hand-drawn or CAD-generated, is its ability to communicate clearly and compellingly both technical information about the intended garment and its overall aesthetic feel.

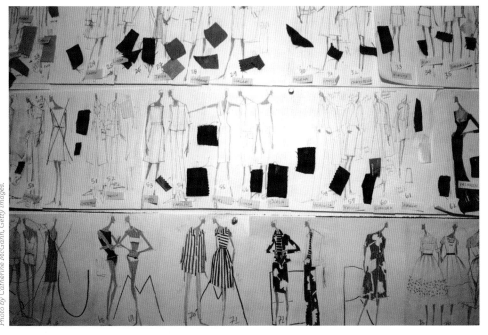

Photo by Catherine McGann, Getty images.

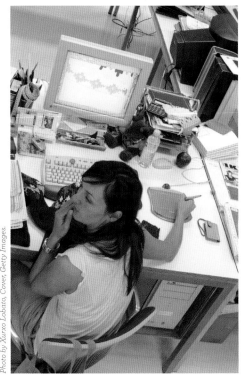

Photo by Xurxo Lobato, Cover, Getty Images.

Above Sketches for a collection, Nara Paz, 2011

Above Top Sketches with fabric swatches, Isaac Mizrahi, 1995 • ***Above*** Sketching with CAD software, Zara, 2005

Color Basics

Color theory derives from the relationships among colors—how they are defined, conceptualized, and applied. Hue refers to a pure color perceived along a visible spectrum of light. Saturation refers to the degree of a hue's intensity. Shades are colors darkened by adding black and tints are colors lightened by adding white. For monochromatic color schemes, fabrics can be dyed with a color in its purest form or at different levels of saturation. Combining the tints and shades of a single hue, such as pink, red, and maroon, creates a tonal palette. All other color combinations can be drawn from the color wheel.

The color wheel sequences the spectrum of hues into a circular diagram. The primary colors are red, blue, and yellow. Mixing two primary colors gives the secondary colors: violet, green, and orange. Mixing a primary and a secondary color produces six tertiary colors: red-violet, blue-violet, blue-green, yellow-green, yellow-orange, and red-orange.

Hue

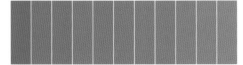

Saturation

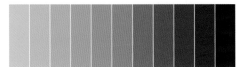

Shades

Tints

Color Wheel

Analogous

Any set of three adjacent hues on the color wheel, such as blue-violet, blue, and blue-green.

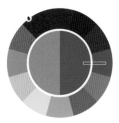

Complementary

Hues directly opposite on the color wheel, such as blue and orange or blue-violet and yellow-orange.

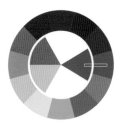

Split Complementary

Hue paired with two others equally spaced from its complement on the color wheel, such as blue, red-orange, and yellow-orange.

Triadic

Any set of three hues positioned equally around the color wheel, such as violet, green, and orange.

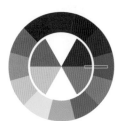

Double Complementary

Any set of two complementary color pairs, such as red and green or yellow and violet.

Left Color and fabric samples in the studio of Sophie Theallet, New York, 2009

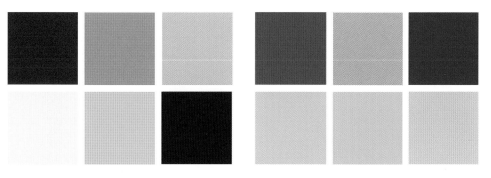

Color Temperature

Colors are grouped by warm hues (reds, oranges, yellows, and some browns/tans), which visually recede, and cool hues (greens, blues, violets, and some grays), which visually advance.

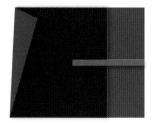

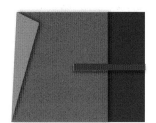

Color Proportion

The same set of colors behaves in profoundly dissimilar ways when combined in varying proportions. Color collections may well encompass more than three hues, but whether within a single garment or on a total look, they fall into three manners of use: foundation, complement, and accent.

Brights

Brights are hues at full intensity. Used entirely or as accents, they can bring power or playfulness to a design.

Photo by Joel Benjamin.

Midtones

Midtones describe the range between bright and pastel colors. They control the volume and intensity of a design.

Photo by Andrew Swaine, courtesy of Nara Paz.

Photo by Andrew Swaine, courtesy of Nara Paz.

Pastels

Pastels are tints of color created by adding white. Pastels speak with a sweet voice and usually appear in Spring/Summer collections.

Photo by Joel Benjamin.

Jewel Tones

Jewel tones are associated with gemstones such as rubies, sapphires, or citrines. Infused with light, they suggest richness and luxury.

Muted Tones

Muted colors are dusty midtones created by adding gray. They imply the patina of age, giving a design a vintage quality.

Photo by Joel Benjamin.

Earth Tones

Earth tones are associated with clay pigments like ochre, umber, and sienna, as well as elements like sand, stone, moss, and bark. They can ground a design in the natural world.

Photo (detail) by Claire Zellar Barclay; hair and makeup by Sarah Brown Roux.

Neutrals

Neutrals comprise the achromatic colors: black, white, silver, and gray. In fashion, camel, khaki, brown, navy, and indigo serve as neutrals for more complex color schemes. They seldom elicit strong responses on their own, allowing for greater focus on the shape, textures, and details of a design.

Photo by firstVIEW; Chloe.

Photo by Tracy Aiguier.

Photo by Chris Moore, Catwalking, Getty Images; Peter Som.

Courtesy of Bottega Veneta.

Color and Texture

Texture greatly affects color. Two cloths of pure cotton in the same shade of blue, one rough woven the other smooth, will elicit different responses. Sequined, satin, and lamé surfaces reflect light, creating a dynamic color that sparkles and shines. Feathered and furred materials, velvets, and felts absorb light, deepening or dulling a color. When layered, sheer fabrics like chiffon, which allow light to pass directly through a color, produce the illusion of multiple color tones.

Photos by Andrew Swaine, courtesy of Nara Paz.

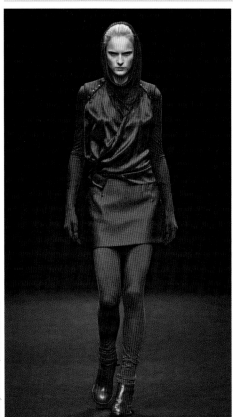

Color Story: Red

Red, the color of blood, symbolizes both death and life. Red arrests attention and signals danger. It is the hue of fire, war, and revolution. It suggests courage but also devilry. An ancient and once costly color (from the cochineal insect), red conveys authority and pomp. Scarlet is provocative: seductively sinful or lustily passionate. Throughout Asia, an intense vermillion is closely associated with prosperity, and some Asian brides wear red as a sign of rebirth into their husband's family. More recently, red has become an emblem of social responsibility. In fashion, red always asserts its presence.

Color Story: White

White is the reflection of all colors. It implies cleanliness and purity. In the nineteenth century, its suggestions of innocence and fresh starts led brides in the West to adopt the color for their wedding day. In Eastern cultures, however, white remains the symbol of mourning. Its associations with ice and snow can give it a psychological chill, but its reflective properties make it cooling in warm climates. For fashion, white is literally a blank canvas.

Photo by Joel Benjamin; Donna Karan.

Photo by konradbak, Fotolia.

Photo by George Mayer, Fotolia.

Photo by Victor Virgile, Gamma-Rapho via Getty Images; Sarah Burton for Alexander McQueen.

Color Story: Black

Black is the absorption of all colors. For many cultures, it has long represented death and mourning. Austere black conveys piety and respectability. The color of the night, it can be darkly sensual and mysterious. Both power and rebellion are clothed in black. Black is the confident uniform of the city, embodying a kind of urban armor. And no garment is more versatile or iconic than the little black dress. Today, elegant or tough, black dominates fashion.

Fibers

Fibers are the most basic component of a textile. Natural fibers can be plant based, like flax and cotton, or animal based, like silk or wool. Referred to as staple fibers, most natural fibers are short and must be twisted together to form yarn. By contrast, silk is a filament fiber, a single cocoon is capable of yielding thousands of yards.

Manufactured fibers can come from minerals, such as fiberglass and foils. They can be formed from regenerated wood pulp or cotton linters, such as rayon and acetate. Or they can be entirely synthetic, such the polymer-based polyester, acrylic, and nylon. These filament fibers can be extruded from machines in infinite widths and lengths.

Each of these fibers has a particular "hand," or feel, and each has certain performance properties. Designers must know a fiber's strength, weight, and absorbency, its resistance to abrasion, wrinkling, or heat, how quickly it dries or wicks, and how well it drapes, retains its shape, or stretches.

Engraving by William Hincks, Library of Congress.

Above Sewing and harrowing flax seeds, Ireland, 1782

Photo by Caroline Vancoillie, iStockphoto.

Photo by Peter Pattavina, iStockphoto.

Photo by laughingmango, iStockphoto.

Above Left Flax plants •
Above Cotton bolls • *Left*
Silkworm cocoons

Photo by Daniel MAR, iStockphoto.

Left Shearing the wool of an angora goat, France, 2008

Photo by Leonid Shcheglov, Fotolia

Above Manufacturing synthetic threads, Belarus, 2011

Yarns

To be woven or knit into fabric, fibers must first be made into yarns. (Threads are finer yarns used for sewing or embroidery.) To transform short staple fibers into continuous strands, they must be spun. The resultant high twist creates a strong yarn, which if broken can rely on the neighboring fibers for support. Filament fibers have a low twist or no twist at all. They make for smoother, more uniform and lustrous yarns but are weaker. A yarn may come in various plies, determined by the number of strands that are twisted together to create it. Plying allows different fibers to be blended together into one yarn. The goal might be to improve performance, reduce costs, or create an aesthetic effect.

Above Spinning yarn, Tamil Nadu, India, 2011

Above Industrial spinner in a textile factory, 2010

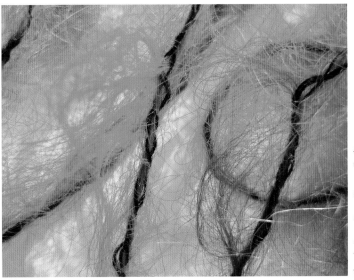

Above Left Homespun wool yarns • ***Above*** Mohair yarns

Above Silk embroidery threads

Wovens

Woven textiles are made on a loom and comprise vertical yarns called the *warp* and horizontal yarns called the *weft*, or filling, that cross at right angles, creating the grain. The three basic weave types are a plain (muslin, voile, chiffon, organza, taffeta), twill (denim, gabardine, tweed, serge,), and satin (satin, sateen, charmeuse).

Pile weaves add extra sets of looped warps or fillings, which are cut (velvet, velveteen, corduroy) or left uncut (terry cloth). Jacquard looms combine plain, twill, and satin weaves into patterns that are integral to the fabric (brocade, damask). The greater complexity adds to their cost, but the designs will not fade or wear out. Woven textiles tend to hold their shape over time, so are ideal for more tailored garments.

Right Burberry, Fall/
Winter 2009/10 • *Below*
Handloom, Ireland, 2006

Photo by *first*VIEW.

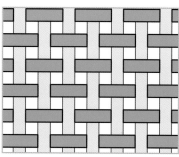

PLAIN WEAVE

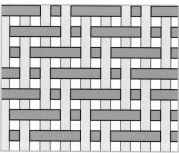

TWILL WEAVE

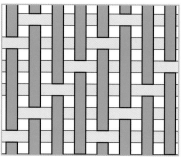

SATIN WEAVE

Photo by Nico Smit, iStockphoto.

Right Back-strap loom,
India, ca. 1965–71

Left Power loom,
Scotland, 2011

Knits

Knitting uses needles to produce consecutive rows of interlocking loops, or stitches. A wale is a column of loops that runs vertically and a course is a row of stitches that runs horizontally. The two basic stitches are the knit and the purl. Knit stitches typically form the face of the fabric, while purl stitches appear on the reverse. Alternating between them creates cables, ribs, and other three-dimensional patterns. Knitting machines can be fully fashioned (shaped panels), flat (unlimited yardage), or circular (long, seamless tubes).

Knit loops can be dense or open, depending on the size of the needles. Knits, too, can be either warp or weft (filling) faced. Knit fabrics include double knit, jersey, and interlock. Knits are warm and wrinkle resistant and provide greater stretch than wovens.

Above Right Missoni, Fall/Winter 2011/12 • *Right* Circular knitting machine, Mauritius, 2007 • *Below* Flat knitting machine, Bangladesh, 2011

Photo by firstVIEW.

KNIT STITCH

PURL STITCH

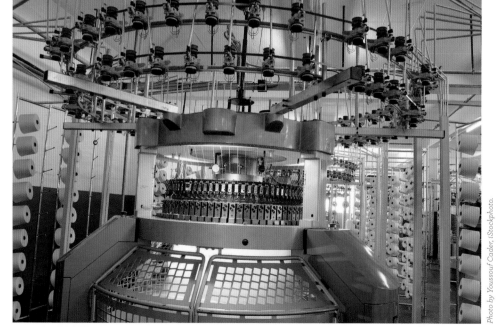

Photo by Youssouf Cader, iStockphoto.

Photo by Cross Design, Fotolia.

Right Christopher Kane,
Fall/Winter 2011/12

Photo by Victor Virgile, Gamma-Rapho via Getty Images.

Crochet

Crochet relies on a single hook to build a chain of loops, which becomes the foundation for additional rows. In crochet, a stitch is supported by and supports the stitch on either side of it. This process creates patterns that can range from tight and flat to open and lacy. Although strongly associated with traditional craftwork, crochet can be combined with other materials to create garments with a more modern look.

Right Roberto Cavalli,
Spring/Summer 2011

Photo by Oliver Morin, AFP, Getty Images.

Macramé

Macramé builds an openwork textile by hand tying yarns or leather cords into square knots and hitching knots. The technique, of medieval origin, traditionally favors fringes and incorporating beads and other decorative items into a garment's design. Cavandoli is a style of macramé known for its geometric patterns and free-form shapes.

Lace

True lace is an openwork textile constructed by looping, twisting, and braiding threads without the benefit of a backing fabric. Needle, bobbin, and cutwork (also called whitework) lace were the three options prior to the nineteenth century. Machine-made varieties such as appliqué lace are manufactured on a fine net, which may or may not be removed. Laces can also employ techniques like knitting, crochet, and macramé or work ribbon or tape into the design.

Photo by firstVIEW.

Left Erdem, Spring/ Summer, 2011

Photo by Nancy Nehring, iStockphoto.

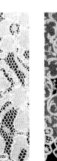

Photo by Roberto Mendolicchio, Fotolia.

Above Left Needle Lace ●
Above Bobbin Lace

Photo by Ruslan Kudrin, Fotolia.

Above Appliqué Lace

Photo by anzeletti, iStockphoto.

Above Cutwork Lace

Photo by firstVIEW.

Felt

Felting is possibly the oldest method for making fabric. Traditionally, heat and moisture combined with pressure and friction would entangle the scalelike fibers of wool into a dense, matted structure of great strength and warmth. Needle felting uses barbed needles to achieve a similar result. Today, many other fibers, including cotton and rayon, can be bonded together using thermal, mechanical, and chemical processes.

Right Viktor & Rolf, Fall/
Winter 2011/12

Courtesy of Filz Felt.

Right Industrial felt rolls

Dyeing

Dyeing may occur at any stage of the manufacturing process. Applying dyes to fiber (stock and top dyeing) or to yarn (skein, package, and beam dyeing) gives the greatest penetration of color. Applying dyes to cloth (jet, jig, pad, and beam dyeing) produces affordable solid-colored fabrics. Simple apparel such as T-shirts and hosiery might be dyed only after they are constructed.

Different fabrics require distinct types of dye, depending on their fiber content. Cellulose-based fabrics such as cotton or bamboo are colored using fiber-reactive, direct/substantive, or vat dyes. Protein-based fabrics such as mohair or cashmere are colored using vat, acid, or indirect/mordant dyes that need a bonding agent. Synthetics have individual demands that might include disperse, pigment, basic, and metal complex acid dyes.

Right Yarn dyeing, Cappadocia, Turkey, 2007

Photo by Alberto Nó, iStockphoto.

Right Unbleached, undyed cotton cloth, De Angeli-Frua factory, Italy, 1947

Photo by Alfred Eisenstaedt, Time & Life Pictures, Getty Images.

Above Textile dyeing, Yunnan Province, China, 2005 • *Left* Drying cloth after dyeing, Kabul, Afghanistan, 1990

Printing

Textile printing is the application of color in specific patterns to a fabric. Printing includes hand blocking, stencil, heat transfer, resist, and discharge processes. The most common practices today are screen, roller, and digital printing.

Screen printing pushes colors through a mesh screen whose perforations form the pattern. Each color requires a separate screen; when two dyes overlap, known as overdyeing, a third color may be produced without an additional screen. With roller printing, designs are first engraved into copper rollers. The process entails greater expense and planning but is efficient for larger runs of fabrics that have fine painterly details.

The photographic quality of digital printing has revolutionized the textile industry. Designers use CAD technologies to quickly develop highly detailed textile patterns, which are sent to ink-jet printers to transfer to fabrics or garment pieces. For now, this process tends to be reserved for small runs of specialty and custom fabric, but it is becoming increasingly accessible.

Photo by Diorgi, Fotolia.

Above Block printing, India, 2011

Photo by Alfred Eisenstaedt, Time & Life Pictures, Getty Images.

Above Machine printing, De Angeli-Frua factory, Italy, 1947

Photo by Franc & Jean Shor, National Geographic, Getty Images.

Above Screen printing, Glarus Canton, Switzerland, 1956

Above Printed cotton
designed by Saul Steinberg,
late 1940s

Right Digital print dress by
Mary Katrantzou,
Spring/Summer 2011

Silhouette

In developing a silhouette, designers must contend with basic geometries. The *x-axis* (horizontal) and *y-axis* (vertical) constitute the width and length of a shape; the *z-axis* (depth) pulls a shape off the two-dimensional plane, transforming it into a three-dimensional volume. These relationships are fundamental to every shape that conforms to or surrounds the human body.

Famous for his dramatic, rounded hourglass silhouette of 1947, Christian Dior introduced a series of collections that he named after the alphabetical impression of their shape. In 1954, the H Line realigned the female figure by dropping the waist, essentially creating a straight line from shoulder to hip. In 1955 the A Line drew a shape that flared out from the shoulder. In 1956, the Y Line flipped this shape, emphasizing the shoulder and tapering to the knee in a narrow skirt.

Cristóbal Balenciaga was another master of redefining the relationship between garment and body. His tunic, chemise, baby doll, and sack dresses were all innovative manipulations of the waist. For his empire line, he cut dresses and coats like kimonos. For his signature cocoon coats and balloon jackets, he boldly enveloped the female figure in abstract sculptural forms.

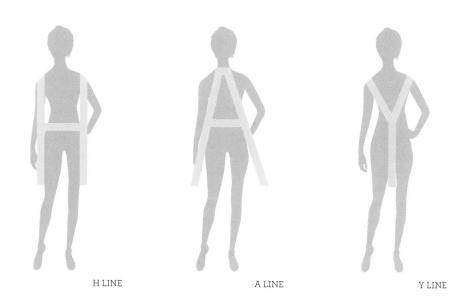

H LINE   A LINE   Y LINE

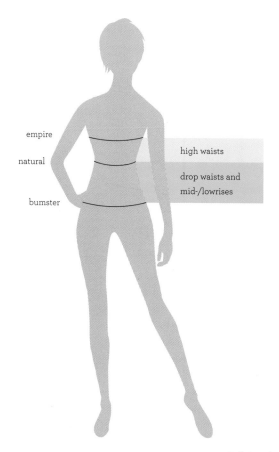

empire

natural

high waists

drop waists and mid-/lowrises

bumster

Left Waistlines

Left Balenciaga, Spring/
Summer 2008

Necklines

CREW

JEWEL

BATEAU

SCOOP

U-NECK

COWL

V-NECK

SQUARE

SWEETHEART

KEYHOLE

SURPLICE

HALTER

Collars

PETER PAN

SAILOR

SAILOR (BACK)

CONVERTIBLE

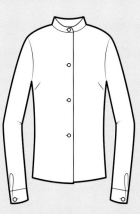

BAND

BUTTON-DOWN

MANDARIN

JABOT

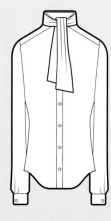

ASCOT

SHAWL

TURTLENECK

MOCK TURTLENECK

Sleeves

CAP

PETAL

THREE-QUARTERS

FLUTTER

BELL

BISHOP

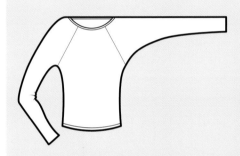

RAGLAN

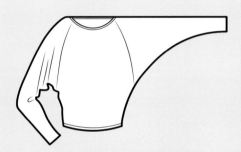

DOLMAN

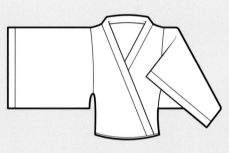

KIMONO

PUFF

JULIET

LEG-O'-MUTTON

Tops and Blouses

BUSTIER

CAMISOLE

SHELL

HENLEY

POLO

TUNIC

BLOUSON

PEASANT

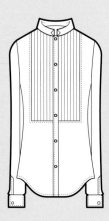

TUXEDO

WESTERN

CAMP

Jackets

BLAZER

DOUBLE-BREASTED

TAILCOAT

TUXEDO

CARDIGAN

BOLERO

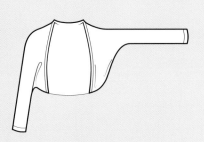

SHRUG

SAFARI

MOTORCYCLE

BOMBER

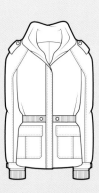

PARKA

Coats

PEACOAT

A-LINE

TRENCH

BALMACAAN

CHESTERFIELD

COCOON

Dresses

SHEATH

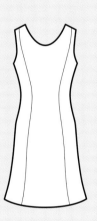

PRINCESS

SLIP

HALTER

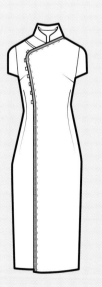

CHEONGSAM

WRAP

TRAPEZE

BLOUSON

WEDGE

EMPIRE

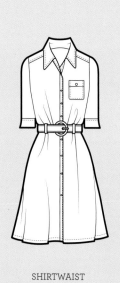

SHIRTWAIST

DROPWAIST

Skirts

STRAIGHT

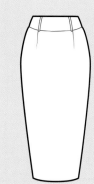

PENCIL

A-LINE

CIRCLE

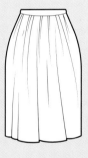

TRUMPET

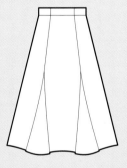

GODET

DIRNDL

TULIP

WRAP

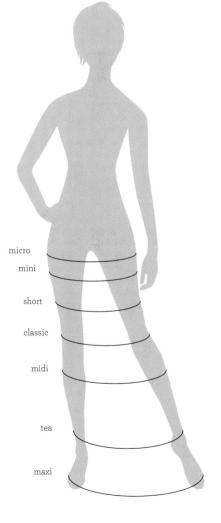

micro

mini

short

classic

midi

tea

maxi

Above Skirt Lengths

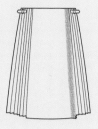

KILTED

SARONG

TIERED

BUBBLE

POUF

HANDKERCHIEF

Pants

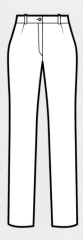

STRAIGHT

TAPERED

FLARED

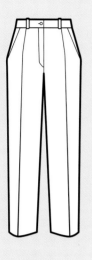

CLASSIC

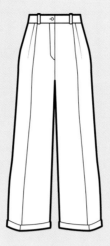

BAGGY

SAILOR

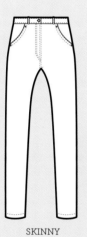

SKINNY

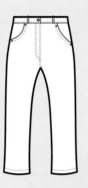

CAPRI

LEGGINGS

PALAZZO

DHOTI

HAREM

Construction

The patternmaking process might start with draping or with drafting. Regardless of which technique is implemented, the precision of the decisions made at this stage will ultimately allow for the clearest expression of the designer's vision. To the untrained eye, it may seem that the designer has already determined every choice, but the value of a good patternmaker cannot be overstated. Patternmakers interpret a design in tangible, three-dimensional terms. By controlling fit, adding ease, adjusting seams, or positioning pockets and other details, they address every imaginable consideration for a successful garment.

Machine and hand sewing are the first necessary skills, but stitchers must develop a considerable level of expertise before they can construct a quality garment. To be adept at fashioning garments, they must know how to prep pieces by ironing and basting; anticipate how fabrics will behave when cut and sewn; plan the most productive order for assembling garment components; master the application of linings, interfaces, interlinings, trims and notions; and understand how to steam and press the garment into shape at every step.

Viktor & Rolf, Spring/Summer 2011
Photo by Pascal Le Segretain, Getty Images.

Draping

For some designers, draping is a form of sketching in three dimensions with fabric, and they use the process to generate their earliest ideas for a garment. More often, designers turn their initial sketches over to drapers, who create "roughs," or *toiles*, on a dress form using cotton muslin or jersey. With these inexpensive materials, drapers can test the designer's concept, making informed choices before committing to the final fashion fabric. Throughout this process, pinning and marking, the draper intuitively places darts and tucks, manipulates fullness, and adjusts other shaping details and any decorative elements. In the end, all information on the *toile* must be transferred and trued on paper to create a flat pattern from which to accurately produce a sample garment.

Right Madeleine Vionnet draping a design on her articulated wooden dummy at a one-fifth scale, 1923

Photo by Thérèse Bonney, Hulton Archive.

Photo by Daniel Acker, Bloomberg via Getty Images.

Above Creating a *toile* on a dress form, Nanette Lapore, New York, 2010

Flat Patternmaking

The flat patternmaker brings to the workroom the skills to engineer a finished garment from the designer's sketch or draped pattern. Whether developed for a single sample or for a large-run production, the math and mapping of a design directly affects the bottom line. Keeping in mind a garment's purpose as well as how it will be maintained, patternmakers must address the overall complexity of a design, the efficient use of fabric, and the time and skill required to construct the garment.

Using pencils and measuring tools or CAD programs, patternmakers draft paper patterns. The pattern pieces show dart placement and seam allowances; they also include grain lines and notches to indicate fabric direction and pattern matching, as well as information for scaling the pattern to other sizes. Many patternmakers develop slopers—basic patterns without seam allowance—that they modify repeatedly for new styles while retaining the ideal fit of their sample size.

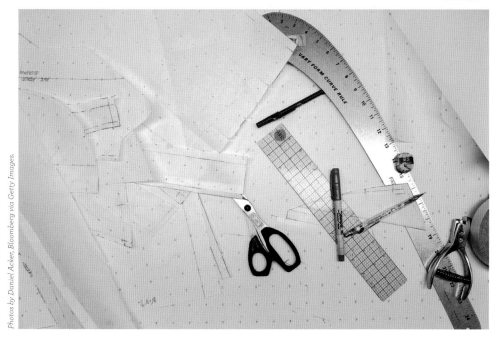

Photos by Daniel Acker, Bloomberg via Getty Images.

Above Top Cutting a paper pattern, Nanette Lapore, 2010 •
Above Patternmaking tools

Fabric Manipulation

Fabric manipulation transforms textiles, increasing the variables involved in the design process. A wide variety of methods can be employed to restrain, release, or redirect the power of the cloth. Skillful draping, stitching, and heat setting help to build new characteristics into couture.

Forgoing traditional tailoring techniques, Madeleine Vionnet created garments that conformed to the body by draping on the bias; that is, against the grain. The same give and ease of fit that is achieved by changing the direction of the grain-line also affects the freedom and flow of movement. Understanding the properties of the bias in draping can mean the difference between flares that ripple gracefully or roll robustly.

Simple tucks, regimented pleats, and complex origami-inspired folding can serve as architectural devices that reinforce, reshape, or reinvent an area. Pleats may be set by hand or secured by stitches for fabrics of almost any fiber content; heat setting is used primarily on synthetic fabrics. Heat-set pleats can run the gamut from crisply creased sunburst pleats to more organic primitive pleats. Designers Mariano Fortuny, Mary McFadden, and Issey Miyake are well known for their innovative interpretations of primitive pleating, effectively resurfacing a garment while retaining the overall silhouette.

Ruching, shirring, and smocking are all controlled methods of crafting fullness into patterns with stitches; gathers, too, are useful in constructing a myriad of silhouettes. Cristóbal Balenciaga, known for the bubble skirt, also gathered fabrics into ruffles, bells, and poufs to create his bold sculptural forms.

Photo by William Albert Allard, National Geographic, Getty Images.

Above Top Creating pleats in fabric • *Above* Issey Miyake, "cicada" pleats created in collaboration with textile designer Makiko Minagawa, first shown Spring/Summer 1989

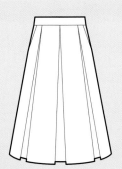

BOX PLEAT

SIDE PLEAT

KNIFE PLEAT

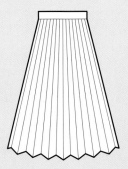

ACCORDION PLEAT

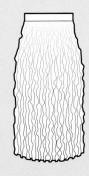

MUSHROOM PLEAT

CARTRIDGE PLEAT

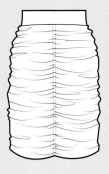

RUCHING

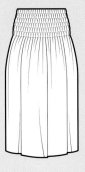

SHIRRING

SMOCKING

CASCADES

FLARES

DRAPES

Dart Manipulation

Building on the foundation, a patternmaker can manipulate measurements and dart placement mathematically. The primary function of a dart is to control fullness. A dart can also be split into multiple darts and repositioned to contribute to the aesthetic of a design.

Above and Left Waistband dart slashed, spread apart, and pivoted to create a shoulder dart

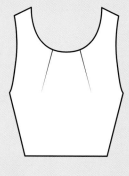

NECKLINE

FAN

INVERTED Y

INVERTED T

SHOULDER

ARMHOLE

BUST

SIDESEAM

WAISTBAND

T

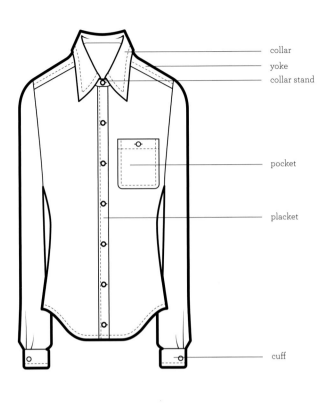

collar
yoke
collar stand

pocket

placket

cuff

Details

The details of a garment can be structural or decorative or both. Tacking and topstitching, for instance, will reinforce an area, but when applied in interesting patterns and contrasting colors, they become aesthetic elements as well. Beyond their practical value, pockets can be instrumental in the overall look of a garment when scale, structure, and placement are considered creatively. For even the simplest design, such as a basic man's dress shirt, different collars or cuffs create subtle shifts in style. Functional closures like buttons, zippers, hooks, toggles, and ties often become focal points.

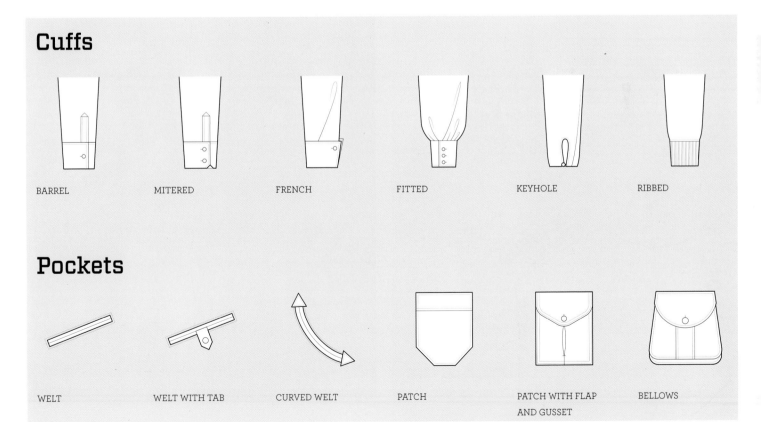

Cuffs

BARREL   MITERED   FRENCH   FITTED   KEYHOLE   RIBBED

Pockets

WELT   WELT WITH TAB   CURVED WELT   PATCH   PATCH WITH FLAP   BELLOWS
AND GUSSET

Digitizing, Grading & Marker Making

Technology allows much of patternmaking to be computerized. Designers can develop a pattern entirely through a CAD system such as Gerber or Lectra or scan existing patterns for redrafting and correcting. These digital patterns transcend language and cultural differences that could later complicate the manufacturing process.

Digital patterns are also used in grading and marker making. Grading is the process by which each sample pattern piece is revised to create the full set of sizes in which a garment will be made available. Marker making maps out the most economical configuration for cutting a garment from the fashion fabric, considering constraints such as grain, nap, and pattern.

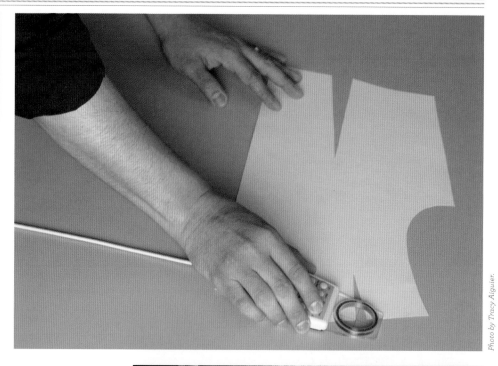

Photo by Tracy Aiguier.

Above Using a Gerber digitizer to scan a sloper

• *Right* Marking bolts of tartan for efficient pattern matching, 1955

Above Grading notations on a pattern piece

Photo by Matteo Natale, Fotolia.

Photo by J. Baylor Roberts, National Geographic, Getty Images.

Cutting

Cutting is the first stage in the fabrication of a garment and helps to ensure that the fit and drape remain true to the original pattern. Designers can continue to experiment with a design at this point, by positioning pattern pieces on different grain lines to produce alternate versions of their concept.

Photo by Ton Koene, Picture Contact BV, Alamy.

Above Cutting the fashion fabric. Note the slopers hanging behind the cutter.

Stitching

The first step in stitching a garment together usually involves basting, a temporary stitch that allows the stitcher to secure areas well enough to determine where adjustments may need to be made. It also serves as a guide for the placement of permanent stitches.

In the couture process, garments are always hand finished and, in some cases, assembled completely by hand. A variety of stitches can be done by hand, including the basting stitch, back stitch, buttonhole stitch, whip stitch, cross stitch, and blind stitch. Some are used to join the components of a garment or to secure a hem, while others are purely decorative.

Industrial sewing machines produce a basic straight stitch and are often favored in mass production and situations that demand strength and durability from each seam. There are specialty machines as well: the buttonhole machine, the embroidery machine, the blind stitch machine for hemming, and the overlock machine, or serger, which finishes seams to prevent raveling. Dressmakers and tailors also use a variety of these techniques and machines to create garments or make alterations and repairs.

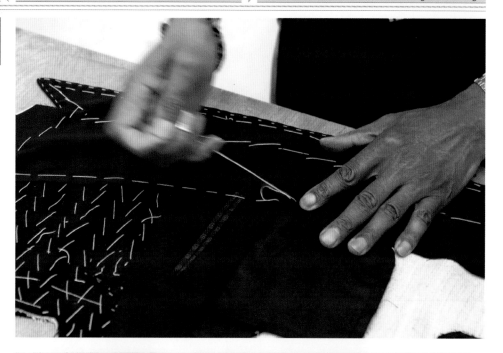

Photos from Bloomberg via Getty Images.

Above Top Tailor stitching a waistcoat at Huntsman Tailors, Savile Row, 2006 •
Above Seamstress putting finishing stitches to a couture gown, Valentino, 2006

Basic Stitches

Basting Stitch

Running Stitch

Back Stitch

Chain Stitch

Finishing Stitches

Whip or Overcast Stitch

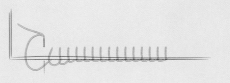

Blanket Stitch

Buttonhole Stitch

Cross Stitch

Hem Stitches

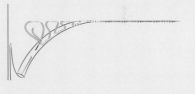

Running Hem Stitch

Vertical Hem Stitch

Slip or Blind Hem Stitch

Catch or Herringbone Stitch

Fitting

Fitting a sample is a measure of quality control, verifying the soundness of the design and the desired fit of each element of the garment. Fit models embody the measurements of a designer's ideal sample size. They allow designers to observe their work in movement and provide direct feedback about issues such as comfort and ease. Designers will arrange for multiple fittings to ensure that every issue has been addressed and that all adjustments have been executed successfully. When establishing the right fit for production, any modifications will make their way back to the original pattern. The goal of fitting may also be to customize a garment for a specific client or for a runway or editorial model.

Photo by Jean-Noel de Soye, Gamma-Rapho via Getty Images.

Photo by Julia Xanthos, New York Daily News via Getty Images.

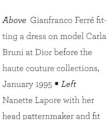

Above Gianfranco Ferré fitting a dress on model Carla Bruni at Dior before the haute couture collections, January 1995 • *Left* Nanette Lapore with her head patternmaker and fit model, February 2010

Finishing

Once a garment is sewn, it must be finished. This may encompass bias binding of seams, removing tacking, adding thread loops for closures or belts, securing buttons or hook and eyes, hemming, and attaching labels. Decorative elements such as hand embroidery, appliqué, sequins, beads, or jewels may be applied postproduction. Quality craftsmanship demands checking for missed stitches, loose threads, or other flaws. The completed garment receives a final steaming and pressing before being properly packed for storage or delivery.

Photo by Jean-Noël de Soye, Gamma-Rapho via Getty Images.

Above Label hand-stitched into a custom-made suit by Giorgio Armani, 2006

Production

188
Specifications

Once the prototype for a garment has met the expectations of the design room, every element involved in producing that first in-house sample must be documented and prepared for use as a reference throughout the entire production process. Regardless of scale, when a design moves into this phase, all pertinent details about the selected fabrics and notions, and all instructions for the proper cutting, construction, and finishing of the garment, must be streamlined and spelled out in a clear manner that can be understood and executed by any domestic or foreign manufacturer. Pre-production samples from the factory ensure that the designer's specifications have been adhered to successfully and that quality garments can be made in quantity.

191
Manufacturing

To select the right manufacturing process for apparel involves numerous considerations. Some large fashion companies have successfully integrated design, prototyping, construction, and distribution into a single operation. In most cases, however, production is outsourced, often to factories in foreign countries. The choice to go overseas may be driven by economics, but it may also be a matter of finding the manufacturer best suited to the specific needs of the job. Always a vital concern, quality control is especially challenging when working internationally. In the end, designers must balance issues of cost, productivity, culture differences, technologies, delivery systems, and ethics.

Worker assembling shirts at the TAL Apparel factory, Hong Kong, 2011
Photo by Daniel J. Groshong, Bloomberg via Getty Images.

Tech Pack

The production process begins when the designer, illustration in hand, meets with the technical designer to work out the design specifications. This encompasses specific details about the garment's construction, such as measurements and choice of fabrics, closures, or trim. In large companies, the manufacturer might produce the sample pattern, but in smaller operations the job often falls to an in-house sample maker.

Once all of the data is gathered, the technical designer creates a technical package, or tech pack, consisting of a technical drawing, a grades-specific sheet (spec sheet), and a construction and trim detail sheet. The technical drawing, known as a flat sketch, customarily represents the garment laid flat. Although the rendering is scaled down, it reflects the relative proportions of design details in the actual garment. It may also contain notes and measurements. The specifications include any pertinent production information, such as cutting, sewing, or finishing instructions.

Most companies use Production Management System (PMS) software to create their tech packs. However developed, the tech pack provides everything necessary for the manufactured garment to realize the designer's vision.

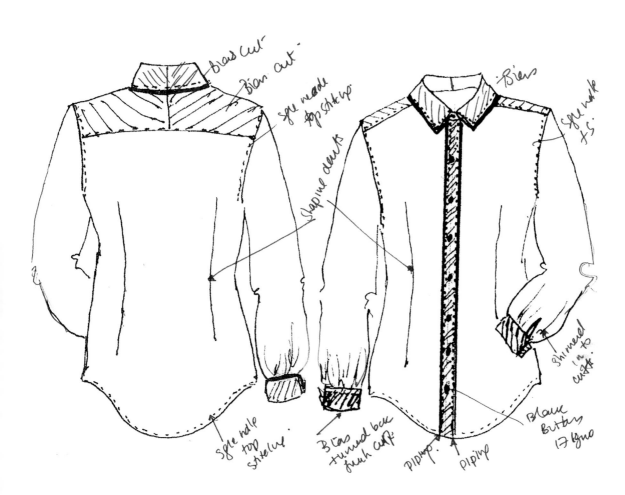

Left Flat sketch of the model "Cindi" with designer's handwritten notes, The Essential White Shirt, Fall 2011

KATITI
the essential white shirt
L/slve shirt with contrast bias piping

GRADED MEASUREMENTS

Style:Cindi F1102

Season: Fall 11   Created: 9/30/10

Modified: Approved:

Front View

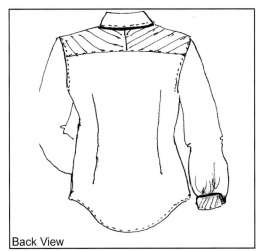

Back View

Description	Tol (-)	Tol (+)	S	[M]	L
Length from HPS	1/2	3/8	27 1/2	28	28 1/2
Across Shoulder -set in**	1/4		15 1/2	16	16 1/2
Across Front 5" below HPS -set in**	3/4		14	14 1/2	15
Across Back 5" below HPS -set in**			15	15 1/2	16
Chest Circ 1" below AH **			36	38	40
Front waist pos from HPS (X)			15 1/2	16	16 1/2
Waist Circ (X) below HPS **			33	35	37
Sweep Circ Straight **			39 1/2	41 1/2	43 1/2
Armhole along curve Circ			17 1/2	18 1/2	19 1/2
L/ Slve Lngth fr AH to edge of turned back cuff	**		22 1/2	23	23 1/2
Muscle Circ 1" Below Armhole			12 1/2	13 1/2	14 1/2
Sleeve Opening Circ LS			7 1/2	8	8 1/2
Sleeve Cuff Height Unfolded			4	4	4
Sleeve Placket Width continuos flap			3/8	3/8	3/8
Sleeve Placket Length			3	3	3
Front Neck depth fr I/L @ CF to seam	1/4		2 3/8	2 1/2	2 5/8
Back Neck depth fr I/L @ CB to seam	1/4		5/8	5/8	5/8
Neck Width HPS to HPS			6 3/4	7	7 1/4
Colar Height at CB incl contrast piping		1/4	2 1/4	2 1/4	2 1/4
Neck Band Height at CB			1 1/2	1 1/2	1 1/2
Colar Point		1/8	2 5/8	2 5/8	2 5/8
Colar Length Point to Point inc contrast piping		1/4	15 3/8	15 7/8	16 3/8
Shoulder Forward at HPS			3/4	3/4	3/4
Shoulder Slope at HPS			1 1/2	1 1/2	1 1/2
Shirt Tail Height F&B			0		0
Hem Depth			1/4	1/4	1/4
Back Yoke Height from CB			3	3	3
Front Placket Width Incl contrast piping**		1/4	1 1/4	1 1/4	1 1/4
Bias cut contrast piping width			1/8	1/8	1/8
Pocket Width			0		0
Chest Pocket Placement from HPS			- 1/4		1/4

Left Tech Pack specs for
"Cindi"

Prepro

Based on the tech pack, pattern, and materials for each garment, the factory makes a pre-production sample, or prepro, either in the contracted fabric or in a fabric with identical quality and thread count. The factory also sends "lab dips"—swatches of the contracted fabric and any artwork (for printed fabrics) or dyed yarns. Bulk fabric purchasing, dyeing, and printing cannot proceed until the designer and technical design team have approved all of the lab dips.

When the prepro arrives in the design studio, the technical designer fits the garment on a model in the presence of the designer (and sometimes the production manager) to make sure that it corresponds to all specifications laid out in the tech pack. The technical designer and production manager will go back and forth with the factory until the sample meets the designer's standards.

Once the prepro is approved, the factory makes a top-of-production sample (TOPS), and once that is approved, bulk production begins.

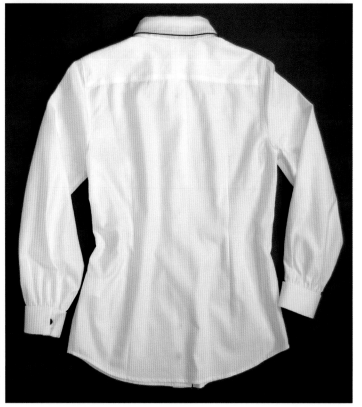

Courtesy of Katiti Kironde.

Left Prepro of "Cindi"

Factories

Most independent factories specialize in a particular category or type of garment. They may also be structured to deal with different scales of production. Factories that are set up for large-scale manufacturing usually impose minimums, while smaller operations can provide the kind of attention and services required to produce small runs. Depending on the garment type, factories may present a choice between piecework or assembly-line production. In the interest of reducing costs, some factories offer an expanded menu of services, from the provision of fabrics and notions to direct distribution.

Production managers in any factory are responsible for overseeing the entire production process. They maintain open lines of communication between the designer and the factory to keep the process on schedule and on budget. When working with overseas manufacturers, fashion houses may contract with local agents to be on site on their behalf to evaluate and report back on a factory's practices and productivity. When language barriers exist these representatives also serve as translators. Global sourcing teams are employed to identify the international manufacturers best suited to a designer's needs and to negotiate agreements between the two. They also ensure that these factories comply with child labor laws and fair working conditions.

Photo by Micky Wiswedel, iStockphoto.

Photo by Rob Crandall, Photo Library.

Top Cutting pattern pieces in a garment factory, Cape Town, South Africa, 2010

• *Above* Stitching Mango jeans in a garment factory, Shenzhen, Guangdong, China, 2010

Vertically Integrated Design

Vertically integrated companies design, test, produce, deliver, and sell their own products. Eliminating middlemen in the supply chain allows them to reduce costs, oversee quality control, and maintain brand consistency throughout the entire process. This business model also reduces the possibility of delays that might be caused by a dependency on other companies. Most large firms that follow this approach still rely on push manufacturing, which involves committing to the production of predetermined quantities at least twelve to sixteen months in advance. This timetable puts them at a disadvantage in a fashion marketplace where speed is as important as style.

One clear exception is Zara, a subsidiary of industry giant Inditex. It has taken vertical integration a step further, by instituting a quick response system at its campus that can take a design from sketch to store in fewer than three weeks. Headquarters sends out prototypes twice a week, solicits feedback from the retail stores worldwide, and produces only the most popular items in small lots, ensuring that each location has a unique mix of goods on hand at any given time. This rapid production cycle provides Zara with a sharp competitive edge, allowing it to answer any trend immediately.

Photo by Xurxo Lobato, Cover, Getty Images.

Above Top Design center of the Zara factory, A Coruña, Spain, 2005 • ***Above*** Pressing finished garments, Zara factory, 2005

Distribution

Once garments have successfully maneuvered through the manufacturing cycle, they are prepared for distribution. When a production run is complete, the factory sends it to a consolidator who works with a customs agent to make sure all the paperwork is in order. Afterwards, the consolidator will sort and pack the merchandise by destination. Shipments can be sent either to a central warehouse or directly to retailers. As soon as goods coming from overseas are on a container ship, known as "freight on board," ownership and responsibility shifts from the manufacturer to the design company. The entire distribution process must be a consistent extension of the fashion brand, from the physical (hangers, shipping boxes) to the logistical (delivery channels, returns).

Photo by Rob Crandall, Photo Library.

Photo by Xurxo Lobato, Cover, Getty Images.

Left Top Preparing finished garments for shipping from a Shenzhen factory •
Left Cargo planes waiting to transport Zara clothing from Spain to Greece, 2005

Working Conditions

As an investigative photographer for the National Child Labor Committee, Lewis Hine documented the working conditions of children in the United States between 1908 and 1924. The environment of the textile mills created serious health problems, from stunted growth and curvature of the spine to chronic bronchitis; long hours of hard work led to high accident rates from physical and mental fatigue. Deprived of an education, children were condemned to a future of illiteracy and poverty. Not until the New Deal was child labor legislation effectively put in place.

Today, around the globe, textile and apparel workers, adult and child, still seek a living wage, safe working conditions, and freedom of association.

Photos by Lewis Wickes Hine, Library of Congress.

Above Young spinner, Mollahan Mills, Newberry, South Carolina, 1908 • *Left* Young doffer in a Lincolnton, North Carolina, mill, 1918

Far Left Ten-year-old spinner, Lincolnton, North Carolina, 1908 • *Left* Fifteen-year-old drawing-in worker, Berkshire Cotton Mills, Adams, Massachusetts, 1916

Photo by Lewis Wickes Hine, Library of Congress.

Photo by Mario Tama, Getty Images.

Above Textile worker, Cheney Silk Mills, South Manchester, Connecticut, 1924, where working conditions were favorable • *Left* Garment workers protesting working conditions at Liberty Apparel, New York, 2004

Life of a Garment

Drawing by
Michael Alexander Guran

2. Designer creates toile

1. Designer sketches dress

11. Dress inspires another designer

10. Owner consigns dress

9. Dress goes to dry cleaners

3. Cutter cuts pattern in fabric

4. Designer fits dress on model

5. Model shows dress on runway

8. Dress is admired

7. Shopper discovers dress

6. Garment worker sews dress

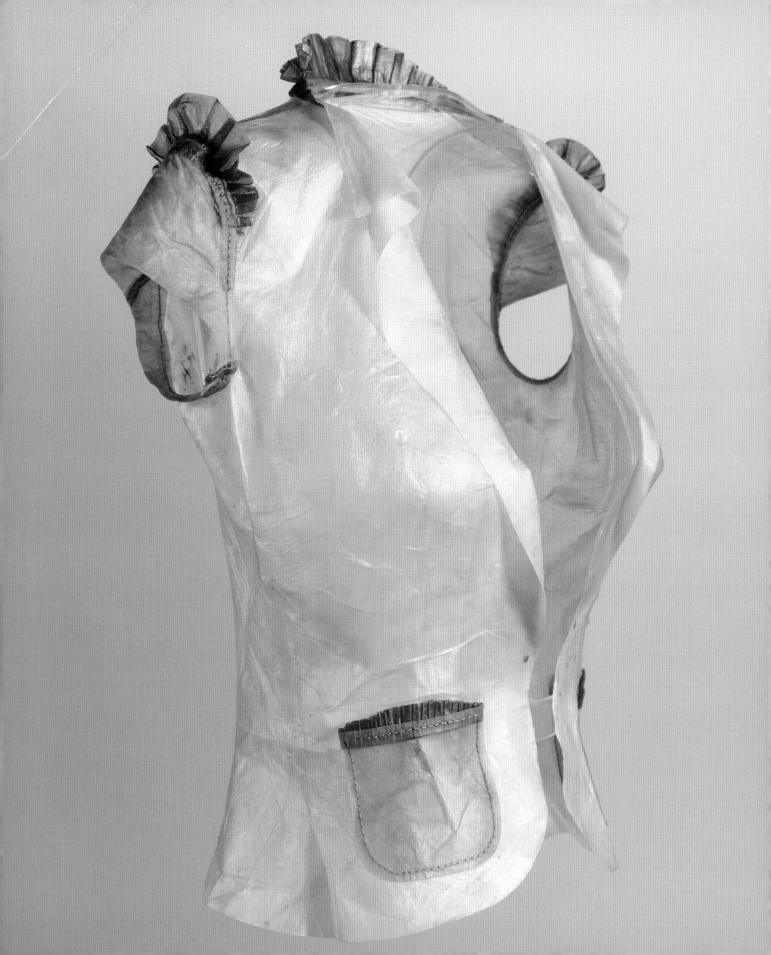

Evolution

200
Sustainability

Sustainability occupies a now-integral but still-evolving position in the fashion conversation. Ecofriendly designers are concerned with the origins, processing, and eventual disposal of their fashion products. Yet the fragmented nature of the apparel business poses real challenges to creating a sustainable strategy. There are many possible, often overlapping approaches, each with advantages and disadvantages for an industry that thrives on consumption. Considerations include practices that reduce energy use and toxic emissions, practices that promote durability over disposability, practices that improve trading conditions in developing countries and that advance social equality everywhere, practices that promote local resources and local talents, practices that eliminate waste through recycling or upcycling. In their search for new materials and processes that play a positive ecological role, designers have turned both to tradition and to science.

210
Technology

Technological innovation has long served to push the frontiers of fashion design. Utilitarian applications have included garments that protect against the weather, enhance performance in sports, and generally make life more comfortable and productive. High fashion has appropriated cutting-edge developments in textiles, from digital prints to flexible molds, from synthetic textures to light-emitting fibers. Smart fabrics and smart clothes are being invented to perform in unexpected ways, to answer desires—for protection, for entertainment, for communication—as yet unimagined by the future wearer. An entirely new dialogue is unfolding: Science uses the soft construction of clothing to experiment with "intelligent" and "sensing" technologies and avant-garde designers explore how far technology can go in creating new building blocks for fashion.

Organic

The Organic label by John Patrick is considered one of the most sophisticated expressions of ethical fashion. The designer's modern, slightly irreverent aesthetic breaks with the blandness of much sustainably produced clothing. Organic cottons and wool, vegetable-tanned leathers and recycled knits serve as the foundation for his sportswear, to which he adds unexpected textiles like recycled nylons and polyesters and repurposed neoprene.

Patrick's target customer has grown up expecting to have sustainable choices in stylish, affordable clothes. The company believes in complete transparency, educating the audience at its runway shows with multimedia presentations about the sourcing and processing of the materials used in the collections as well as the conditions of the workforce.

Photo by Victor Virgile, Gamma-Rapho via Getty Images.

Left Organic by John Patrick, Fall/Winter, 2012/13

Clean

Called the "Vivienne Westwood of eco," Linda Loudermilk makes high-end fun-with-an-edge sustainable clothing. Most of the fashion from the Los Angeles–based company is made in the United States and hand finished. Loudermilk has, in fact, trademarked the term *luxury eco*, positioning it as a certification of earth-friendly practices joined with quality craftsmanship.

Her designs employ a wide sweep of the available environmentally conscious fabrics: bamboo, wool, vegan silk, hemp, soya, organic cotton fur, Oeko-Tex fabrications, Ingeo, SeaCell, Eco-Spun, and reclaimed textiles. The Loudermilk brand crusades for clean couture, building relationships with companies that produce fibers without pesticides and heavy mineral dyes. Clean water is a particular concern, and the company contributes a percentage of sales from its Mission Wear line to initiatives around the world.

Photos courtesy of Organic by John Patrick.

Left and Above Organic by John Patrick, Resort, 2011

Left Linda Loudermilk,
Spring/Summer 2006

Local Design

Although much of the fashion industry's production has moved overseas, some fashion businesses are finding ways to reclaim manufacturing on a scale that allows them to produce locally. In 2000, Natalie Chanin started a line of one-of-a-kind T-shirts under the label Project Alabama, for which she hired talented stitchers and quilters from her local community. Many of the women involved in the creation of those first pieces still work with the company, now known as Alabama Chanin.

The entire production process for the Alabama Chanin brand remains a regional concern. The fiber for their certified-organic cotton jersey is farmed in Texas, spun into thread in North Carolina, and knitted in South Carolina. The fabric returns to North Carolina to be dyed, then heads to the company's studio in Florence, Alabama, to be cut, painted, embellished, and constructed by hand.

Photos by Robert Rausch, courtesy of Alabama Chanin.

Both Pages Alabama Chanin, Spring/Summer 2011

Photo by Robert Rausch, courtesy of Alabama Chanin.

Slow Fashion

Slow fashion is a movement that invests in the quality of a craft and the people who make it, providing a meaningful alternative to fast, disposable fashion. Chanin was championing slow fashion before the concept had entered the lexicon of the fashion industry. Alabama Chanin uses high-grade organic and recycled materials to fashion unique garments that are numbered and signed by the artisans who craft them.

The brand's success is often attributed to Chanin's ability to build community, providing a platform for talent that might otherwise go unrecognized. The company's fresh take on homespun style also encourages a do-it-yourself personal approach to fashion, and they hold regular immersive workshops.

Photo by Lisa Eisner, courtesy of Alabama Chanin.

Zero Waste

Between 15 and 20 percent of the fabric used in making new garments ends up in landfills. In response, designers like Susan Dimasi, Chantal Kirby, Mark Liu, Holly McQuillan, Timo Rissanen, Julian Roberts, David Telfer, and Yeohlee Teng have been developing new pattern-cutting techniques—such as Roberts's subtraction cutting—to generate their designs. The patterns for these garments fit together like a puzzle within the dimensions of the fabric, eliminating scraps. In some designs, the fabric is not cut, but instead draped, tucked, and tacked into place, all without letting the fashion quotient drop.

With the ultimate goal of zero waste, forward-thinking designers have already begun to repurpose, recycle, and reinterpret fashion as part of their core design process.

Repurpose

Instead of answering fashion's imperative for the constant generation of novelty by creating a new object, some designers challenge the assumption by repurposing an existing one. Maison Martin Margiela's Artisanal collections preserve discarded garments, accessories, and fabrics, reinventing their original functions, to make entirely new garments and accessories. Old gloves, belts, wigs, combs (even vinyl records) have been preserved in one-of-a-kind textiles that are then fashioned into garments, each piece requiring a unique plan for its construction. The Artisanal collections employ intelligent, zero-waste practices throughout the design process; sustainably produced, these newly transformed garments are presented as valuable objects in the discourse of high fashion.

Above Maison Martin Margiela, Artisanal, Spring/ Summer 2001

Courtesy of Sheena Matheiken.

Above Four days in the
life of the Uniform Project,
2009/10

Reinterpret

Consumers have also advanced zero-waste strategies. In 2009, Sheena Matheiken vowed to wear the same black button-down, reversible A-line dress for an entire year, effectively redefining the "little black dress" as an agent of social change. Her daily photo posts for the Uniform Project showed the garment worn forward and backward, as a dress, a tunic, and a jacket, reimagined and reaccessorized over and over. The dress became so popular that Matheiken released a limited-edition run of 365 copies, which sold out in less than a week, and posted the pattern online for her DIY followers. In the space of a year, she proved the long lifespan, and greater value, of a single garment when it is creatively reinterpreted rather than replaced.

New Frontiers: Catalytic Clothing

In an industry that contributes so greatly to polluting the globe, the imperative to protect the planet has led some designers into the domain of science. Designer Helen Storey has collaborated with chemist Tony Ryan on an innovative biomedical and environmental project in partnership with the University of Sheffield and the University for the Arts, London. In late 2010, they showed Herself, the first iteration of an air-purifying dress.

Catalytic Clothing applies photocatalytic technology, currently used in industrial products like paint and cement, to textiles intended for clothing. The nanoparticles of the photocatalyst bond easily to fabric when laundered. When exposed to light, the photocatalyst rearranges the electrons in the fabric, making them more reactive. The electrons then interact with water in the air, breaking down into radicals, which in turn interact with airborne pollutants, reducing them to harmless chemicals.

To effect air quality substantially, the technology will need to be incorporated into the mass production of many different fashion products, across many different brands. Meanwhile, the idea that individuals can actively change their environment by what they wear is a compelling step forward.

Photos courtesy of Catalytic Clothing.

Above Still from *Herself: Catalytic Clothing* directed by Adam Mufti • **Left** Detail of Herself, prototype air-purifying dress, 2011

Right BioCouture, women's jackets, September 2007 ●
Far Right Microbial cellulose biomaterial after ten days of growth

New Frontiers: BioCouture

Bacteria, the future of fashion? In the pursuit of alternative methods of textile production, Suzanne Lee, a senior research fellow at Central Saint Martins, London, is working at the forefront. First conceptualized in 2003, and developed in collaboration with the scientific community, her BioCouture project proposes, in essence, to grow clothing.

Creating this primordial soup of style involves a sugary green tea solution to which is added a mixed culture of bacterial cellulose, yeasts, and other microorganisms. The bacteria feed on the sugar and produce fine threads of cellulose that adhere to one another, forming a skin on the liquid's surface. The resulting cellulose mat, whose texture resembles a vegetable leather, can be molded into a three-dimensional shape or dried flat, then cut and sewn like traditional cloth.

The biomaterial is natural, nontoxic, compostable, and requires less dye than commonly used fibers. Lee envisions repurposing waste from the food and beverage industry to fuel production on a larger scale and to an even more sustainable effect. The biomaterial does face challenges before it can be introduced to the market: Research is ongoing to produce the microbial cellulose in a specific shape, maintain its flexibility, make it water resistant, and control the rate at which it breaks down. Nonetheless, its implications for the fashion industry are powerful.

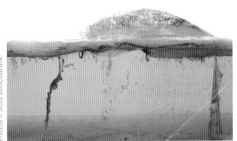

Photos © 2012 BioCouture.

E-Textile Explorations

Since the 1990s, designers at the intersection of fashion, technology, and art have been working to showcase what fashion is capable of in the twenty-first century. Fashion and textile designers have joined forces with engineers, chemists, and physicists to find ways of incorporating into traditional textile practices new electronic technologies such as LEDs, fiber optics, conductive thread, and electroluminescent wire in order to expand fashion's boundaries.

Maggie Orth helped to pioneer the field of e-textiles while working on her Ph.D. at MIT's Media Lab from 1997 to 2001. In one of her first garments, the ethereal Firefly Dress of 1998, conductive materials, an embroidered power plane, and sensors complete a circuit that causes LEDs suspended in the tulle to flicker with the movement of the wearer. Orth is currently working with the U.S. military to develop camouflage clothing that reacts to its immediate surroundings: a soldier's clothing might mimic the bricks in a wall or the blades of tall grass.

With degrees in neurophysiology and architecture, Lynne Bruning began experimenting with e-textile components in 2006. Her creations incorporate LEDs, the LilyPad Arduino (an electronic microcontroller board conceived by Leah Buechley for wearables), conductive threads, black light–reactive fibers, and ultrasonic sensors. Her disco-feel Day-Glo Dress is woven from surveyor's string; the more formal Mrs. Mary Atkins-Holl Dress integrates traditional Japanese dying techniques with luminescent angelina fiber and LEDs.

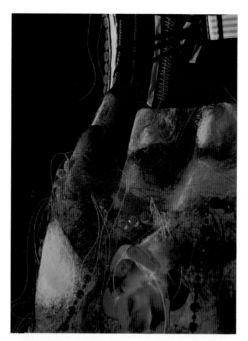

Courtesy of Maggie Orth.

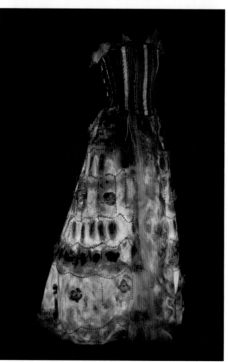

Above Lynne Bruning, Mrs. Mary Atkins-Holl Dress

Photos by Lynne Bruning.

Above Top Maggie Orth, Firefly Dress and Necklace, 1998 ▪ *Above* Lynne Bruning, Day-Glo Dress

Right Undercover,
Fall/Winter 2009/10

Techno Couture

Not all technological advances belong to fashion's future. Science and technology have always played a part in the evolution of clothing, providing designers with new ways to answer specific design issues. Today, smart fabrics that resist abrasion, staining, or fire, that protect against environmental extremes, that offer the wearer greater mobility and convenience are readily available. Thus, a designer like Jun Takahashi will integrate NASA-engineered fabrics and other space-age textiles not only into his practical high-performance gear for Nike, but also into the fashion-forward clothing for his Undercover label. The challenge is to incorporate the new technologies into a seamless aesthetic.

For some designers, technological innovation has become a means to push the conceptual side of their work. The undisputed leader of this approach to fashion is Hussein Chalayan. His experiments with wearable electronics, from digital-display to remote-controlled morphing garments, have allowed him to explore more fully the themes of transformation and flux that have always been integral to his designs. His striking fusions of advanced science and haute couture have elevated the proposition that fashion renews itself through technology.

Photos by firstVIEW.

Right Hussein Chalayan,
Fall/Winter 2007/2008

DISSEMINATION

Dissemination completes the cycle of the fashion. A design house employs multiple channels of display, distribution, and communication to deliver its product to the consumer in a way that is consistent with the brand. Every choice regarding the type of runway exhibition or photographic image is vital to the successful delivery of both ideas and products. Each presentation aims to put a collection within a context that best tells the designer's story. The media provides a way for designers to magnify and transmit these stories to a larger audience, or more crucially, a targeted one. The scale and approach of different corporate structures and models of retail operations also set the stage for how customers engage a brand. In the end, the power of early adopters and champions of style can influence the perception of, and drive public opinion around, any product. Fashion mavericks and bloggers are among the arbiters of taste who resonate with today's consumer, giving a heterogeneous, democratizing voice to the world of fashion.

Presentation

218
Runways

Runway shows have evolved over time to meet the needs and desires of designers and buyers, the press, and the public at large. While commerce lies at the heart of putting on a fashion show, there is no denying that society expects more from the catwalk than just clothes. Any kind of presentation must reflect the culture of the day. Audiences of certain eras demanded reserved elegance, while the thrill of the unexpected is more in line with the present. Regardless of how the runway is interpreted, it will always be an important tool for framing a designer's concept and connecting with the client through a shared experience.

221
Beyond

The demand for new and improved runway experiences seems to grow exponentially each season. In an effort to keep up, designers continue to explore alternative ways of reaching audiences, connecting their collections with their mode of delivery. Thinking outside the box is vital. Some designers delve into technologies to make their shows accessible instantly and globally; others scout for unusual locations or employ media that push the conceptual envelope. Still others look to the past, revisiting and refreshing earlier presentation styles, understanding that everything old is new again for the next generation. Meanwhile, the showmen of fashion design elevate the catwalk to a full-immersion theatrical event that can approach the level of performance art.

Louis Vuitton, Spring/Summer 2011
Photo by François Guillot, AFP, Getty Images.

Salon to Catwalk

Life-size dolls captured the imaginations of the fashion cognoscenti as far back as 1391, when Queen Isabella of Bavaria is said to have given one to Queen Ann of Bohemia to share the latest styles. Fashion dolls continued to serve as instruments in the dissemination of trends until the birth of the haute couture salon. Their importance was briefly reestablished after World War II with the Théâtre de la Mode, a collaborative industry endeavor used to reassert Paris's position as the leader of couture.

Charles Frederick Worth was among the pioneers of the runway, hosting fashion parades in his salon to showcase his collections for clients. Another English designer, Lucile (Lady Duff Gordon), is said to have trained the first professional fashion models in 1897. Live *mannequins* became an industry standard by the 1920s; as a result, many fashion houses employed in-house models.

In the early twentieth century, designers like Jeanne Paquin and Paul Poiret introduced themed presentations with dramatic finales, opened them to the fashion press, and moved their productions out of the salon. In 1921, Jean Patou hosted the first private preview for press, buyers, and private clients, the standard model for fashion shows used today. The greater the exposure, the more creative designers became about protecting their ideas. Legend has it that the rapid glide and distinctive gestures of Christian Dior's models were meant to thwart any attempt to copy design details.

By the 1960s, the move away from the haute couture salons and toward the youth-focused ready-to-wear market led to a speeding up and energizing of the traditional fashion show. In London, Mary Quant at Bazaar, like other designers and owners of hip boutiques, created fashion "happenings" with loud music and a partylike ambience. The 1970s brought dancing and the occasional somersault as the catwalk became more playful. Although the ultimate goal of the show is to sell the collection, throughout the 1970s and into the 1980s the runway presentation and its entertainment value became as important as the designs themselves. Some designers began to show in alternative spaces like lofts, restaurants, and galleries while others, especially in Paris, were mounting large, theatrical spectacles. A perfect storm of influential buyers, prominent clientele, A-list celebrities, doyens of high society, powerful media personalities, and supermodel royalty became the benchmark of fashion shows of the 1990s and 2000s.

Photo by Keystone-France, Gamma-Keystone via Getty Images.

Photo by Ralph Crane, Time & Life Pictures, Getty Images.

Photo by Lichfield, Getty Images.

Opposite Page Top
Modeling a coat for
private clients in the salon,
Maison de Jean Patou,
1934 • *Left* Fashion show
staged by Christian Dior
on an elevated catwalk
at the Villa Hügel, Essen,
Germany, 1953

Above Annacat fashion
show held in the boutique,
London, 1965. Visible in the
audience are photographer
David Bailey and his then
wife, Catherine Deneuve.
• *Right* Fashion show
in the salon, Maison de
Christian Dior, 1955. Visible
in the front row are Louise
Bousque, Paris editor, and
Carmel Snow, editor in chief,
of *Harper's Bazaar*; and in
the second row Alexander
Liberman, art director of
American *Vogue*.

Photo by John Chillingworth, Getty Images.

Above Christian Lacroix's lavish haute couture presentation, Fall/Winter 1987/88 • *Left* Playfulness on Kenzo's catwalk, Spring/Summer 1972

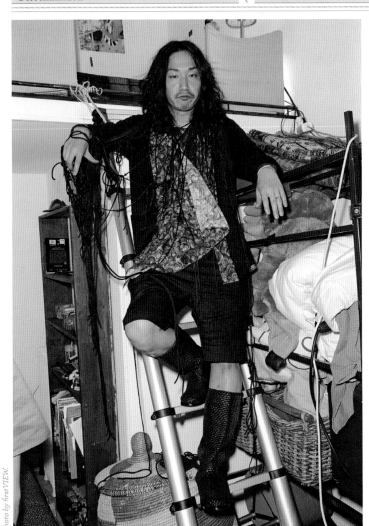

Photo by first-VIEW.

Out of the Box

Courting clients, buyers, and the press becomes harder every season. The race to impress and entertain has some designers returning to the experience of the *défilé de couture*. Designers from Azzedine Alaïa to Ricardo Tisci for Givenchy have been opting for the simplicity, glamour, and intimacy of salon shows. Tom Ford made news when his return to womenswear in 2010 was a private presentation with a single photographer in attendance.

Sometimes the venue is a cheeky shock to the system, as when Imitation of Christ in 2000 showed in a funeral salon. Other times, designers are defining a context for their practice, as when Bless presented their Spring/Summer 2011 collection as an informal night at home with friends.

Short films and videos have increasingly come into play. Their use might be frankly commercial, as when in 2010 Ralph Lauren projected beautifully edited optical illusions—product shots, runway and lifestyle clips—on the exteriors of his flagship stores on Madison Avenue and Bond Street. Or they might be more atmospheric or conceptual in nature, as with the extraordinary collaborative work of Nick Knight, Ruth Hogben, and others at SHOWstudio out of London.

The Internet has allowed designers to break down the barriers to traditional shows, providing a global audience with a virtual all-access pass to their presentations courtesy of live video streaming.

Photo by Tullio Puglia, WireImage.

Top Left Bless, Spring/ Summer 2011 show • *Far Left* Film by Ruth Hogben for Gareth Pugh, projected on a ceiling during the Pitti Immagine Uomo, 2010/11 • *Above Left* Still from Hogben's film • *Left* Live feed of Alexander McQueen's Plato's Atlantis collection, October 2009

Theatre of Fashion: Galliano

Ever since his days at Central Saint Martins, John Galliano has been known as a performer. The designer immersed himself in his themes, frequently undergoing personal transformations meant to complement the work. Often, he designed his presentations for shock and awe.

The theatre of fashion was woven into the fabric of his collections, sometimes literally as well as figuratively. His tenure at the House of Dior from 1996 to 2011 especially afforded him opportunities to stage elaborate narratives. Galliano's extensive research into history and different cultures often resulted in flamboyant interpretations of those themes. Although set design always played an important role in his productions, the clothes themselves become larger-than-life characters in the stories he told.

Galliano's lavish Fall/Winter 2005/06 haute couture collection, for example, featured gowns designed to lift the veil on the intricate underpinnings of how the clothes were constructed, as an homage to Monsieur Dior on the centennial of his birth. Inspired by the French Revolution, his Spring/Summer 2006 collection for Dior opened to a polished steel stage, bathed in a sanguine light and echoing with the sound of clattering horse hooves. The year 1789 featured prominently throughout the collection, as did fabrics that gave the impression of being blood soaked. In another nod to the house's founder, for his Fall/Winter 2010/11 collection at the Rodin Museum, Galliano sent out bouquet after bouquet of exotic living flowers, complete with cellophane wrapping. Imaginative high drama was the hallmark of the designer's fantasies.

Photo by Pool Bassignac/Benainous, Gamma-Rapho via Getty Images.

Above Right Dior haute couture, Spring/Summer 2006 • *Right* Dior haute couture , Fall/Winter 2010/11

Photo by François Guillot, AFP, Getty Images.

Left Dior haute couture,
Fall/Winter 2005/06

Theatre of Fashion: Lagerfeld

All the world's a stage for Karl Lagerfeld. Perhaps the two most consistent attributes of a Lagerfeld production are scale and opulence. He has also described his inspiration as coming in waves that will often suggest the presentation for a collection, along with its initial direction.

In one instance, inspired by Sweden's Ice Hotel, Lagerfeld transformed the Grand Palais in Paris into a frigid auditorium with a large box covering the stage. The lights came down, the box went up, and the scene was set for Chanel's Fall/Winter 2010/11 ready-to-wear collection. An enormous iceberg, nearly 30 feet (9 m) high and weighing 240 tons (217.7 mt), became the unforgettable centerpiece for a show in which models stomped through puddles of melting ice in the latest Chanel finery. Although a glacier might seem like a tough act to follow, the next season, for Chanel's Spring/Summer 2011 ready-to-wear collection, the Grand Palais hosted a full orchestra and a sprawling garden set that paid tribute to the 1961 film *L'Année dernière à Marienbad*.

Lagerfeld is also responsible for the first fashion show that, in theory at least, could be seen from space. A 660-foot (201 m) section of the Great Wall of China became the ultimate runway for the Fall/Winter 2007/08 Fendi collection. Under his masterful direction, the realm of fashion as theatre becomes a magical, once-in-a-lifetime moment, every time.

Photo by Andrew H. Walker, Getty Images.

Above Special presentation of Fendi's Fall/Winter 2007/08 collection, Beijing, China • *Left* Chanel, Fall/Winter 2010/11

Above Chanel, Fall/Winter 2011/12 • *Left* Chanel, Spring/Summer 2011

Theatre of Fashion: McQueen

Alexander McQueen pushed the fashion show beyond extravagant fantasy into the realm of conceptual and performance art. In one ground-breaking show after another, he splattered his models with blood and dirt, surrounded them with fire, drenched them with rain, sent them through water, over a bed of nails, into wind tunnels, and soaring above the audience, had them escort wolves down the catwalk, iceskate in a snowy landscape, and wage battle around a giant chessboard. For one collection in 2001, beautiful madhouse figures inhabited a two-way mirrored box out of which suddenly emerged a tableau vivant of a Joel-Peter Witkins moth-covered nude; for another in 2009, twisted blow-up dolls circumnavigated a blackened scrapyard of props from past shows.

The technical wizardry that McQueen brought to his stagecraft created indelible images: Shalom Harlow spinning in a white strapless trapeze dress, slowly spray painted by robotic guns; Kate Moss's holographic figure in floating organza materializing within a pyramidal structure; the other-worldly creatures of Plato's Atlantis quietly parading past the camera tracks that streamed them live online.

The discomforting narratives of McQueen's dramatic mise-en-scènes, balanced against the exquisiteness of his clothing, challenged as much as enthralled his audience. One particularly evocative show, in 2004, reenacted Sydney Pollack's *They Shoot Horses, Don't They?*, a film set against a Depression-era dance marathon. Relentlessly circling the dance floor, couples shimmied, strutted, raced, staggered, and finally collapsed in exhaustion. Never one to water down the raw emotion of his productions, McQueen tantalized with what fashion might have to say about the human condition.

Photo by Eric Ryan, Getty Images.

Photo by Dominique Charriau, WireImage.

Photo by firstVIEW.

Top Alexander McQueen, Fall/Winter 2006/07 • *Middle* Fall/Winter 2009/10 • *Above* Spring/Summer 1999

Left Alexander McQueen,
Spring/Summer 2010

Media

230
Publications

The printed page has long been a valuable tool for persuasion and influence in the fashion world. From volumes of fashion plates to commercial glossies, periodicals have sold fashion and the fantasies that inspire it and driven its public discourse. Some serial publications have emerged with a distinct editorial voice, capturing the fashion *zeitgeist* and distributing content across targeted audiences. Even the pages of advertising that make publishing possible inform fashion's narrative at any given point. Magazines continue to evolve with interactive, multimedia, digital presences on websites and mobile devices.

252
Image Makers

Images rule fashion. They are the primary delivery system for a designer's creation. Fashion illustrators and photographers play a unique role in the fashion industry. While capturing the essence of a designer's collection on a page or a screen to sell and inspire, they are simultaneously interpreting style from a personal perspective that filters through social history and contemporary culture—whether they realize it or not. As a result, illustrators and photographers have become a vital part of the evolution of fashion, often influencing designers, media, and consumers through innovative advertising and artistic editorial work.

262
Commentators

The increasing speed and scope of the fashion industry, coupled with unprecedented access to technology, has created not just an interest in, but a demand for, a wide array of fashion voices, ones that authentically represent many different types of consumers and that move beyond traditional media models. Bloggers are some of today's most influential fashion commentators because they concentrate on very specific, at times niche, perspectives when it comes to telling the story of fashion. Both the public and industry professionals tap into these valuable information streams as they deliver texts, images, audio, and video in real time.

Photograph by Toni Frissell, 1939
Toni Frissell Collection, Library of Congress.

Fashion Plates

Among the earliest vehicles for spreading trends, engraved prints that reproduced portraits of powerful, and presumably stylish, subjects made their way throughout Renaissance Europe. Superseding these in fashion reporting were plates that showed an entire figure, often front and back, wearing the latest styles. In the seventeenth century, hand-colored plates by artists like Abraham Bosse, Wenceslaus Hollar, and, later, the Bonnart brothers became highly prized for their detailed renderings. The plates, which served no other purpose than to promote fashions, might be displayed in shop windows to inform and entice the public.

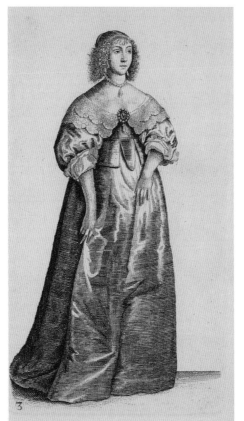 

Above Wenceslaus Hollar, 1639 • *Above Right* Hollar, 1640 • *Right* Hollar, 1640, front and back views

Left Abraham Bosse, ca.
1630–40 • *Middle* Bosse,
ca. 1630–40 • *Right* Bosse,
mid-1600s

Left Nicholas Bonnart,
late 1600s • *Middle* Henry
Bonnart, 1694 • *Right*
Henry Bonnart, 1690s

Fashion Periodicals

Le Mercure Galant, founded in Paris in 1672 by Jean Donneau de Visé, was the first (though short-lived) fashion periodical, adding descriptive texts to the illustrative plates. A later incarnation included the names of shops where such styles might be found. During the eighteenth century, fashion journalism continued to grow. The large-format *Galerie des Modes et Costumes Français*, compiled and published by Jacques Esnauts and Michel Rapilly sporadically between 1778 and 1787, featured work by artists like Jean Antoine Watteau. Le Brun Tossa produced *Le Cabinet des Modes* twice a month from 1785 to 1789, the first to appear regularly. Meanwhile, newspapers began to report on seasonal fashions.

Fashion periodicals survived the French Revolution and picked up again with *La Journal des Dames et des Modes*, created in 1797 and published by Pierre Antoine Leboux de La Mésangère from 1801 to 1839. He also bought *Observateur des Modes* in 1823. In the early nineteenth century, whether monthly or quarterly, the journals were featuring engraved prints of men's, women's, and, increasingly, children's fashions by some of the finest fashion artists of the period: Paul Gavarni, Antoine Charles Horace Vernet, Pierre Charles Baquoy, and Louis-Marie Lante. Available by subscription from 1797 to 1801, *Heideloff's Gallery of Fashion* was the top English publication. Later, British periodicals, such as *La Belle Assemblée* and *Le Beau Monde*, adopted French titles for greater cachet.

Above Left Le Cabinet des Modes, 1786 • Above Right Observateur des Modes, 1820 • Right Le Beau Monde, 1831

All plates private collection.

Left Fashions in *New London Magazine*, 1786
• *Below* Le Journal des Dames et des Modes, 1808 • *Below Right* Le Journal des Dames et des Modes, 1812

French Sources

During the second quarter of the nineteenth century, advances in printing technology enabled larger runs in the production of plates and triggered a boom in French fashion periodicals. These publications disseminated Parisian styles to provincial and foreign readers, establishing the city as the center of influence for the next hundred years. *Le Moniteur de la Mode*, for instance, was a celebrated women's fashion journal that from 1843 to 1913 presented the latest developments in style, including coiffures and home furnishings, often drawn by Jules David. As in the similar *Modes Parisiennes*, the clothes were modeled in environments that reflected everyday activities for fashionable women, gathered in a parlor or walking in a park, and were styled with accessories and hairdos that complemented each look. Plates included the names and addresses of the houses that produced or sold the garments depicted. Although packaged as French, many fashion publications were actually published in Germany or Belgium.

LES MODES PARISIENNES

Above "Amazone" from *Les Modes Parisiennes*, 1857

● *Left Le Moniteur de la Mode*, 1860

Above Spread from *La Mode Illustrée*, October 1865 • *Far Left* Le *Journal des Dames et des Demoiselles*, 1878, copied from *Le Moniteur de la Mode*, 1877 • *Left* Le *Moniteur de la Mode*, 1883

American Adaptations

Lax or nonexistent copyright enforcement throughout Europe allowed English and American magazines to modify and adapt French and German fashion plates for their readers. In the United States, one of the most influential magazines designed for the "woman's sphere" was *Godey's Lady's Book*, which appeared from 1830 to 1898. Editor Sarah Josepha Hale crafted a publication that addressed women's domestic and intellectual life by juxtaposing recipes, handcrafts, sheet music, and color fashion plates, along with essays, poetry, and short stories by Harriet Beecher Stowe, Edgar Allen Poe, Nathaniel Hawthorne, and Henry Wadsworth Longfellow. *Peterson's Magazine* was another important women's periodical to feature fashion plates, though often of a lesser quality than their European counterparts. Introduced in 1842 and published until 1898 by Charles J. Peterson and Ann Sophia Stephens, it distinguished itself by making a noticeable effort to include the work of female writers. Both *Godey's Lady's Book* and *Peterson's Magazine* were published in Philadelphia, Pennsylvania.

Right Godey's Lady's Book, 1840

GODEY'S COLOURED PARIS FASHIONS AMERICANIZED.

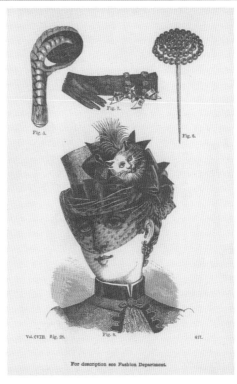

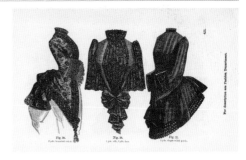

Left and Above Godey's
Lady's Book, 1884

Right "Les Modes
Parisiennes," *Peterson's
Magazine,* 1875, 1880,
1888, and 1889

Gazette du Bon Ton

Lucien Vogel first published the extraordinary *Gazette du Bon Ton* in Paris in 1912, then suspended it during the First World War; he reintroduced the journal in 1920, continuing until its purchase in 1925 by Condé Nast. Designed for an elite audience, this definitive journal of good taste set the format and elevated tone for magazines that followed, including stories on theatre, travel, and gossip. Full-color fashion pochoirs by the premiere artists of the day—Georges Barbier, Paul Iribe, Pierre Brissaud, André-Edouard Marty, Thayaht, Georges Lepape, Etienne Drian, Edouard Garcia Benito, Soeurs David, Pierre Mourgue, Erté, Robert Bonfils, Bernard Boutet de Monvel, Porter Woodruff, Fernand Siméon, Maurice Leroy, and Zyg Brunner—became the centerpiece of every issue. Vogel also created the less rarified, yet very successful, *Jardin des Modes* in 1922, which underwent several incarnations over the next seventy years.

Gazette du Bon Ton. — Nº 7   Septembre 1920. — *Pl. 48*

Right Fernand Siméon, "Bourrasque," 1920

All plates private collection.

Far Left Georges Lepape, "L'Embarras du choix" (Poiret), 1912 • *Middle* Lepape, "Dieu! Qu'il fait froid" (Poiret), 1913 • *Left* Pierre Brissaud, "Ta maman va bien?" (Lanvin), 1914

LA FEMME À L'ÉVENTAIL
Robe du soir, de Worth

LA COIFFURE ESPAGNOLE
Robe du soir, de Doeuillet

LE PARC EN DÉCEMBRE
TAILLLEUR DE DŒUILLET

N° 10 de la Gazette   Année 1921. — Planche 77

BONJOUR !

Above Etienne Drian, "La femme à l'éventail" (Worth), 1920 • *Above Right* Drian, "La coiffure espagnole" (Doeuillet), 1920 • *Far Right* André-Edouard Marty, "Le parc en décembre" (Doeuillet), 1921 • *Right* Porter Woodruff, "Bonjour!" (Camille Roger hat), 1921

LES BELLES DAMES DU PARAVENT
ROBES ET MANTEAUX, DE DOUCET

Le Jardin des Modes

Lucien Vogel, Directeur

ROBE NOUVELLE ET VIEILLE COMMODE

Far Left "Les belles dames du paravent" (Doucet), 1924–25 • *Left* Pierre Brissaud, cover of *Le Jardin des Modes*, 1923

Harper's Bazaar

America's first fashion magazine debuted in November 1867 as a newsprint weekly titled *Harper's Bazar: A Repository of Fashion, Pleasure, and Instruction*, catering to middle- and upper-class women. Although it drew on fashions from Paris and even Germany, *Harper's* devoted space to American designers even before the turn of the century.

In 1901 *Harper's* became a monthly, and in 1929 the title changed to *Harper's Bazaar*. In 1915, Erté began a twenty-two year relationship with the magazine, producing many of its covers.

During the 1940s and 1950s, led by editor Carmel Snow, fashion editor Diana Vreeland, and art director Alexey Brodovitch, the magazine pushed fashion journalism and design forward, showcasing some of the brightest talents on its pages. Under Vreeland's creative direction, and through the lens of photographers such as Louise Dahl-Wolfe, Toni Frissell, and Richard Avedon, *Harper's Bazaar* took the fashion photo shoot out of the studio.

In the 1990s, under the editorship of Liz Tilberis, the magazine once again became a force within fashion publishing. Edited for the past decade by Glenda Bailey, with a turn toward glamour and romance, *Harper's Bazaar* is a home to photographers such as Patrick Demarchelier, Peter Lindbergh, and Terry Richardson.

Harper's Bazaar, 13 January 1872, ed. Mary L. Booth

Harper's Bazaar, 28 July 1900, ed. Elizabeth Jordan

Harper's Bazaar, March 1927, ed. Charles Hanson Towne; illustration by Erté

Harper's Bazaar, July 1949, ed. Carmel Snow; photo by Louise Dahl-Wolfe

Harper's Bazaar, January 1965, ed. Nancy White; Katherine Denzinger

Harper's Bazaar, November 1970, ed. White; photo by Hiro

Harper's Bazaar, February 1999, ed. Elizabeth Tilberis; photo by Patrick Demarchelier

Harper's Bazaar, August 2009, ed. Glenda Bailey; photo by Peter Lindberg

Below Harper's Bazaar, December 2010; photo by Alexi Lubomirski

Harper's Bazaar, April 2009; photo by Mark Seliger

Harper's Bazaar, March 2011; photo by Terry Richardson

Right Photos by Tim Walker in *Harper's Bazaar*, October 2009
• *Far Right* Photos by Camilla Akrans in *Harper's Bazaar*, July 2010

Vogue

Arthur Baldwin Turnure founded *Vogue* in 1892 as a weekly journal of high society. The publication struggled until Condé Nast purchased it in 1909. Under his direction, it became a world-class fashion magazine, which evetually led to editions in England, France, Spain, and Germany, each designed to appeal to its country's unique aesthetic. Over the years, *Vogue* has cultivated a discerning editorial eye and invested in narratives about women within the larger cultural context. Its masthead has hosted a roll call of legendary editors—Bettina Ballard, Diana Vreeland, Grace Mirabella, and Anna Wintour—each of whom has reshaped the publication to be relevant to her time. Its pages have showcased every major fashion photographer, from Cecil Beaton to Mario Testino.

The popular publication (with numerous global editions) influences readers on many fronts, covering lifestyles, society, and the arts, as well as fashion trends and developments. And having set the standard for over a century, *Vogue* has earned its position as a fashion authority. In its most recent incarnation, Wintour has focused on reaching a broader audience with more accessible ideas about fashion. She has also leveraged the power of the magazine to encourage new talent, collaborating with the Council of Fashion Designers of America in 2003 to create a fund that provides money and mentorship to at least two emerging designers each year.

Below Photos and text by
Cecil Beaton in *Vogue*,
February 1938

Vogue, 15 November 1926, ed. Edna Woolman Chase; drawing by Eduardo Garcia Benito

Vogue, March 1947; drawing by René Bouché

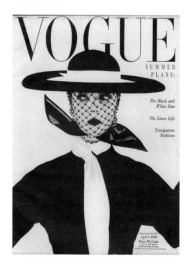

Vogue, April 1950; photo by Irving Penn

Vogue, July 1953, ed. Jessica Daves; photo by John Rawlings

Right *Vogue*, February 1969, ed. Diana Vreeland; photo by Bert Stern

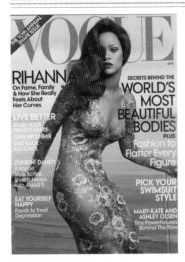

Vogue, April 2011, ed. Anna Wintour; photo by Annie Lebovitz

Vogue (British), April 2011, ed. Alexandria Shulman; photo by Mario Testino

Vogue (Russian), December 2009, ed. Aliona Doletskaya; photo by Sølve Sundsbø

Vogue (German), November 2009, ed. Christiane Arp; photo by Sølve Sundsbø

Vogue (Spanish), March 2011, ed. Yolanda Sacristán; photo by Alex Lubomirski

Vogue (Brazilian), July 2010, ed. Daniela Falcão; photo by Jacques Dequeker

Vogue (Japanese), June 2008, ed. Kazuhiro Saito; photo by Inez van Lamsweerde and Vinoodh Matadin

Vogue (Chinese), February 2011, ed. Angelica Cheung; photo by Patrick Demarchelier

Right Photo by Annie Leibovitz in *Vogue*, December 2009 • *Far Right* Photos by Peter Lindberg in *Vogue*, January 2011

Elle

Pierre Lazareff and his wife, Hélène Gordon Lazareff, founded *Elle* in Paris in 1945. Daniel Filipacchi and Jean-Luc Lagardère purchased the magazine in 1981, after which it was launched in the United States. Today, with forty-two international editions representing sixty countries, it is the world's the best-selling fashion publication. Unlike many other magazines that focus on high society and the elite of fashion, *Elle* integrates fashion, beauty, health, and entertainment coverage in an accessible way for the smart consumer with a sense of style. The publication sees its mission as guiding the *Elle* reader to self-expression and empowering her endeavors. Editor in chief of the American edition Robbie Myers describes her readers as "young enough to think about life as an adventure and old enough to have the means to live it."

Elle, March 2011, ed. Franck Espplasse-Cabeu; photo by Jean-Baptiste Mondino

Elle (American), December 1989, ed. Régis Pagniez; photo by Gilles Bensimon

Right and Below Elle, February 1955, ed. Françoise Giret; photos by Kazan–Studio Chevalier •
Far Right "First Look," *Elle* (American), March 2010, ed. Roberta Myers

Quatre lignes avancées   quatre couturiers hardis

GQ, August 1979, ed. Jack Haber; photo by Albert Watson

GQ, March 1980; photo by Jean Pagliuso

GQ

GQ began life in 1931 as a menswear trade publication called *Apparel Arts*. After gaining popularity with consumers, in 1958 it became *Gentlemen's Quarterly*, published as a quarterly supplement to *Esquire* magazine. When Condé Nast purchased it in 1980, editor Art Cooper broadened the scope of the publication, going beyond fashion to include coverage of food, fitness, sex, books, entertainment, travel, sports, and technology. The name was simplified to *GQ* in 1983, an acronym that has come to symbolize the magazine's position as an authority on men's fashion and culture. After Cooper's retirement in 2003, Jim Nelson became editor in chief. Nelson and design director Fred Woodward have attracted a younger readership that prefers a more casual interpretation. The term "meterosexual"—coined by journalist Mark Simpson after visiting a *GQ* exhibition—in many ways defines its style-conscious reader, a man concerned with culture, travel, fitness, grooming, and fashion. The magazine now has eighteen international editions.

Above Photos by Paola Kudaki and Tom Schierlitz in *GQ*, September 2010
• *Left GQ*, September 2010, ed. Jim Nelson; photo by Ben Watts

WWD

W

Edmund Fairchild founded *Women's Wear Daily* in 1910 as an offshoot of his menswear-focused trade journal *Daily News Record*. His grandson, John Fairchild, was instrumental in elevating the profile of the publication during his tenure as European bureau chief of Fairchild Publications, starting in 1955, and in his role as publisher of *WWD*, from 1960 to 1996. Covering their social lives along with those of their clients, John Fairchild helped to transform designers into celebrities. He was notorious for his capricious whims, uncompromising tactics, and legendary feuds with designers, which could result in banning any reference to them in the publication—sometimes for years. Patrick McCarthy took over from Fairchild with a fairer, more even-handed reporting style; he retired in 2010.

Known as "the bible of fashion," the daily trade newspaper is geared toward executives and professionals hailing from every sector of the industry, including design, manufacturing, retail, finance, media, and advertising. *WWD* provides coverage of the latest news and trends in fashion, beauty, and commerce. Style leaders also use it to keep apprised of shifts in the trade. The Walt Disney Company sold Fairchild Publications to Advance Publications (the parent company of Condé Nast Publications) in 1999, but the publication continues to be operated independent of other Condé Nast properties.

W began in 1972 as a monthly full-color broadsheet focused on fashion and society. Its founder, John Fairchild, intended for the magazine to serve as a complement to its sister publication, *Women's Wear Daily*. Patrick McCarthy, who became the magazine's chairman and editorial director, reintroduced it in 1993 in an oversized glossy format, with the *W* standing for the "world of style"—one that includes fashion, art, society, celebrity, beauty, design, cinema, music, technology, politics, and travel. Purchased by Condé Nast Publications in 1999, the periodical has positioned itself as a leader in the luxury market, both reflecting and influencing the global fashion elite. It has also become the most boundary-pushing publication in the company's portfolio, with many of the world's most prestigious photographers creating elaborate award-winning editorial spreads for its pages. *W* also has a history of inviting controversy, regularly running provocative imagery and polarizing stories.

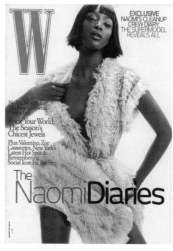

W, June 2007, ed. Bridget Foley; photo by Steven Klein

W, November 2009; photo by Pierpaolo Ferrari

Left Women's Wear Daily, 2010, ed. Edward Nardoza

i-D

Terry Jones, a former art director for *Vogue*, started *i-D* in 1980. From its modest beginnings as a cut-and-paste, hand-stapled fanzine that covered London's punk scene to the sophisticated glossy it is today, the magazine has focused on street style. After a period from 1984 to 2004 when Tony Elliott was a publishing partner, Jones and his wife, Tricia, regained full control of *i-D*. Early on, the magazine built a reputation for innovation with inventive typography and experimental photography. It was an ideal environment for cultivating new talent, and Wolfgang Tillmans, Nick Knight, Dylan Jones, Juergen Teller, Caryn Franklin, and Craig McDean all launched their careers there. *i-D* pioneered a documentary-style fashion coverage called the Straight Up, posing subjects against a wall and photographing them head-to-toe. *i-D* was also the first publication to feature the likes of John Galliano, Alexander McQueen, Helmut Lang, Raf Simons, and Rick Owens as well as Madonna, Franz Ferdinand, Kanye West, Chloë Sevigny, and Scarlett Johansson. To this day, the many models and celebrities featured on its covers sport a winking smile that pays tribute to the magazine's unique logo. It continues to reinvent itself, spinning off books and exhibitions dedicated to documenting innovators from every creative field.

Above Left i-D, October 2006; photo by Richard Bush • *Above* i-D, Spring 2011; photo by Emma Summerton • *Above Right* i-D, July 1985, ed. Terry Jones; photo by Robert Erdman • *Left* Photos by Luke Smalley in i-D, May 2007

Visionaire

Founded by Stephan Gan, Cecilia Dean, and James Kaliardos in 1991, *Visionaire* challenges the conventional format for fashion magazines. Published three times a year in limited-edition, concept-driven albums, it serves as a tribute to inspiration and creativity. These expensive, highly collectible journals of fashion and aesthetics use unconventional materials and innovative packaging to develop "paper and ink as performance art," as the *Washington Post* put it. *Visionaire*'s primary means of communication is visual, keeping text to a minimum. It showcases the work of both masters and emerging talents from the worlds of art, theatre, design, fashion, photography, and film, to tease out the theme behind each issue. *Visionaire* invites this league of creatives to reimagine and reinterpret the boundaries of crafting a publication.

Edited by Gan, *V* was launched in 1999 as the "ready-to-wear" spin-off from the couture *Visionaire*. It serves as an accessible large-format glossy covering fashion, music, film, and art for a global audience. The *V* aesthetic relies heavily on the chemistry produced by forging unpredictable collaborations between the worlds of high art and celebrity and those of underground culture and total unknowns. *V*'s success has led to its own offshoot, *VMAN*.

Below and Below Right
Visionaire 27, "Movement," 1999; lenticular-printed cover photos by Nick Knight, interior photo by Marucs Mâm with drawing by Thierry Perez

Right and Above Right
Visionaire 26, "Fantasy," 1998, ed. Stephen Gan; cover photo by Inez van Lamsweerde and Vinoodh Matadin

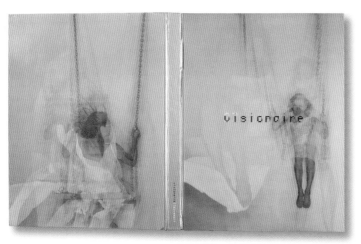

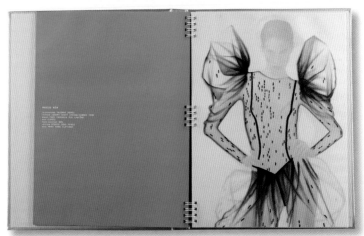

Left, Above, and Below Left Visionaire 29, "Woman," 1999; case design by Greg Foley, cover photo by Nick Knight, interior photos by Mario Testino

Below V, Summer 2009, ed. Stephen Gan; photo by Mario Testino

Twentieth-Century Illustrators

The earliest hand-colored fashion plates were, by definition, one of a kind. Each artist translated color differently; in some instances by choice, in others by necessity. Technological advancements and the standardization of color printing made it possible to mass-produce fashion drawings. Long after the invention of the camera in the nineteenth century, illustrations were still used for editorials and advertising. Commercial and fine artists could capture the spirit of style. Like a heavily manipulated photograph, a fashion sketch fabricates a fantasy because it represents a moment that has never truly existed.

Fashion illustrators have always been important interpreters of the aesthetics of their age. Correlations can often be made to major art movements. In the 1920s Paul Iribe's work for Jeanne Lanvin conveyed a modernist's flair. During the same period, Erté's work embodied the art deco sensibility, while Thayaht (Ernesto Michahelles) projected a futurist vision in his rendering of Madeleine Vionnet's designs. In the 1940s Salvador Dalí pushed the relationship between surrealism and fashion in his collaborations with Elsa Schiaparelli. From the 1940s and throughout the 1950s, the sketching style of popular artists like Christian Bérard, Eric (Carl Erickson), and René Gruau avoided specific details, suggesting instead the essential mood of a garment.

Right Logo by Paul Iribe for the House of Jeanne Lanvin, 1923

ROBERT PIGUET

NINA RICCI TISSUS LABBEY

Le Roy Soleil

Schiaparelli

Above Left Illustration by Pierre Mourgue, *La Femme Chic*, 1945 • *Above* Illustration by André Delfau, *La Femme Chic*, 1945 • *Far Left* Illustration by Salvador Dalí for Elsa Schiaparelli's perfume Le Roy Soleil, 1947 • *Right* Illustration by Marcel Vertès, *Vogue*, April 1950

Right Illustration by Eric
(Carl Erickson), *Vogue*,
November 1956

Chanel news: complete evening coverage

Just two of the dinner-evening dresses from Chanel's new collection—but they tell everything
about her new love of coverage: arms are sleeved, necklines high,
skirts flared (from the hipbone) to the ankle—or almost.

132   VOGUE, DECEMBER, 1954

The beautiful
American—
new byplay for
her navy blues

VOGUE, FEBRUARY 1, 1960

Above Illustration by René
Gruau, *Vogue*, December
1954 • *Right* Illustration
by René Bouché, *Vogue*,
February 1960

Although interest in fashion illustration declined in favor of fashion photography throughout the 1960s and 1970s, illustrators like Rene Bouché and Joe Eula contributed valuable bodies of fashion artwork, influencing fashion as they rendered it. The 1980s enjoyed the resurgence of the fashion illustrator, with widely different artists like Steven Stipelman, Antonio Lopez, and Tony Viramontes achieving legendary status within the industry.

At the century's turn, fashion illustration has produced some memorably distinct styles. Jean-Philippe Delhomme's work often takes a witty, satirical approach to the glamour of fashion. Ruben Toledo, husband of fashion designer Isabel Toledo, commits his fashion impressions to the page in a precisely graphic, but quirky, aesthetic. And a couturier's mastery of the stylized fashion sketch has allowed Karl Lagerfeld to incorporate his drawings into editorials as well as advertising.

Above Illustration by Steven Stipelman, 1980s
• *Left* Illustration by Joe Eula for Geoffrey Beene, September 1969

BARNEYS
NEWYORK

Serge and Lana weren't co-dependent, they were in love.

Clothing by Giorgio Armani

Left Illustration by Jean-Philippe Delhomme for Barney's New York, 1994
• *Above* Illustration by Antonio Lopez for Missoni, October 1983
• *Below* "L'armes bleues," illustration by Tony Viramontes of a Stephen Jones hat for Gaultier, 1984

Photographers

Once photography moved beyond basic documentation and classic portraiture, the photographer could focus on the artistry of capturing an image, making statements and telling stories. As early as the 1900s, photographers like Baron Adolph de Meyer had begun to elevate fashion photography to an art form. Photographers Edward Steichen, Cecil Beaton, George Hoyningen-Huene, and Horst P. Horst soon followed during the 1920s and 1930s, developing exquisitely lit, perfectly posed, highly stylized images. Meanwhile, surrealist/dadaist Man Ray was applying conceptual art techniques to his fashion shoots.

As photography continued to evolve technically, the fashion photographer could manipulate images in new ways that reflected the times. Fashion moved out of the controlled studio during the 1940s and 1950s. Toni Frissell, William Klein, Louise Dahl-Wolfe, and Richard Avedon were among a new generation of photographers who would shoot on location, allowing them to infuse images with movement and vitality. Youth culture and the sexual revolution of the 1960s and 1970s inspired photographers to break the refined and restrained standards of the fashion establishment, to let their images reflect a culture that was both rebellious and erotically charged. David Bailey and Helmut Newton are among the period's most provocative image makers.

The 1980s and 1990s became a time of excess and celebrity, providing fertile creative ground for fashion photographers like Herb Ritts, Annie Leibovitz, Bruce Weber, David La Chapelle, Mario Testino, Patrick Demarchelier, Steven Meisel, Sara Moon, and Nick Knight, all whom have become celebrities in their own right. Technology continues to provide new tools for the photographer. In much the same way the earliest fashion photographers were described as artists who painted with light, today's photographers can paint an image with pixels. For better or for worse, the image makers can use computer software to correct, redefine, enhance, or completely distort a photograph.

Fashion photography has become such an important part of the business that creating these shots often requires complex collaborations. Behind the photographer and the designer, large teams of fashion professionals—creative directors, stylists, makeup artists, and hair stylists— all contribute to the images that will influence the public's perception of fashion and, in the best of cases, move the industry in a new direction.

Above Photo by Man Ray, *Harper's Bazaar*, 1937

Street Photographers

Already in the late 1800s, photographers like George Hendrik Breitner and Jacques Henri Lartigue were pioneering street photography, capturing the fashions of the day for posterity. The work of Henri Cartier Bresson and Lisette Model in the 1930s and Robert Doisneau in the 1950s has also inspired contemporary street photographers. The 1980s saw a stronger focus on street fashion with Amy Arbus's monthly fashion feature for the *Village Voice*, "On the Street." In the 1990s Shoichi Aoki was among the first to take an interest in documenting street style in Tokyo's Harajuku district. Each of these photographers was instrumental in laying the groundwork for the present generation. Today, none is more famous than Bill Cunningham. With two weekly columns for *The New York Times*, he encapsulates fashion's big picture: "The main thing I love about street photography is that you find the answers you don't see at the fashion shows. If you just cover the designers in the shows, that's only one facet. You also need the street and the evening hours. If you cover the three things, you have the full picture of what people are wearing."

The Sartorialist

Scott Schuman is the creator of the Sartorialist. In 2005, after fifteen years of retail and marketing work, he decided to take two of his passions, fashion and photography, to the street and online. The Sartorialist has become an inspiration to a whole generation of bloggers, as well as a go-to resource for consumers and the fashion industry. The blog's popularity has established Schuman as an authority on fashion and styling, and he now contributes to GQ magazine and style.com. He relates his shooting style to the way designers hunt for inspiration. Selecting subjects is about more than the currency of their clothes. Equally important is their unique combination of color, pattern, proportion, and attitude.

Garance Doré

Garance Doré takes a decidedly artistic approach to her visual diary, which she started as *Une Fille Comme Moi* (A girl like me) in 2006, while living in Marseille, France. She incorporates street-style portraiture, fashion drawings, and commentary to illustrate her "five ideas per week." Unlike many of her contemporaries, she opts not to take candid images, instead carefully posing her subjects—friends, fashion insiders, and stylish strangers—on the street or in their homes. These fashion portraits benefit from Doré's fresh, understated approach, which leans toward what she describes as the modern woman: natural, minimal, and real.

Bloggers

Fashion entered the blogosphere in the early 2000s. Initially, blogs were regarded as little more than literary hobbies for the fans of fashion. But, over the past decade, they have become a significant part of how fashion information is processed and perceived both by the industry and by mainstream fashion consumers. The success of many high-profile blogs has attracted the attention of advertisers and investors, potentially making blogging a lucrative endeavor. These online fashion journals provide readers with a new way to filter through an overwhelming amount of information, follow like-minded experts, and interpret the data to fit their personal lifestyles. Fashion blogs are generally geared to a specific area of fashion: insider industry information, clothing and accessory trends, personal style, celebrity gossip, or shopping advice. Although usually associated with independent and aspiring writers, the popularity of the platform has encouraged large corporate retailers and media outlets to create their own promotional blogs.

On the Runway

Cathy Horyn's On the Runway: All Things Fashion reports fashion news, events, and runway shows. Her professional yet provocative blog is an extension of the work she has done for *the New York Times* since 1999. Horyn is a leading fashion journalist who has also written for *Vanity Fair* and the *Washington Post*.

AdR

AdR reflects Anna Dello Russo's reputation for being a "passionate fashionista," as well as her ability to identify cutting-edge trends. Formerly an editor of Italian *Vogue*, she is currently editor-at-large and creative consultant for the Japanese edition. Her avant-garde writing style has been compared to that of fashion icon Diana Vreeland.

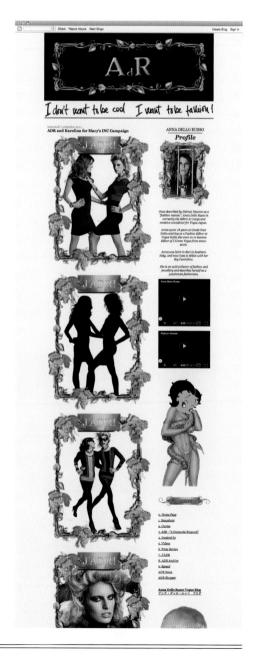

Style Bubble

Susanna Lau, aka Susie Bubble, posts three times a day in Style Bubble, the blog she started in 2006. This popular visual diary is known for featuring young, undiscovered talent as well as Lau's daily ensembles and fashion observations. Lau has written for *Elle* magazine, dazzeddigital.com, and *The Daily Rubbish*.

Style Rookie

Tavi Gevinson began Style Rookie at the age of eleven. Within two years, the industry began to look at her as a something of a fashion prodigy. Before long, this teen from the suburbs of Chicago was on the radar of leading fashion designers such as Karl Lagerfeld and Rodarte's Mulleavy sisters. Gavinson has gone on to create *Rookie* magazine.

Talk2myshirt

Talk2myshirt is a fashion-tech blog launched in 2006 by Erich Zainziger. Having worked for companies like Philips Electronics, Zainziger has an interest in innovations and advancements involving smart textiles and wearable technology. Talk2myshirt features DIY projects, research, and reviews and serves as a community platform for fashion techies.

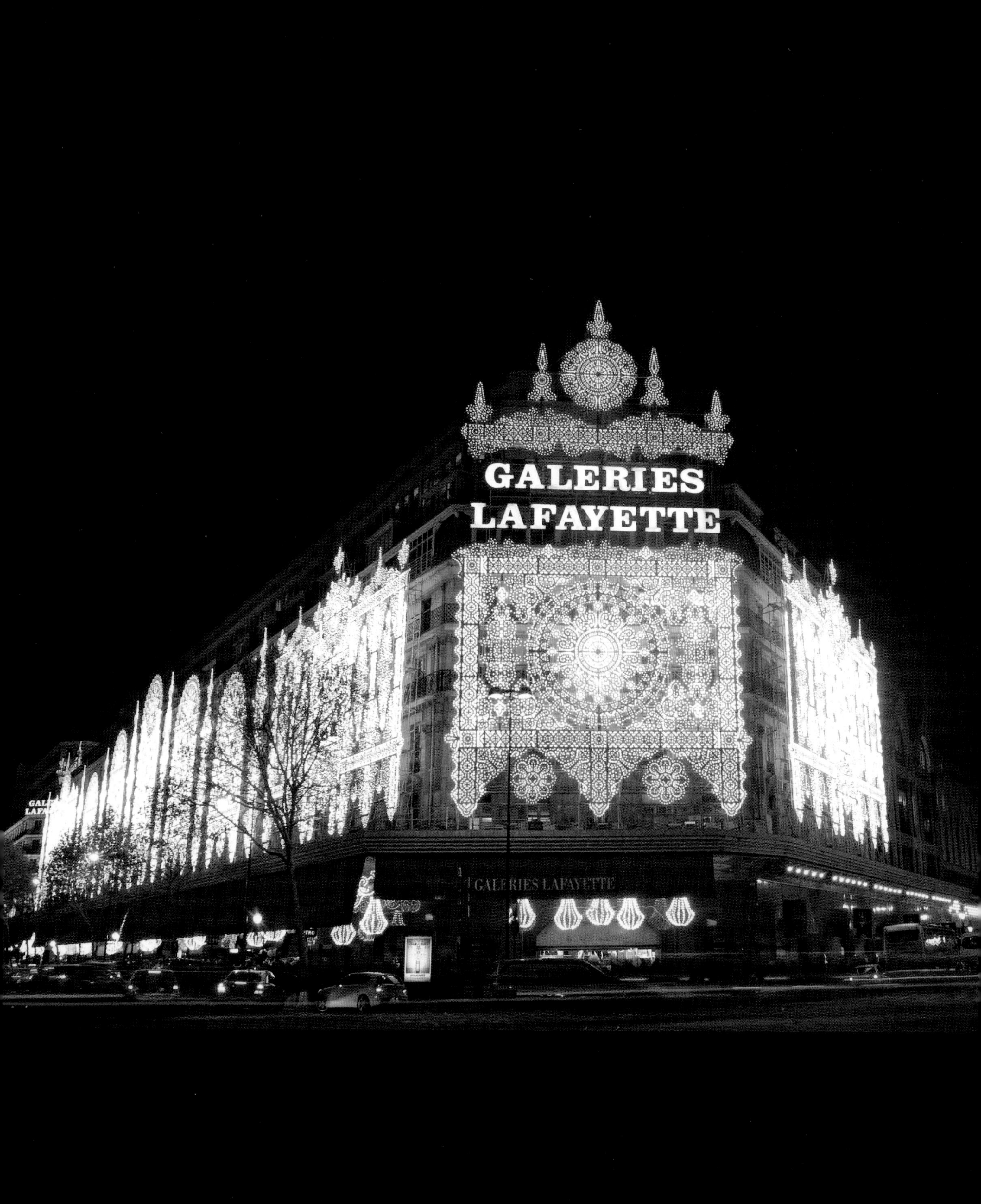
GALERIES
LAFAYETTE
GALERIES LAFAYETTE

Market

266
Ownership

The ownership model behind a fashion label directly affects how that company operates. Designers who choose to retain complete control over their business may serve their desire for creative freedom but will usually limit how far and how fast their brand can expand. Although designers that follow this route find it increasing difficult to compete with mega-firms, some like Dries Van Noten and Rei Kawakubo have built successful international businesses without sacrificing their power or their philosophy. In selling a controlling interest of their fashion house to a large conglomerate, designers must answer to boards and shareholders, but it also affords them access to valuable resources not otherwise within reach. Somewhere in the middle lies a compromise, an ownership model that can offer financial stimulation and still allow the designer a level of autonomy. With creativity and commerce falling into distinctly different camps, designing around the divide becomes as crucial to the success of the brand as each new collection.

268
Branding

Traditionally, a brand indicated ownership. It has since shifted from mere label to mighty symbol of everything a design house stands for. Didier Grumbach, president of the Chambre Syndicale, eloquently describes the current importance of the brand: "Creativity is more important than marketing; creativity is tied to a brand. The brand is more important than the product itself. When you buy a Hermès necktie for a gift, you do not care that it is twice as expensive as another necktie, because you have an entire universe in it that you relate to." Increasingly, designers themselves are perceived as less important than their brands and may leave or return to their fashion house or leave again without necessarily disturbing the brand's forward momentum.

271
Retail

Retail is what closes the loop in the fashion cycle. If designers are to remain financially viable, they must find the right sales model. Relationships have become more important than transactions in a highly competitive marketplace. To cultivate authentic relationships and build a solid base, any strategy for engaging the consumer must reflect their needs and desires, as well as those of the distribution channel and the designer. Sales take place on many different platforms. Retail environments range from intimate boutiques to sprawling department stores. They can be brick-and-mortar operations or virtual ones. Carefully designed environments and experiences are an extension of the brand and can add actual or perceived value to whatever is being sold.

Galeries Lafayette, Paris, 2009
Photo from Bloomberg via Getty Images.

Luxury Conglomerates

Although it may seem a fairly recent phenomenon, having financiers fund fashion brands is nothing new. Entrepreneur Marcel Boussac financed Christian Dior after the Second World War, and his backing set the stage for a fashion enterprise that still thrives today, unlike those of many of Dior's contemporaries. Fashion became big business in the 1990s thanks to the surge of major conglomerates taking controlling interests in luxury labels. The combined power of these consortiums of couture has been responsible for the revitalization of older fashion houses like Balenciaga, Givenchy, Gucci, and Louis Vuitton as well as the growth of many new ones, including Alexander McQueen, Marc Jacobs, and Stella McCartney. Despite the dangers of monopoly and designers' loss of creative control, the conglomerates now drive the fashion industry.

LVMH

A leader among the conglomerates is LVMH (Louis Vuitton Moët-Hennessy) run by Bernard Arnault, whose Groupe Arnault owns a majority share. This global arbiter of taste controls an enormous piece of the couture and luxury ready-to-wear industry and is aggressively trying to buy controlling shares in stand-alone, family-run businesses such as Hermès, of which LVMH now holds over 20 percent. Dior is not technically part of LVMH; rather it belongs to the Groupe Arnault.

PPR

Challenging LVMH is PPR, headed by the entrepreneur François-Henri Pinault. In 1999, Pinault's father, François, CEO of Pinault-Printemps-Redoute, entered the luxury sector by acquiring 42 percent of the Gucci Group in a bitter battle with his former friend Arnault of LVMH, which then owned just over 20 percent. Other high-end fashion labels soon joined the Gucci Group, and in a takeover bid in 2004, the Pinaults acquired the remaining equity in the company. In addition to the luxury sector, PPR, as the larger holding company has been known since 2005, also maintains a controlling interest in Fnac, the electronics/cultural goods retailer; its growing sports and lifestyle division owns 75 percent of Puma.

Photo by Mehdi Fedouach, AFP, Getty Images.

Photo by Thomas Samson, Gamma-Rapho via Getty Images.

LVMH Holdings

10 Cane • Ardbeg • Acqua di Parma • Belvedere • Benefit Cosmetics • Berluti • Bodegas Chandon • Bulgari • Cape Mentelle • Céline • Chaumet • Château D'Yquem • Château Cheval Blanc • Cheval des Andes • Cloudy Bay • Connaissance des Artes • De Beers • DFS • Dior Watches • Dom Pérignon • Domaine Chandon • Donna Karan • eLuxury • Emilio Pucci • Emilio Pucci Parfums • Fendi • Fendi Parfums • Fred • Fresh • Givenchy • Glenmorangie Company • Groupe les Echos • Guerlain • Hennessy • Hublot • Investir • Kenzo • Kenzo Parfums • Krug • Le Bon Marché • Les Echos • Loewe • Louis Vuitton • Make Up For Ever • Marc Jacobs • Mercier • Miami Cruiseline Services • Moët & Chandon • Montaudon • Newness • Newton • Numanthia • Parfums Christian Dior • Parfums Givenchy • Perfumes Loewe • Radio Classique • Rossimoda • Royal van Lent • Ruinart • Samaritaine • Sephora • Stefanobi • TAG Heuer • Terrazas de los Andes • Thomas Pink • Veuve Cliquot • Wenjun • Zenith

PPR Holdings

Alexander McQueen • Balenciaga • Bottega Veneta • Boucheron • Brioni • Girard-Perregaux • Gucci • JeanRichard • Sergio Rossi • Stella McCartney • Yves Saint Laurent

Luxury Groups

Unlike the large-scale brand portfolios acquired by conglomerates, luxury groups focus on a smaller number of holdings. Whereas larger groups may diversify beyond fashion goods, most smaller luxury groups focus on related products. While in some cases the reasoning behind the acquisition of similar labels suggests the desire to eliminate the competition, most luxury groups are built with the intent of bringing together successful brands that complement one another.

Valentino Fashion Group

Textile manufacturers in Italy since 1836, the Marzotto family expanded into the clothing market in 1991 when they purchased a controlling share of Hugo Boss, which they maintained until 2009. In 2002 the Marzotto Group purchased Valentino and began to focus on the various brands within the Valentino empire and on licensing M Missoni and MCS Marlborough Classics. Three years later, the company split its fashion holdings from its textile businesses. In 2007 the Permira private equity fund took a controlling interest in the Valentino Fashion Group. The same year, VFG purchased 45 percent of the American design house Proenza Schouler, in which it still holds a minority interest after selling much of its stake to a group that includes Theory founder Andrew Rosen. In 2012, VFG was purchased by Mayhoola for Investments S.P.C., a private luxury group owned by Qatar's royal family.

Prada Group

The Prada label, started by Mario and Martino Prada in 1913 as Fratelli Prada, specialized in the sale of leather goods, handbags, and steamer trunks. Six years later, it became an official supplier to the Italian royal family. Miuccia Prada inherited the company from her mother Luisa Prada in 1978, after working at the company for eight years. Together, with Patrizio Bertelli, who would become her husband, she began to move the company in a new direction, which included the acquisition of other brands. The new luxury group secured a controlling stake in Helmut Lang in 1999, followed by Jil Sander a few months later. The same year, they joined forces with LVMH to acquire a 51 percent interest in Fendi. Then came the shoemakers Church's and Car Shoe in 2001. All this put Prada on top of the European luxury goods market. The investments proved unsuccessful, however, and the Prada Group began to pull back, first selling their stake in Fendi in 2001, then Helmut Lang and Jil Sander in 2006. The Prada Group currently consists of Prada, Miu Miu, Church's, and Car Shoe.

Privately Owned Labels

In the world of fashion conglomerates, few luxury labels have been able to maintain ownership of their name. Among those that remain are family-owned Hermès and Chanel.

Hermès

Thierry Hermès established Hermès in 1837 as a harness workshop that catered to the aristocracy in Paris. In 1880, his son Charles-Émile took the reigns and moved the shop to 24 rue du Faubourg Saint-Honoré, where it remains today. The first couture apparel collection was introduced in 1929, and today the brand is famous for silk scarves and the iconic Kelly and Birkin bags. Hermès is a prime example of a high-profile luxury brand that has managed to retain private ownership. The Hermès family retains over 73 percent control, with an estimated 6 percent free-float (outstanding shares available to the public for trade). LVMH, which holds a 21 percent interest, has been slowly acquiring more stock in the company each year, a sign that could signal interest in a takeover. As a countermeasure, in 2010 the Hermès family set up a holding group with over 50 percent of the company's capital.

Chanel

The House of Chanel began as Gabrielle "Coco" Chanel's millinery shop in 1909. The label has produced iconic fashion items, from Chanel No. 5 perfume to the quilted Chanel bag. The Wertheimer family became a part of the Chanel legacy in 1924 when Pierre Wertheimer invested in Parfums Chanel, in exchange for a 70 percent share of the company. Although Chanel resented his stake in the business, the brand has been in the Wertheimer family's care since her death in 1971. They hired Karl Lagerfeld in 1983 to update the house for the contemporary fashion consumer. Under Lagerfeld's direction, in 2002 Chanel established the Paraffection company to preserve small specialty haute couture ateliers. Wertheimer grandsons, Alain and Gerard, currently control the luxury brand.

Opposite Page Above
Bernard Arnault (right), CEO of LVMH, 2009 •
Below François Pinault, CEO of the PPR Group, 2010

Licensing

Couturiers have used licenses to build their brands, broaden their markets, and significantly increase their bottom line. Licensing agreements permit manufacturers to produce products under a designer's label for a set period of time in a specific region. One such arrangement in 1925 resulted in the creation of arguably the most recognized perfume in the world, Chanel No. 5. Unlike many of his contemporaries, Christian Dior exercised great control over his licenses, maintaining the quality and creativity associated with his brand. This ensured that after his death the House of Dior could go on doing business at the same level. Ralph Lauren is an example of a contemporary designer who has successfully diversified into every conceivable fashion-related category, including restaurants. Pierre Cardin, by contrast, created a system of licenses in the 1960s that generated profits, but diluted the strength of the label because so many products bearing his name failed to meet the brand's perceived standards. Halston provides another cautionary tale of allowing ungoverned licenses, in his case, agreements with low-cost J.C. Penney, to undermine his reputation.

Nº 5

CHANEL

THE MOST TREASURED NAME IN PERFUME...

CHANEL

Bonwit Teller   Harzfeld's

I. Magnin   Neiman-Marcus

The Shoes of Christian Dior

designed in Paris by Roger Vivier   about $27.00

Above Left Advertisement for Chanel No. 5 • *Left* Advertisement for Christian Dior shoes by Roger Vivier

Brand Marketing

Calvin Klein, already head of an established fashion house in the mid-1970s, gained fame by placing his name on the back pocket of a pair of jeans. An early example of the logo as brand marketing, it triggered the designer jeans trend of the 1980s. Louis Vuitton, of course, had long embraced this strategy, applying its logo as a pattern to practically every imaginable surface.

Another tactic is intentionally to remove any evidence of branding (including logos), creating the perception of an insider status. Countering the tyranny of logos, items from Maison Martin Margiela's show collections are marked with a blank tape label held by four pick stitches. Visible from the outside, and recognizable from a distance, the stitches have in fact become the logo, an international "badge of cool."

Product placement works best when extremely relevant to or seamlessly integrated into an environment. Inserting products into entertainment vehicles (films, television programs, and live performances) and special events increases visibility and engenders trust when it makes sense. Giorgio Armani, for instance, has mastered dressing celebrities on the red carpet without sacrificing the integrity of his brand.

Photo by David Corio, Michael Ochs Archive, Getty Images.

Private collection.

Above Subtle mark of the blank label on a Maison Martin Margiela jacket, 1989/90 ▪ *Right* Mary J. Blige in logo-covered pants by Fendi, early 1990s

Photo by Paul O'Driscoll, Bloomberg via Getty Images.

Left Giorgio Armani couture fitting room at the Cannes Film Festival, 2006

Capsule Collections

Today's fashion consumers shop across many retail platforms and most contemporary wardrobes include both luxury and mass-market items. Capsule collections allow designers to partner with retailers to bridge the gap between high and low, making their brand accessible by having a presence at various price points in multiple markets. This strategy allows both the designer and the retailer to build new audiences. A history of highly successful fashion diffusion teams and the growth of cost-conscious shopping seem to have laid to rest fears of brand diminishment.

Swedish H&M has led the charge in high-profile alliances, with sometimes unexpected designers: Karl Lagerfeld, Stella McCartney, Viktor & Rolf, Roberto Cavalli, Comme des Garçons, Matthew Williamson, Jimmy Choo, Sonia Rykiel, Lanvin, Versace, Marni, and Maison Martin Margiela. It has also leveraged the celebrity of pop stars Madonna and Kylie Minogue, fashion blogger Elin Kling, and fashion editor Anna Dello Russo. Topshop in the United Kingdom has partnered with some of the brightest British fashion design stars, including Celia Birtwell, Louise Goldin, Christopher Kane, Meadham Kirchhoff, Alexander McQueen, Jonathan Saunders, Sophia Kokosalaki, and model Kate Moss. eBay, the online auction and shopping website, has established exclusive partnerships with Norma Kamali, Derek Lam, and Narciso Rodriguez. And Target, which has worked with Jean Paul Gaultier, Alexander McQueen, Missoni, Isaac Mizrahi, Zac Posen, Rodarte, Proenza Schouler, and Anna Sui, entered into an unprecedented relationship with Neiman Marcus to create a holiday collection for 2012 that featured twenty-four of the CFDA's leading designers.

Photo by Mark Large, Alamy.

Photo courtesy of H&M.

Above Top Launch of Kate Moss for Topshop, 2007 • *Above Middle* Launch of Sonia Rykiel for H&M, 2010 • *Left* Derek Lam for eBay, 2011

The Store

Private collection.

Right Bonwit Teller advertisement, 1928 • *Far Right* Filene's French Shops advertisement, 1951

Photo by Isabelle Ogoula.

Photo by Dominik Pabis, iStockphoto.

Photo by Michael Alexander Guran.

Above Middle Sonia Rykiel store, Paris, 2011 • *Right* Louis Vuitton store, Budapest, 2009 • *Far Right* Prada store, Singapore, 2011

Even in an age of online shopping, nothing can replace the unique experience of walking into a space, being immersed in that store's particular combination of display, merchandising, and customer service, and the immediate gratification of leaving with a purchase. Traditional retail models include the boutique, the designer brand store, and the department store. Each has a different strategy for making a sale. The boutique depends greatly on a consistent personal vision, usually that of the owner and/or buyer, which caters to a customer in an intimate environment. The brand store is an extension of the designer's aesthetic, where every aspect of the shopping experience reflects the concept behind the label. The department store serves as an umbrella for many shopping niches, offering a broad variety of products that appeal to a wider audience.

Essential to any retail strategy are store buyers who can grasp operational goals, budgets, timelines, and perhaps most important, their customer base. Buyers are instrumental in translating what designers put on the runway into retail-friendly purchases. Buyers edit designer collections based on their experience of what will sell and can sometimes request modifications to a design that will better suit their customer. In reality, every decision buyers make regarding who and what and how much to carry will define a store's target customer and what they will buy.

The Curated Store

The retail experience continues to evolve. The modern fashion store is being reimagined and reinvented by visionary merchants to serve unique philosophies about culture and commerce. These alternative stores set themselves apart from their contemporaries by experimenting with different approaches to engaging the fashion consumer. Dover Street Market (DSM) is a retail concept created by Rei Kawakubo that shifts focus every six months. It carries numerous labels alongside Comme des Garçons merchandise and serves as a space for artistic collaborations of all kinds, including ones with Nike, Paco Rabanne, Louis Vuitton, and Yayoi Kusama. It also provides a home for exclusive content and innovative fashion newcomers like Christopher Kane, Gareth Pugh, and Jun Takahashi of Undercover. A second DSM has opened in Ginza and a third is planned to launch in New York City. Similarly, Colette has been described as Paris's temple of cool, combining the sale of fashion and accessories with an exhibit space, bookshop, and water bar. It has achieved cultlike status among dedicated fashion connoisseurs due to its reputation for offering cutting-edge, hard-to-find products, with limited stock that changes regularly. Colette also boasts over 150 collaborations with stylish celebrities, designers, and the Dover Street Market. In New York, Opening Ceremony is a multifaceted fashion business that includes a retail space, showroom, and private-label collection. It has built a impressive history of collaborations with fashion brands like Pendleton, Levi's, Timberland, Keds, and Robert Clergerie, as well as actress Chloë Sevigny and filmmaker Spike Jonze. Every year, Opening Ceremony adopts the consumer experience of a different country to explore the culture and commercial character of that locale.

The Pop-up Shop

The pop-up shop serves several functions. As a marketing strategy, it draws the attention of the media and the community. Carefully chosen locales might act as catalysts for introducing fashion retail into otherwise underserved areas. Real estate companies and landlords can offset the cost of empty properties with short-term leases. From a business perspective, the pop-up creates a sense of urgency for consumers who understand time-sensitive shopping experiences. It also allows brands to move unique stock and one-of-a-kind samples that might not be available anywhere else. The first of these short-term sales spaces, called Vacant, appeared in Los Angeles in 1999 with a simple idea: the store would close once all the merchandise was sold, then move onto another location. Comme des Garçons adopted the strategy in 2004 with its one-year-expiration-date Guerilla Shop. Other big labels like Gucci, Kate Spade, Louis Vuitton, and Puma have since embraced the trend. The next logical step in this retail revolution is the pop-up mall. Boxpark Shoreditch, a mall constructed of recycled shipping containers in East London, was the brainchild of British entrepreneur Roger Wade. Launched in 2011, the five-year project provides affordable spaces to innovative brands by invitation only. That same year, Popuphood was introduced in Oakland, California, a flash-retailing initiative that also serves as an incubator program for small businesses and a street-by-street revitalization project for struggling neighborhoods.

Photo by Jeff Gilbert, Alamy.

Above Dover Street Market, London, 2007

Photo by Richard B. Levine, Alamy.

Above Tommy Hilfiger pop-up store, Meatpacking District, New York, 2011

Event Space

Photo by Neilson Barnard, Getty Images.

Long before Daphne Guinness dressed for the Metropolitan Museum of Art's Costume Institute Gala in the windows of Barneys on Madison Avenue in 2011, go-go dancers took the place of mannequins in the windows of Carnaby Street shops. London in the 1960s made shopping an event, with boutiques becoming venues for "happenings" where customers could socialize, get informed, and be entertained.

Today, multipurpose retail space can enhance a brand, as well as magnify the fiscal and cultural value of its store within the community. Prada's New York "epicenter" is appropriately housed on the former site of the Guggenheim Museum's Soho branch. Designed by Rem Koolhaas, the 23,000-square-foot (2,139 sq m) space easily transforms into an amphitheater/exhibition hall/event space. Retail resides within culture as it plays host to lectures, performances, art exhibits, and other activities. Prada's commitment to added-value retail experiences extends to its Miu Miu label. Miu Miu Musings, an intellectual salon often hosted by socialite and style icon Shala Monroque, attracts industry leaders like Andrè Leon Tally, Suzy Menkes, and Imran Amed.

Photo by Chad Buchanan, Getty Images.

Above Daphne Guinness dressing for the Costume Institute Gala in a window of Barneys New York, 2011
• *Left* Gathering for a performance by the Raconteurs at the Prada Epicenter, New York, 2006

e-Commerce

"Brick and click" or "click and mortar" are terms used to describe real-world retailers that also have an online shopping presence. "Bricks, clicks, and flips" are operations that add a physical catalogue to the mix. E-commerce has transformed the fashion business, making it possible for designers to build a global customer base, sometimes eliminating the need for a physical location completely. In the United States, Black Friday, the kick-off to the holiday shopping season, is now accompanied by Cyber Monday, because of how much of an impact it has on the bottom line. Technology continues to make the process faster, more efficient, and increasingly interactive. David Lauren was a pioneer when he began to lead the Ralph Lauren brand into the digital age with what he called "merchan-tainment." Rather than launch the equivalent of an online catalog, he managed to build a virtual environment that reflected the lifestyle branding that is an essential component of Ralph Lauren store design and advertising campaigns, two of the company's most important branding tools. Although there are perceived downsides to shopping online—the inability to touch the product, lack of confidence regarding fit and quality—savvy online merchants can create innovative business models that reward the client in other ways. Moda Operandi is an online service that photographs the latest collections both on the runway and in showrooms, then allows clients to prepurchase products during virtual trunk shows, often with pieces that would never otherwise be made available. Thecorner.com is another online outlet that creates individually tailored ministores for unique, avant-garde, and hard-to-find designer brands.

Polyvore

Mood boards and communities set Polyvore apart from other fashion sites. Visitors are encouraged to channel their inner fashion editor to create "sets" of their favorite fashions and accessories with images pulled from all over the Internet, mixed and matched to reflect individual style, and then shared with visitors from every corner of the globe. These boards often influence trends and stimulate sales because each image of an item is linked to a source where it can be purchased. In addition to fan-based shopping, the site offers designer spotlights, "how they wore it" features, and fashion advice.

Photo by Dave M. Benett, Getty Images.

Top Ralph Lauren celebrating ten years of digital innovation with 3-D projections onto the London flagship store, 2010

Net-a-Porter

Net-a-Porter focuses on the latest "must haves" for women and is considered one of the world's premier online luxury fashion retailers. Launched in 2000, the site features magazine-style spreads of international labels that are updated weekly. In addition to cutting-edge editorial merchandising, the company is known for its great packaging and excellent customer care. Net-a-Porter's style destination for men, Mr. Porter, also sells luxury goods. It offers uncluttered layouts, real-life men as models, and a streamlined, well-edited selection. Although these sites cater to an affluent clientele, they democratize access to high-caliber products in contrast to most of their brick-and-mortar counterparts.

Gilt Groupe

Gilt Groupe is a members-only merchant that brings the thrill of the sample sale to online shopping. This first-come, first-served fashion site serves up time-sensitive daily deals. A heightened sense of urgency and competitiveness fuels purchases. In addition to apparel, Gilt Groupe sells home decor and food, city-based services, and one-of-a-kind travel packages. Although all products are promoted under the heading of discounted designer goods, Gilt Groupe also works with brands to produce products exclusively for the site that will never hang in stores. Previews of upcoming sales, featured designers, and must-have pieces are meant to make the buyer feel like an industry insider.

Of a Kind

"Know and own" is the philosophy behind Of a Kind, a site that's meant to appeal to fashion consumers who are interested in the processes and personalities behind the products they buy. Of a Kind focuses on discovering, supporting, and promoting emerging fashion talent with well-crafted and affordable limited editions. Early adopters can help launch careers and support small fashion businesses around the world. They are rewarded with insider information about the designers, insights into how the products are made, and the knowledge that they are among only a handful of people in the world who own one of these special pieces.

Fashion/Art

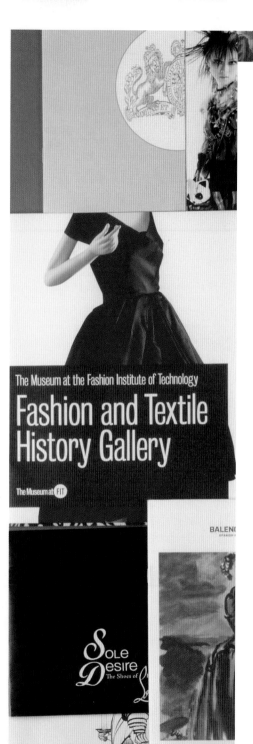

To ask whether fashion is art is not the right question. The more pertinent query is, *When* is fashion art? In an interview with Ingrid Mida, Harold Koda, curator-in-charge of the Costume Institute of the Metropolitan Museum of Art, stated: "I like to point out, just as not all photographs are art, not all fashion is art, but what constitutes an important work in either field is not necessarily established by the intention of its creator or the reason for its creation." Two fundamental measures of art are form and content. Fashion designers apply the elements of art and the principles of design to a specific set of materials, which meets the first criteria. They also infuse their work with ideas and messages designed to move fashion beyond mere utility. But who decides whether these benchmarks are enough?

Does the designer's intent or the reception of the work establish how fashion is defined? Does the authority of the curator trump public perception, and is that opinion powerful enough to broaden the definition of art, pushing past historical and societal constraints? Some designers easily embrace the label of artist. Cristóbal Balenciaga said that "a couturier must be an architect for design, a sculptor for shape, a painter for color, a musician for harmony, and a philosopher for temperance." While others, even those whose work might seem most aligned with conceptual art practices, draw a clear distinction. Martin Margiela denies any association: "Fashion is an inspiration, a craft, a technical know-how and not, in our opinion, an art."

The business of fashion can be sited as a factor in undermining fashion's status as an art form. Clothes, however artfully crafted, remain a commodity to be bought and sold. An entire industry is built on the production of fashion, with success being measured at the cash register. Miuccia Prada makes her position clear: "Definitely fashion for me isn't art. Art is a place for ideas without any other direct concerns. If I'm a good fashion designer, it's because I sell." But if commercial viability negates fashion's standing as art, other forms of aesthetic practice must come under scrutiny, with the line between art and commerce having become very blurred over the years. The distinctions must be examined in degrees, understanding that business is but one of the many facets of either fashion or art, next to craft, science, technology, and performance.

Design ist Kunst, die sich nützlich macht (design is art that makes itself useful) is the motto of Germany's Die Neue Sammlung, the largest design museum in Europe. The phrase helps to frame the discipline of fashion within a contemporary context of art. From this perspective, the value of art is not lessened for also serving a function. If no object is endowed with artistic significance until one assigns it such a meaning, then art is truly in the eye of the beholder, regardless of the medium, whether it falls under the heading of fine, performing, decorative, or applied arts.

The recognition of a medium as an art form has often required advocates stepping up to raise standards and awareness. In the early twentieth century, led by Alfred Stieglitz and F. Holland Day, the Photo-Secession promoted photography as a fine art, given the subjectivity of manipulating an image. Rudolf Arnheim, Béla Balázs, and Siegfried Kracauer developed some of the earliest theories about film as an authentic art form. As late as 1987, the Jazz Preservation Act was instrumental in establishing jazz music as a unique, black American musical art form. Fashion as art has its own champions in creative communities of scholars, writers, educators, curators, and avid collectors.

The histories of art and fashion have long been closely intertwined. Art regularly documents fashion while fashion often references art. Mariano Fortuny and Madame Grès looked to Greek statuary. Paul Poiret commissioned Raoul Dufy to create textiles. Madeleine Vionnet studied the choreography of dancer Isadora Duncan to better understand the body in motion. Elsa Schiaparelli collaborated directly with artists Salvador Dalí, Alberto Giacometti, and Jean Cocteau to create masterworks of fashion surrealism. Ralph Rucci has used his own paintings as the foundation for collections of original fabrics. Exploring the places where art and fashion intersect provides greater insight into whether fashion is art by association or simply a kindred spirit.

Yohji Yamamoto describes museums as "where fashion goes to die." But in recent decades, museums have played an important role in analyzing and interpreting fashion (Yamamoto's among them). Diana Vreeland was, of course, a pioneer in this realm when she joined the Costume Institute in 1972. Her exhibits were true experiences, filled with scent and music as well as clothing, capturing the theatre of fashion. Fashion exhibitions continue to proliferate and become more impactful. "Alexander McQueen: Savage Beauty" was the Met's eighth most attended show in 141 years. It is also important to note that many museums today no longer segregate traditional works of art, furnishings, and fashion, instead choosing to put them together in context, demonstrating their close relations.

In the end, asking *when* fashion becomes art is a more useful way to bridge the gap between converts and nonbelievers, simply because it serves as an invitation to continue exploring the subject, rather than becoming entrenched on one side or the other. Or perhaps one should take a cue from the Baz Luhrmann film of a simulated dialogue between Schiaparelli and Prada for the Met's recent "Impossible Conversations" exhibition. Prada has the final, fittingly ambiguous, statement: "Fashion is art, fashion is not art. But at the end, who cares?"

Tastemakers

280
Stylists

Traditionally, the fashion conscious have taken their cues from fashion designers or fashion editors. Today, every wardrobe choice a socialite or celebrity makes is documented and scrutinized in the tabloids and on the Internet within moments. The value of having a trusted advocate dedicated to developing their fashion personae has led to the growing importance of the fashion stylist. Beyond selecting clothes, they are charged with keeping ahead of trends, while understanding what works for a specific individual or situation. Many stylists in the public eye, like Rachel Zoe and Patricia Field, have achieved their own level of celebrity status as wardrobe gurus. Grace Coddington is an excellent example of a visionary stylist with the ability to influence the creative direction of high-profile editorials and ad campaigns, while Michaela Angela Davis works across multiple platforms—television, film, music videos, performances, and public appearances—to make her statements about style.

282
Arbiters

Whereas most follow fashion, some definitely lead. Every visible facet of society—politics, privilege, music, film, the media, and of course the fashion industry—has produced, sometimes inadvertently, authentic arbiters of style. Their impact and relevance can often be measured by how their sartorial expression enters the fashion vernacular. To refer to something as being very Jackie O. is a universally understood description. There are messages in the manner of dress. David Bowie made a career of communicating different ideas of himself by experimenting with his image, while Patti Smith could serve as a study in the evolution of a single theme on how clothing conveys identity. Whether they represent a way of life or the attitude of an era, whether they speak of elegance, rebellion, or eccentricity, icons have staying power.

Tilda Swinton in Haider Ackermann, Fall/Winter 2009/10
Photo by Sean Gallup, Getty Images.

Grace Coddington

Photo by Solve Sundsbø

Left Grace Coddington in *i-D*, March 2009

Grace Coddington's relationship with *Vogue* began early in life. As a teenager living in Wales, outdated copies of the fashion magazine were her only link to the glamorous world of style. When she was seventeen, her photographs were submitted to a *Vogue* model competition. Winning the Young Idea category launched her modeling career, which included a stint as house model for Vidal Sassoon. A car accident left her disfigured at the age of twenty-six, derailing her career until five reconstructive surgeries allowed her to return to modeling in 1963. Five years later, over lunch with Beatrix Miller, editor of British *Vogue*, she was hired as a junior editor for the magazine. She rose to the level of senior fashion editor before moving to New York and becoming design director for Calvin Klein Collection in 1987. A year later, she joined Anna Wintour at American *Vogue* as fashion director.

On a fashion shoot in 1971, Coddington met her mentor, fashion photographer Norman Parkinson, whom she credits for her dedication to the art of creative collaboration. She has earned a reputation for working very closely with photographers to produce her trademark, theatrical fashion fantasy photo narratives. In 2002, the CFDA honored her illustrious career with their Lifetime Achievement Award. Coddington has in fact been shaping the perception of fashion for over fifty years. With the release of R. J. Cutler's 2009 documentary *The September Issue*, the true impact of her work as creative director for American *Vogue* has been celebrated not just by the industry, but by all fashion aficionados.

Patricia Field

Photo by Davis Surowiecki; Getty Images.

Left Patricia Field at the DKNY Fall/Winter 2003/04 show

Time magazine named Patricia Field one of the 100 Most Influential Fashion Icons of All Time. She has touched the fashion world as retailer, a stylist, a costume designer, and a fashion designer. Field opened her eponymous Greenwich Village boutique in 1966. Currently located on the Lower East Side, her shop offers an eclectic mix of edgy, theatrical fashions and accessories, an aesthetic that pays homage to 1990s club kids and drag queens.

Field is perhaps best known for the flavor she brought to the HBO series *Sex and the City*, on which she collaborated with Rebecca Weinberg. The show became as famous for the fashions worn each week by its four leading ladies as for the steamy storylines. Her work earned her five Emmy Award nominations and one win as well as six Costume Designers Guild Award nominations with four wins. When the series moved to the big screen she followed, crafting the sexy, sartorial style for two movies. Her costume work also includes *Ugly Betty* and the film *The Devil Wears Prada*, which led to an Oscar nomination for best costume design.

Her own fashion line, the House of Field, is popular with celebrities like Jennifer Lopez, Paulina Rubio, Shakira, and Mary J. Blige. She has produced numerous fashion projects in collaboration with other companies, including Candie's Shoes, Rocawear, Pro-Keds, Seiko Japan, Payless Shoes, Mattel's Barbie, Marks and Spencer, HSN, and Coca-Cola.

Rachel Zoe

Right Rachel Zoe at the Couture Council of MFIT awards luncheon, 2010

Self-taught celebrity stylist Rachel Zoe's motto is "Be Glamorous. Everyday." That applies to herself as well as to her Hollywood A-list clients: Kate Beckinsale, Cameron Diaz, Jennifer Garner, Anne Hathaway, Kate Hudson, Keira Knightley, Lindsay Lohan, Eva Mendes, Debra Messing, Demi Moore, Nicole Richie, Molly Sims, and Liv Tyler. Zoe is known for a sexy, laid-back glamour that defines red carpet dressing.

She began her career as a fashion journalist for *YM* and *Gotham* magazines, but her work as a freelance stylist put her on the map. In 2007 with Rose Apodaca, she published *Style A to Zoe: The Art of Fashion, Beauty, and Everything Glamour*, a *New York Times* best seller with insider styling tips and advice about all aspects of a fashionable life. In 2008, she became a reality television star with the launch of *The Rachel Zoe Project*, which follows her efforts as a celebrity stylist. Her comprehensive blog serves up The Zoe Report, AccessZOEries, and Zoe Beautiful, through which she continues to share her successful formula for style. She launched Luxe Rachel Zoe, an accessories collection for QVC, which she followed with the Rachel Zoe clothing collection sold at high-end retailers such as Nordstrom and Neiman Marcus. Zoe is also the chief style consultant for Piperlime.com.

Michaela Angela Davis

Right Michaela Angela Davis at Harlem's Fashion Row, 2010

Michaela Angela Davis describes herself as an "image activist," having built a career founded on expanding the narrow narratives of women and celebrating African American culture. Prior to her first job as associate fashion editor at *Essence* magazine in 1991, she assisted her aunt, stylist Joanne Buffer, on photo shoots for big ad campaigns and for *Vogue* magazine, working with photographers like Avedon and Hiro.

Davis went on to help launch *Vibe* magazine as fashion director, then became editor in chief of *Honey* magazine, before returning to *Essence* as the executive fashion and beauty editor in 2004. She is a regular contributor to *Full Frontal Fashion* and has worked with *Ebony*, *Vanity Fair*, *Clutch*, *The View*, E!, VH1, and Metro TV. As a stylist, her high-profile subjects have included Oprah Winfrey, Beyoncé, Prince, Diana Ross, Donald Trump, Mary J. Blige, and Maxwell. Her focus on urban culture and the empowerment of women has provided her with unique opportunities to affect change in the media and within brands as they position themselves in the influential global urban market.

In an interview for WatchHerWork.org, a mentorship program for young women of color, Davis explained how she had to "figure out how to be an activist and not give up these other things that I think are important, like fashion, and style, and culture, and amazing shoes," realizing that, "when I have on amazing shoes those young girls listen to me in a totally different way."

Jacqueline Kennedy Onassis

Photo by Art Rickerby, Time & Life Pictures, Getty Images.

Left Jacqueline Kennedy at the Taj Mahal, India, 1962

Jacqueline Kennedy, well known for her discernment in all aspects of life, particularly when it came to culture and fashion, is said to have "revolutionized the taste of a nation." As First Lady, she was expected to wear the work of American designers as a symbol of support for the domestic fashion industry. Her passion for French couture strongly influenced the clothes that she had American designers, Oleg Cassini, among them, create for her.

All her selections took into consideration how she would be perceived by the public, as well as the press. She wore white at the president's inaugural ball, automatically standing out in a room of dark dresses. On a trip to Canada, she wore a red Pierre Cardin suit that mirrored the uniforms of the Royal Canadian Mounted Police. Traveling through India, she embraced the country's culture of color and made sure to have dresses constructed of fabrics that could withstand the heat. During her time in Washington, the name Jackie became synonymous with elegant but relaxed garments, often sleeveless, whose clean lines so suited her modern style.

After life in the White House, she was followed just as closely. Marrying Greek billionaire Aristotle Onassis, she became Jackie O. and set off a new phase of fashion influence that included her signature oversized sunglasses as well as a return to many of her favorite international designers. In the years that followed, her clothing always reflected the time in which she was living with great subtlety and grace.

Shala Monroque

Photo by Pascal Le Segretain, Getty Images.

Left Shala Monroque in Paris, 2009

Born on the Caribbean island of Saint Lucia, Shala Monroque made her way to Greenwich Village in her twenties. Her relationship with billionaire gallerist Larry Gagosian has since given her an entry into the inner circles of the international art community and has allowed her to become a high-end fashion client. Jetting around the world with Gagosian and in her new role as creative director of *Garage* magazine (recently launched with Dasha Zhukova), what shines forth is Monroque's self-confidence and unconventional turn of mind.

Her eclectic balancing of the elegant and the bold has made her a favorite among street photographers and bloggers. Monroque displays an instinctive fashion sense. While she leans toward a classic silhouette, with a pronounced fondness for 1950s-inspired clothing and kitten heels, she is playful with her accessories. She also has a keen eye for vivid colors and strong prints.

Monroque treats fashion as a form of self-expression and favors designers who are about more than making pretty frocks. Although she wears edgy brands like Rodarte with ease, she especially connects with Prada and Miu Miu. In fact, Miuccia Prada has become a role model and close friend. Monroque, for her part, hosts Miu Miu Musings, a salon-style gathering at stores around the globe and serves as an unofficial ambassador for the brand. With her artful blend of thoughtfulness, daring, and femininity, the fit seems perfect.

David Bowie

Photo by Peter Still, Redferns.

Right David Bowie at the Hammersmith Odeon, London, 1983

By definition, the power of a fashion icon is rooted less in the clothes he wears than in how he wears them. Central to David Bowie's career as a musician has been his experiments with larger-than-life identities for the stage. With each new persona, Bowie's visual presentations have expressed a facet of his personality within the context of his music and society, usually pushing the boundaries of both.

Bowie's most recognizable personality was Ziggy Stardust, the personification of Glam Rock. Ziggy's flamboyant style was steeped in androgyny. A shock of red hair, makeup, fitted jumpsuits, and platform shoes all served to blur the lines between the sexes. Later, came the Thin White Duke, who could be seen as equally rakish and aristocratic. The look also evoked the cabarets of the early twentieth century: slicked-back hair, a flawless white shirt, black trousers, and waistcoat.

Bowie has always been an aficionado of the suit, usually streamlined and narrow to accentuate his lean physique and often in white. In the 1980s, he reinvented himself by adopting a pompadour and a big suit. With age has come polish, repositioning himself as an English gentleman in Savile Row suits. A certain confidence, control, and measured eccentricity characterize the core of Bowie's aesthetic. Being married to supermodel Iman officially ties him to the fashion world, but his sartorial influence has been firmly ingrained upon our culture and the story of fashion for quite some time.

Patti Smith

Photo by Morena Brengola, Getty Images.

Right Patti Smith in Milan, 2007

Patti Smith, poet, painter, and performer, is the muse of many a downtown kid and designer alike. In 1967 she moved from rural southern New Jersey to New York City. There, she met Robert Mapplethorpe, with whom she began living and working on her art. Smith already had a discerning eye toward style—a rangy, disheveled gamine channeling Rimbaud and Baudelaire. Her poetry readings eventually led her into music, and in 1975 she recorded her debut album, *Horses*. The record, a startling mélange of rock, improvised sound, and incantatory poetry, sent up sparks that would ignite the punk explosion. Equally influential was Mapplethorpe's cover photograph of Smith: an androgynous figure with hacked-off locks, in black pants, white shirt, undone skinny tie, black jacket thrown over the shoulder, gazing forward in a declaration of independence.

Over time Smith pared her look down to a few key gestures: a worn T-shirt or white shirt (cuffs unbuttoned), broken-in boots, men's jeans, a leather jacket or boxy blazer, a slouchy hat, and a devil-may-care attitude. Smith stepped out of the performing spotlight, reemerging in the mid-1990s. In her return to music and writing, her aesthetic has remained constant. If her clothes seem more tailored today, it's in part a result of wearing the designers her style has influenced; foremost Ann Demeulemeester, who asked Smith to walk her menswear show in 2006, a year before she would be inducted into the Rock and Roll Hall of Fame. As always, Smith is conscious of what she conveys, and there's a sweetness to her swagger.

Daphne Guinness

Photo by Nick Harvey, WireImage.

Left Daphne Guinness in London, 2010

A muse to many artists, designers, and photographers, Daphne Guinness is a direct descendant of Arthur Guinness, who founded the famous brewery in 1755. Her childhood was spent at the family's country homes in England and Ireland. Family holidays were celebrated at an eighteenth-century monastery in Cadaques, Spain, where Salvador Dalí, Marcel Duchamp, Richard Hamilton, Man Ray, and Dieter Roth were neighbors.

The fashion realm has embraced Guinness as a visionary. In 1994, she joined the ranks of sartorial savants when she was inducted into the International Best Dressed Hall of Fame. Her carefully cultivated approach to fashion has inspired equally considered, bold dressers such as Lady Gaga. Her friendships with designers like Alexander McQueen have been deeply productive. Tom Ford asked her to close the show that marked his return to womenswear in 2011.

Guinness has become a prolific designer in her own right, often creating pieces she imagines but can't find elsewhere. She has collaborated on many design projects, including a clothing line for Dover Street Market, as well as accessories, jewelry, and scents, and developed a line for MAC cosmetics in 2011. Guinness is an avid collector of couture. The Museum at the Fashion Institute of Technology worked with her in 2011 to curate an exhibition of approximately 100 personal fashion objects, as a tribute to how she thinks about fashion and the art of dressing. In addition to her contributions to the fashion industry, she has worked in film as an actress, producer, and editor of three shorts.

Kate Moss

Photo by Mark Boland, Getty Images.

Left Kate Moss in London, 2011

The legend of Kate Moss begins with being discovered at John F. Kennedy Airport in New York at the age of fourteen. She was described as the antisupermodel because of her demure stature and childlike features. Her career took off five years later as part of a Calvin Klein advertising campaign that ushered in the controversial "heroin chic" look of the early 1990s. She was also closely associated with the introduction of grunge. Today, Moss's style off the runway is a mix of relaxed rock'n'roll, vintage, and bohemian luxe. Her fashion radar consistently puts her ahead of the adoption of new trends.

After twenty years in the business, the waif supermodel has maintained her presence in the fashion press, at times as much for her party-girl antics as for her style. Moss received the CFDA award for Fashion Influence in 2005 and was inducted into the International Best Dressed Hall of Fame in 2006. She recently reinvigorated her career with a series of high-profile contracts with luxury brands Burberry, Bulgari, Roberto Cavalli, Christian Dior, and Louis Vuitton.

Moss made the transition from model to designer when she launched her own fashion line, sold exclusively at Topshop in 2007. The successful vintage-inspired collection was based on her personal style, giving her fans the chance to emulate her iconic flair for fashion. She has also released four fragrances (Kate, Vintage, Vintage Muse, and Lilabelle) for Coty and designed a selection of handbags for Longchamp.

Chloë Sevigny

Photo by Donato Sardella, WireImage.

Right Chloë Sevigny in
New York, 2006

In the mid-1990s, Chloë Sevigny was just a trendsetting teenager with
an internship at *Sassy* magazine when Jay McInerney dubbed her the
new It Girl—one of the "coolest girls in the world"—in his seven-page
profile in *The New Yorker*. Hanging out on the Lower East Side, in the
company of skateboarders, ravers, and club kids, she became a symbol
of the rule-breaking, underground street scene.

Although Sevigny grew up in the preppy town of Darien, Connecticut,
she prided herself on a creative wardrobe largely composed of finds
from flea markets and thrift shops. She was frequently featured in the
pages of publications like *Sassy*, *Details*, *i-D*, and *Interview*. She also
appeared in music videos for alternative rock bands the Lemonheads
and Sonic Youth. Her 1995 acting debut in the film *Kids* led to roles in
independent films and mainstream projects like *Boys Don't Cry* and
American Psycho. In her career as an actress, she has embraced many
controversial characters on stage, film, and television.

Sevigny has played muse to both filmmakers and fashion designers.
Marc Jacobs told *Harper's Bazaar*: "The fashion world is fascinated by
her. Because not only is she talented, young and attractive, she stands
out in a sea of often clichéd looking actresses." Her involvement in
the fashion industry began as a model in her teens, but it has grown
progressively larger. She has been brand spokesperson for Chloé and
creative consultant for Imitation of Christ. She has now developed her
own line of eccentric clothing for Opening Ceremony.

Susie Bubble

Photo by Caroline McCredie, Getty Images.

Right Susie Bubble in
Sydney, 2011

Susie Bubble is a London-based fashion blogger with a devoted
international fan base. Born Susanna Lau in Hong Kong, she developed her fashion sense in rebellion against popular conventions of
style, favoring instead innovative and uncompromising designers.
She admittedly spends a large portion of her income on the acquisition of fashion. Bubble is a passionate connoisseur of fashion, with an
unapologetically quirky flair, inspiring women around the world who
first and foremost dress to please themselves.

Her blog Style Bubble attracts over 25,000 visitors a day and is credited with being among the first to help make the world of fashion more
accessible and democratic. She uses this platform to share her unique
point of view, posting photographs of her ensembles, or what she
describes as her "outfit experimentations." Bubble has also lent her
avant-garde take on style as a contributor to media outlets like *POP*,
The Guardian, *Elle Collections*, SHOWstudio, and dazeddigital.com.

The industry's embrace of her highly influential voice has earned her
coveted invitations to the runway presentations of leading fashion
houses like Gucci, Chanel, and Lanvin. She was asked to collaborate
with Google on Boutiques.com, their fashion-centric search site. In
2010, her sartorial celebrity landed her a spot in a Gap holiday advertising campaign and led to her selection as one of *Elle* magazine's
favorite twentysomethings.

PRACTICE

288

Icons

350

Artisans & Innovators

The designers who help to set the standards in the practice of fashion may usefully be grouped into three distinct categories: the icon, the artisan, and the innovator. Of course, some practitioners cut across such divisions. By the very scope of their vision and their commitment to excellence, these designers are bound to influence fashion simultaneously on multiple fronts. Each of the designers presented here has established a clear voice; many have introduced new definitions into the language of fashion or have steered the evolution of the industry onto a new trajectory. Some belong to the bright center of the fashion world, others occupy its borderlands. What these designers have contributed may be clear—clothes that capture the *zeitgeist* and the imagination. Why and how they have done so, the intent and methodology that inform their work, gets to the heart of fashion practice. A fashion professional is simply someone who works in the industry, while the diverse cross section of true fashion practitioners defines its direction. These designers represent a core sampling of the fashion visionaries, craftspeople, and inventors who have consistently motivated fashion—defined as a material object and as a system—to move forward.

Icons

290

Icons

Fashion designers reach iconic status along many routes. They may innovate construction techniques or reemploy a fabric type; they may encapsulate a concept of beauty or anticipate a change in lifestyles; they may push boundaries of taste or establish a powerful brand; they may be craftsmen or showmen. All become industry touchstones because they represent an aesthetic ideal at a pivotal point in time. Merely getting there first does not ensure a distinguished place in fashion history. Be it a marketing strategy or a silhouette, legends transcend timelines based on how well they distill the essence of an idea.

Alexander McQueen, Spring/Summer 2010
Photo by firstVIEW.

Adrian

1903–59 (United States)

Adrian, born Adrian Adolph Greenburg, was the reigning costume designer during the golden years of Hollywood's influence on the fashion world. While still in design school at Parsons, he worked on Broadway and in Paris theatre, before relocating to Los Angeles to design for Rudolf Valentino. During his tenure at MGM from 1928 to 1941, he costumed over 200 films, among them *The Wizard of Oz* of 1939 and *The Philadelphia Story* of 1940, creating couture garments for the era's leading ladies. Many of his film designs were manufactured and marketed to a public hungry to dress like their favorite stars. In 1932, Macy's sold over half a million copies of the frothy white evening dress that Adrian designed for Joan Crawford's role as Letty Lynton.

Adrian left MGM in 1941 to pursue a career as a fashion designer in Beverly Hills. Though his business included custom design, he excelled at high-end ready-to-wear, selling to department and specialty stores across the country. He designed eveningwear, often incorporating animal prints or references to modern art movements like surrealism or cubism. But he became famous for impeccably tailored suits that followed the V silhouette he had come to love while working in film, with specially designed padded shoulders and a slim skirt. Adhering to wartime L-85 regulations that restricted fabric use, Adrian created collarless knee-length skirt suits with extraordinary dressmaker details, such as precisely matched stripes. Even after the introduction of the New Look, the designer refused to give up on the style that he felt best suited a woman's figure. He retired in 1952.

Above Joan Crawford in *Letty Lynton*, 1932 •
Opposite Page Adrian suit modeled at Neiman Marcus, 1945

Photo by George Hurrell, John Kobal Foundation, Getty Images.

"When Garbo walked out of the studio, glamour went with her, and so did I."

Giorgio Armani

1934– (Italy)

Giorgio Armani perfectly captured a moment when men and women were seeking a new way of dressing that conveyed a relaxed assurance, creating an identity that continues to be desired around the world. In 1957, he left medical school and took a job as a buyer for the Milan department store La Rinascente, where he honed his styling skills. In the mid-1960s, the textile manufacturer and designer Nino Cerutti asked him to restructure the menswear collection for his company Hitman. There and later as a freelancer for other Italian fashion houses, he began to develop the unstructured, unlined jacket for which he would become celebrated.

In 1975 with his business and life partner, Sergio Galeotti, Armani founded a high-end ready-to-wear company based on a new model of tightly coordinated design and production. In his first collections, he struck an elegantly casual note. He introduced a softer menswear look—in luxurious textiles and a signature palette of earth tones like *greige* (a mixture of grey and beige), mushroom, and moss—easily adaptable, in the age of the power suit, for women.

Famously clothing Richard Gere in *American Gigolo* in 1980 and providing the men's wardrobe for *The Untouchables* in 1987, he was among the first designers to open a Los Angeles office to dress celebrities for red-carpet events. To date, he is among the few to be president, CEO, and sole shareholder of their own fashion house. Armani has expanded his lifestyle brand, one of Italy's largest, to encompass numerous retail lines at varying price points as well as an haute couture collection.

Photo by Pool Bassignac/Benainous, Gamma-Rapho via Getty Images.

Photo by Pool Bassignac/Benainous, Gamma-Rapho via Getty Images.

Above Left Giorgio Armani haute couture, Spring/Summer 2006 • *Left* Emporio Armani menswear, Spring/Summer 2012

"*I design for real people. I think of our customers all the time. There is no virtue whatsoever in creating clothing or accessories that are not practical.*"

Left Giorgio Armani
haute couture, Fall/Winter
2011/12

Cristóbal Balenciaga

1895–1972 (Spain)

Called by Dior "the master of us all," Cristóbal Balenciaga is widely recognized as the most innovative couturier of the second half of the twentieth century. Born in the Basque region to a seamstress mother, he first apprenticed to a tailor, then opened fashion houses under the name Eisa in San Sebastián, Madrid, and Barcelona. Forced during the Spanish Civil War to close his establishments, he relocated (via London) to Paris, where he debuted his first collection in 1937. His masterfully cut designs paid homage to his Spanish heritage, including signature elements like black lace flamenco flounces. The tight bodices and wide skirts of his Infanta gowns of 1939 resembled the dress of young princesses in seventeenth-century paintings by Velázquez.

His salon and ateliers are still remembered for their acute austerity and palpable silence. Unlike many of his contemporaries, Balenciaga was involved in every aspect of the creation of a garment, ensuring that each piece left the couture house precisely as he intended. He experimented with volume to create abstract silhouettes that seemed to float around the body. In the mid-1950s, he introduced the tunic, chemise or sack, and baby-doll styles, as well as seamless cocoon coats. He also worked with textile mills to develop fabrics that behaved in ways that suited these new shapes, such as lightweight silks—most famously, silk gazar—with body and texture that he could sculpt.

His clientele were extremely wealthy, sometimes titled, and deeply devoted. His elegant, decorous designs flattered a maturing body, with details such as wide-standing collars and seven-eighths-length sleeves that covered aging arms and chests and showed off fine jewels. Balenciaga never craved the spotlight, rarely giving interviews. He closed his business in 1968, claiming that fashion had become "a dog's life."

Private Collection.

Above Balenciaga evening gowns, drawn by Benito, *Vogue*, 1939

Right Balenciaga, ensemble drawn by Eric, *Vogue*, March 1951 • *Far Right* Balenciaga double-breasted suit, *L'Officiel*, October 1960

Photo by Philippe Pottier.

"No woman can make herself chic if she is not chic herself."

Left Balenciaga cocktail dress and coat, 1950

Pierre Cardin

1922– (Italy)

Born in Venice to French parents, Pierre Cardin would pave the way for modern fashion design in France. Despite family opposition, he apprenticed to a tailor in Vichy at the age of fourteen. In 1945, he moved to Paris and entered the world of haute couture, working first with Jeanne Paquin and then with Elsa Schiaparelli. In 1947, as head of the *atelier tailleur* at the newly created House of Dior, he helped to create and construct the famous Bar Suit.

Cardin founded his own fashion house in 1950 and began to create architecturally innovative forms. His bubble dress of 1954 remains one of his iconic silhouettes. With a unisex collection in 1958 he crossed into menswear, though haute couturiers traditionally did not design for men. Ahead of the curve, in 1959 he designed a ready-to-wear collection for the department store Printemps, for which he was temporarily expelled from the Chambre Syndicale.

In the early 1960s, Cardin radically changed the look of menswear with collarless high-buttoned suits, which the Beatles, and their London tailor, would soon adopt; he later introduced the Nehru jacket. Throughout the decade, he produced colorful, boldly geometric garments that celebrated youth culture. Inspired by scientific developments, Cardin became one of the first couturiers to use synthetic materials, and in 1968 he developed his own bonded fiber, Cardine, to hold his sculptural shapes.

During the 1970s Cardin, following the early example of Dior, began to acquire licensing deals. An astute businessman, he soon used his name to sell everything from makeup and hosiery to cars to housewares. Although the unrestrained marketing may have diluted his image, his brand became known worldwide and the business continued to thrive. Cardin retired in 1996.

Right Pierre Cardin, Fall/Winter 1958/59 • *Far Right* Pierre Cardin, Fall/Winter 1972/73

Photo by Keystone, Getty Images.

Photo by RDA, Getty Images.

"A great designer must have an ideal to create for and mine is to create for the young."

Photo by Gamma-Keystone via Getty Images.

Left Pierre Cardin, collarless suits, 1960

Gabrielle "Coco" Chanel

1883–1971 (France)

Gabrielle Chanel was more than a fashion designer. She was perhaps the first designer to market a lifestyle: her own, the New Woman of the twentieth century. Following an orphanage education, a brief stage career, and a stint as a demimondaine, Chanel emerged with a new name, "Coco," a penchant for self-mythologizing, and a fundamental understanding of her personal style—all of which are deeply entangled in the Chanel aesthetic.

With the support of her lovers, Étienne Balsan and Arthur "Boy" Capel, Chanel opened a small millinery shop in Paris in 1910. Her work as a *modiste* proved successful. By 1913, she opened a boutique in Deauville, where she sold sportswear, and the following year launched a *maison de couture* in the resort town of Biarritz. Her popularity continued during the war as her clients came to appreciate her designs for their modernity, neutral color palette, and elements of simplicity and ease borrowed from menswear. By the late teens, she had revolutionized couture by making garments out of jersey, a material formerly reserved for men's underwear.

In 1921, she introduced her perfume, Chanel No. 5, whose bottle was meant to evoke a men's cologne. Similarly understated was her most recognized achievement: popularizing the little black dress. During the 1930s, her fashion moved away from the *garçonne* look of the previous decade and evolved into a more romantic, feminine silhouette that incorporated white fabrics, lace, flowers, and bows. It was also during this period that she began to wear, with her typical swagger, lavish combinations of real and costume jewelry.

She closed her couture house in 1939, remaining in Paris for much of the Occupation; given her Nazi sympathies, she then chose self-exile in Switzerland. In 1953, more than a dozen years after retirement, Chanel returned to fashion and in February of the following year she unveiled her comeback collection. Chanel showcased boxy tweed suits that offered a comfortable alternative to Dior's wasp-waist frocks. The collection received many negative reviews in Paris, but the look found immediate success in the United States. The cardigan suit would go on to become a Chanel signature, along with two-tone shoes and quilted shoulder bags.

Photo by Sasha, Getty Images.

Far Left Chanel with Lady Abdy in 1929 • *Left* Chanel organdy evening gown, drawn by Eric for *Vogue*, 1939

Left Chanel at home in the Ritz, ca. 1937 • *Below Left* "Chanel Surprise," *Vogue*, March 1954 • *Below* Chanel putting the finishing touches on a cocktail dress, 1959

"I don't like people talking about Chanel fashion. Chanel—above all else, is a style. Fashion, you see, goes out of fashion. Style, never."

André Courrèges

1923– (France)

In 1950, André Courrèges applied his training as an engineer to haute couture, working for the next decade alongside Cristóbal Balenciaga. As chief cutter, he perfected the master's disciplined, innovative approach to design. In 1961, with the support of his mentor, he opened his own couture house where he turned his skills to creating a futuristic fashion for a new generation.

His miniskirts, pantsuits, and coats were sparely architectural; decorative details, such as welt seaming, came from their construction. His young models could move freely in his outfits, aided by the flat-heeled, mid-calf boots that would become a Courrèges signature. Along with his preferred double-knit wool, he employed new synthetics to keep the crisp lines of his simple geometries. White dominated, set off by vivid touches of color. Haute couture truly entered the space age with his Moon Girl collection of 1964, which would become enormously influential. He also rewrote the rules of appropriate eveningwear when he paired revealing blouses with pants.

Courrèges closed his house in 1965, after showing his first collection on the couture calendar, only to reopen in 1967 with a more playful, colorful line called Prototype. In 1969, in addition to his custom work, he offered Couture Future, a luxury ready-to-wear line that was a continuation of his sharp modern style. By the 1970s, however, Courrèges's vision seemed out of sync with the times. The business continued with launches of fragrances, menswear, and a mass-market line, but was sold in 1985 to a company in Japan, where he had remained popular. The 1990s saw a revival of the Courrèges name.

Photo from Everett Collection, Alamy.

Above Right Courrèges ensembles, 1965 • *Right* Courrèges's Couture Future, *Vogue*, March 1969

"A woman's body must be hard and free. Not soft and harnessed. The harness—the girdle and bra—is the chain of the slave."

Above André Courrèges,
Fall/Winter 1968/69

Christian Dior

1905–57 (France)

Christian Dior built what was arguably the most famous fashion house in the world, whose dictates were eagerly awaited each season. Descended from a Norman manufacturing family, he began his career as a dealer of contemporary art. A series of setbacks led him to study illustration, and in the late 1930s he began selling his sketches to Paris couture houses. In 1938, he was hired by the couturier Robert Piguet, for whom he designed three collections before being called to military service in southern France. When he returned to Paris in 1941, he found work at the house of Lucien Lelong where he designed alongside Pierre Balmain.

Marcel Boussac, an important textile manufacturer and entrepreneur, agreed to finance Dior's own couture house. In February 1947 in an elegant new salon, Dior debuted a collection that he called Corolle to celebrate the bountiful beauty of flowers after years of wartime austerity. A fitted bodice and slim pencil skirt defined one look; another, characterized by the Bar Suit, had sloped shoulders, a nipped-in waist, and a wide, cartridge-pleated skirt. Romantic and historicist, this silhouette became better known, in Carmel Snow's coinage, as the New Look. It would also become the dominant silhouette of the next decade.

The highly stylized body of the Dior woman required interior corsetry and padding. Her proportions changed constantly, as with each collection Dior introduced a new named silhouette such as Zig-Zag, Oblique, Trompe-l'oeil, Longue, Sinueuse, Tulipe, Vivante, Muguet, Flèche, or Libre. In fact, any one collection would show many variations that emphasized either cut or textile.

From the very beginning, Dior thought globally and broadly. He established subsidiaries in New York, Caracas, London, and other cities around the world, and became the first designer to attach his name to a wide range of accessories and products in carefully controlled licensing agreements that brought his taste to a whole new customer. Dior also understood the value of publicity, touring his collections and giving interviews and lectures. At the time of his sudden death in 1957, the House of Dior was responsible for half of France's haute couture business.

Photo by Roger Wood, Getty Images.

Above Dior reviewing a design in his studio, 1952 • **Above Right** Bar Suit of 1947, reconfigured for a presentation at the Sorbonne, 1955

Photo by Keystone-France, Gamma-Keystone, Getty Images.

"Clothes are my whole life. Ultimately everything I know, see, or hear, every part of my life, turns around the clothes which I create. They haunt me perpetually, until they are ready to pass from the world of my dreams into the world of practical utility."

Photo by Loomis Dean, Time & Life Pictures, Getty Images.

Left Varying silhouettes from Spring/Summer 1957, shot in the *grand salon*

Domenico Dolce & Stefano Gabbana

1958– & 1962– (Italy)

Domenico Dolce and Stefano Gabbana consistently mine tropes of Italian culture to produce universally desired collections. The designers met while working at Giorgio Correggiari in 1980 and two years later started a consulting studio that they transformed into a fashion house. Their first showing, as part the New Talent group at Milano Collezioni in 1985, was enthusiastically received. They debuted their Real Women collection the following year and quickly added knitwear, swimwear, lingerie, and menswear lines. In 1993, the partners designed fifteen hundred costumes for Madonna's Girlie Show tour and in 1994 they launched D&G, a younger, street-trending collection.

Dolce and Gabbana revel in the unapologetic eroticism of the female form, tempered just enough by a sense of Catholic propriety. Isabella Rossellini perfectly captures the aesthetic: "They find their way out of any black dress, any buttoned-up blouse. The first piece of theirs I wore was a white shirt, very chaste, but cut to make my breasts look as if they were bursting out of it." The sirens of mid-twentieth-century Italian cinema—Claudia Cardinale, Sophia Loren, Anna Magnani, Anita Ekberg—are recurring sources of inspiration. In their advertising campaigns, contemporary actresses like Rossellini, Monica Bellucci, and Scarlett Johansson, whose strong, voluptuous figures embody the brand, feature in lush vignettes of family, church, history, and seduction.

The designers' constant evocation of the sensual carries with it a touch of mischief. Dolce and Gabbana play with oppositions: tradition and iconoclasm, chic and kitsch, femininity and masculinity, an animal print and a cardinal's cloak, a black lace corset and a pin-striped suit.

Photos by Chris Moore, Catwalking, Getty Images.

Far Left Dolce & Gabbana menswear, Fall/Winter 2006/07 • *Left* Dolce & Gabbana, Spring/Summer 2007

"It's about redesigning a point of view—molto sexy."

Left Dolce & Gabbana,
Fall/Winter 2011/12

Tom Ford

1961– (United States)

Perfectionist Tom Ford brings to fashion a provocative glamour and keen sense of how to sell a brand. Raised in Texas and New Mexico, he studied architecture at Parsons in New York before realizing that he wanted to pursue a career in fashion instead. In 1990, he found the ideal match in Gucci, where he was hired to design the women's collection. Two years later, he rose to design director and two years after that to creative director, responsible for both design and marketing.

Ford turned around the once-ailing company by giving it a clear direction that wedded Italian craftsmanship to a savvy commercialism. He made accessories desirable, retooling classics like the Gucci loafer and streamlining the brand's license agreements. He revamped Gucci's image with advertising campaigns, shot by photographer Mario Testino, that were unabashedly risqué. The clothes themselves were sleek and sexy with a retro flavor. His seventies-inspired Fall/Winter 1995/96 collection was pivotal to the brand's success. When the Gucci Group acquired the House of Saint Laurent in 1999, Ford took charge of the Rive Gauche collection. He quickly laid to rest any doubts about an American heading such an iconic French brand, updating the YSL woman for the new millennium with a powerful luxe sexiness.

In 2004, Ford dramatically split from the Gucci Group after PPR had gained control of the company, and in 2005, with his former boss Domenico de Sole, established his own brand, offering eyewear and beauty lines. In 2007, he launched a menswear line and opened a flagship store on Madison Avenue, then turned his attention to directing the luminous film *A Single Man*. In September 2010, he returned to women's clothing with a salon-style presentation to a closed audience. The thirty-two looks, each created for the muse who wore it, harked back to his last days at YSL but with a glamorousness that was more refined and individual.

Photo by Fred Duval, FilmMagic.

Above The designer with Julianne Moore wearing Tom Ford, London, 2011 • **Right** Advertisement for *Gucci*, Fall/Winter 1995/96

"I'm lucky, I have mass-market tastes."

Left Gucci, Fall/Winter
1996/97 • *Below* Yves
Saint Laurent, Fall/Winter
2001/02

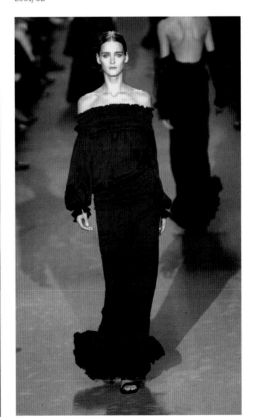

John Galliano

1960– (Gibraltar)

The couturier-provocateur John Galliano first captured the imagination of the fashion world with his 1984 graduation show at Central Saint Martins, inspired by the *merveilleuses* and *incroyables* of Revolutionary France. Although critically successful, his label struggled until his breakthrough collection of black bias-cut gowns shown in Paris in 1994. The following year, Bernard Arnault of LVMH named Galliano creative director of Givenchy's haute couture and ready-to-wear lines, the first British designer to head an established French fashion house. Two seasons later, Arnault offered him the reins at Dior.

Galliano's debut collection for Spring/Summer 1997, impeccably glamorous clothing infused with his own audacious spirit, coincided with the fiftieth anniversary of the House of Dior. The fit was a good one, for Galliano shared Dior's deep romanticism. His tenure reinvigorated the couture house not only creatively but also financially, and the designer became involved in advertising and marketing as well. All along, he continued to show his eponymous label. The dream came crashing down in 2011 when Arnault fired Galliano after a series of anti-Semitic rants, a crime in France of which he was later convicted.

Galliano's research and travels yielded an abundance of references: from Masai tribesmen to Sisi, Empress of Austria, from Wonder Woman to the Little Tramp, flamenco to hiphop, an opera by Puccini to a photograph by Penn. From his remixes came a kaleidoscope of eras, places, and sensibilities. He also never shied away from controversial material, to which his Spring/Summer 2000 couture collection for Dior, subsequently known as *Les Clochards* (loosely, the homeless) attested. Galliano's inventiveness with fabric and cut set him apart. Having perfected both his beloved bias cut and the tailoring synonymous with Dior, he could rearrange the pieces of a garment or ensemble into something altogether new. Beyond the clothes, he was a master of theatrical staging and his extravagant shows regularly took his audience into a place of pure enchantment.

Photo by Jean-Pierre Muller, AFP, Getty Images.

Photo by François Guillot, AFP, Getty Images.

Above Christian Dior haute couture, Spring/Summer 2000 • *Left* John Galliano, Fall/Winter 2004/05

"Haute couture is relevant whatever the economy or mood of the moment. It's poetry from the heart and soul. I dare and I challenge people to dream."

Left Christian Dior haute couture, Spring/Summer 2011

Jean Paul Gaultier

1952– (France)

Embracing the moniker of *enfant terrible* of French fashion, for over three decades designer Jean Paul Gaultier has been drawing on the eccentricities of the Parisian street. He began his career in the 1970s, working with Pierre Cardin and Jean Patou before showing his first ready-to-wear collection in 1976. His iconoclastic spirit has led him to overturn conventional ideas of gender and sexuality, pioneering underwear as outerwear in his corset dress of 1982 and sending men down the runway in lace skirts in 1984. His Frenchness is fused with a love of foreignness: His designs regularly mix elements from cultures across the globe—London punks, Hassidic Jews, Aztec Indians—and his witty shows employ a diverse cast of models.

Despite his lack of formal training, his playful, but well-executed designs and inventive use of new fabrics got him noticed throughout the 1980s and 1990s. Since designing the iconic cone-shaped bra that Madonna wore with men's suiting for her 1990 Blonde Ambition tour, Gaultier has continued to create costumes for both stage and film. In 1997, at a time when many couture houses were closing, he launched his first haute couture collection, earning accolades for his designs' marriage of imagination and technical expertise.

His success has continued into the twenty-first century: The French luxury house Hermès acquired a stake in Gaultier's business in 1999, and from 2003 through 2010 Gaultier served as creative director of womenswear, where he merged the brand's conservative equestrian-influenced style with his own tropes of underwear as outerwear and menswear for women. His explorations of traditional garments (variations on the striped mariner shirt, the trench coat reimagined as a billowing silk dress) appear in his eponymous collections as well. In 2011, Gaultier's designs became the subject of a lively exhibition, organized by the Montreal Museum of Fine Art and touring worldwide.

Right Jean Paul Gaultier haute couture, Spring/Summer 2002. • *Far Right* Hermès, Fall/Winter 2004/05

Photo by Jean-Pierre Muller, AFP, Getty Images.

Photo by François Guillot, AFP, Getty Images.

"Fashion is not art. Never. I am not a painter or a sculptor. My role is to do clothes. Fashion is a reflection of the times, and that's hard enough to do."

Left Jean Paul Gaultier haute couture, Fall/Winter 2011/12 • *Below* Jean Paul Gaultier menswear, Spring/ Summer 2010

Hubert de Givenchy

1927– (France)

Born to an aristocratic French family, Hubert de Givenchy knew from an early age that he wanted to be an haute couturier. He studied at the École des Beaux-Arts in Paris and apprenticed with Jacques Fath in 1945. He went on to work for Robert Piguet, Lucien Lelong, and finally Elsa Schiaparelli, designing her boutique line.

Givenchy opened his own couture house in 1952. Unlike many of his contemporaries, he understood that head-to-toe dressing was on its way out and presented clothing—even his eveningwear—as separates that could be mixed and matched. He also showed a blouse of inexpensive white cotton shirting; named after the model Bettina, this simple, fresh-looking garment became a signature. In 1954, alert to another shift in the industry, Givenchy became one of the first couturiers to offer a high-end ready-to-wear collection.

A chance meeting with Cristóbal Balenciaga led to a deep, lifelong friendship; sharing an aesthetic sensibility that put line before decoration, the two designers would regularly critique one another's work. When Balenciaga closed his doors in 1968, he referred many of his staff and clients to his colleague. Another figure important to Givenchy was Audrey Hepburn. After the designer created her transformative wardrobe for the 1954 film *Sabrina*, she became his muse and one of his most famous clients. The two went on to collaborate on seven more major motion pictures, including *Funny Face* of 1957 and *Breakfast at Tiffany's* of 1961.

Hubert de Givenchy is a tall, handsome, and debonair man. In 1973, he began designing a menswear collection, called Gentlemen Givenchy, based on his own personal style. Although LVMH purchased his company in 1988, the grand couturier continued to head the house until his retirement in 1995.

Right Givenchy sheath dress, drawn by Bernard Blossac, 1955 • *Below* Givenchy separates collection, 1952

Photo by Nat Farbman, Time & Life Pictures, Getty Images.

Private Collection.

"I consider the beauty and artistic value of a fashion, not its utility."

Left Audrey Hepburn in Givenchy, *Breakfast at Tiffany's,* 1961 ● *Below* Silhouettes from 1956

couturier   d'avant-garde

La ligne lampion

La ligne chasuble

La ligne chemise

Madame Grès

Madame Grès was born Germaine Emilie Krebs to a middle-class Parisian family, who discouraged her from further pursuing her education in the arts. Haute couture allowed her to sculpt with textiles, instead. Around 1933, after a brief apprenticeship at the House of Premet, she began to design for a couturière who, acknowledging the phenomenal success of her assistant, changed the name of her house to reflect the one by which Grès now went: Alix.

At the height of the German Occupation, she sold the rights to the name Alix and launched her own couture house as Madame Grès (an anagram of her husband's name). In 1944, the Nazis closed her down for not adhering to wartime restrictions on fabric; when she was allowed to reopen later that year, she showed a collection on the eve of the liberation of Paris composed entirely of patriotic red, white, and blue. Her business thrived throughout the 1950s and 1960s.

Grès, unlike many designers, preferred to drape directly on a live model. She loved the female form and saw her work as a way to enhance the body without restricting it. She was most famous for her long gowns that resembled Grecian columns: uncut panels of silk jersey or silk crepe, swirling loosely in the skirt, tucked and pleated through the waist and bodice (reinforced by subtle corsetry), and often resolved in a twist. Later, she would create geometries based on ethnic dress that eschewed cutting.

In 1972 she was elected president of the Chambre Syndicale and became the first recipient of its Dé d'Or award. Her artisanal designs did not easily translate into a system of mass production, and Grès held out on designing ready-to-wear, which she long viewed as artless, until 1980. Although regarded as one of the twentieth century's finest couturiers, by 1988 she was nearly bankrupt. She retired without fanfare, and her death was not reported for a year.

Manteau en velours de laine marron; béguin de loutre de S. Talbot.

Right Alix coat, drawn by André Delfau, *Images de France*, 1941 ▪ *Far Right* Madame Grès, evening gown, 1948

Photo by Philippe Pottier.

"From the beginning I didn't want to do what others were doing in any way; I wasn't able to because I didn't have the knowledge. That was one reason I took the material and worked directly with it. I used the knowledge I had, which was sculpture."

Left Madame Grès, yellow wool coat, 1951

• *Below* Madame Grès ensemble, drawn by Eric, *Vogue*, March 1951

Halston

1932–90 (United States)

Born Roy Halston Frowick, in Des Moines, Iowa, the designer's movie-star looks and elegant physique gave him an alluring aura. Known simply as Halston, he became as famous as the clothing he created for a swirl of celebrities and international jet setters like Bianca Jagger, Liza Minnelli, Babe Paley, Lauren Hutton, Elsa Peretti, and Elizabeth Taylor.

While studying fashion illustration at the Chicago Institute of Art, he worked as a window dresser and began designing hats. In 1958, he relocated to New York to work with milliner Lily Daché. Two years later, he left to become head milliner at Bergdorf Goodman, where the young Jacqueline Kennedy became his client. By 1966, he was also designing the department store's first ready-to-wear line. He formed his custom design and ready-to-wear business, Halston Ltd., in 1968; within four years, he had taken over the building that housed his New York show-room, opening a three-floor retail boutique, each level of which featured a different Halston collection at a different price point.

In the 1970s, Halston redefined American dressing with a pared-down aesthetic made luxurious with fine textiles and a meticulous cut. His classic pantsuits and shirtwaists, often rendered in signature Ultra-suede, gave women a clean, modern uniform for day, while his many variations on the minimalist dress—strapless, halter, and asymmetrical, draped, spiraled, and wrapped—gave her a glamorous look for dancing through the night at Studio 54.

By the early 1980s, unrelenting work pressure (eight collections a year, numerous divisions, and private commissions) and increasing drug use combined to undermine the designer's success. When he licensed an affordable line for the J.C. Penney discount chain in 1982, many high-end retailers dropped his label and high-profile clients fled. In the end, Halston lost control of his own name in several hostile takeovers. He died of complications from AIDS in 1990.

Photo by RDA, Getty Images.

Photo by Irving Penn.

Above Jacqueline Kennedy in a Halston pillbox hat, Paris, 1961 • ***Left*** Halston pantsuit in *Vogue*, 1969

"A designer is only as good as the people he dresses."

Left Beverly Johnson in a Halston gown, 1975

Marc Jacobs

1964– (United States)

Marc Jacobs is a genuine arbiter of cool, with an uncanny intuition for what people want to wear. In the early 1980s, the on-trend New York boutique Charivari produced a collection of oversized polka-dot sweaters designed as part of Jacob's graduate collection at Parsons. Robert Duffy was among those who took note, hiring the young designer to work at Sketchbook by Ruben Thomas. In 1986, they formed a business partnership, and two years later the Perry Ellis company came calling. Jacobs reinvigorated the American sportswear house with witty collections in imaginative color combinations. He became head designer in 1989, but was dismissed in 1993 after showing his now legendary Grunge collection, which interpreted street style as luxury wear and unnerved company executives.

Jacobs and Duffy were refocused on building the Marc Jacobs label when in 1997, after eighteen months of negotiations, LVMH named Jacobs artistic director of Louis Vuitton, the heritage leather goods company. Charged with producing its first ready-to-wear collection, he has since turned it into one of the world's most profitable fashion houses. Contributing to his success are the bold collaborations he has forged with artists like Stephen Sprouse, Takashi Murakami, Richard Prince, and Yayoi Kusama. Meanwhile, LVMH's stake in Jacobs's own brand has allowed it to expand, with other lines such as Marc by Marc Jacobs.

A talented, sophisticated appropriator, Jacobs joyfully and impudently plays with high and low. He has a taste for pastische, but his wackiness is perfectly controlled. His look can be whimsical, feminine, daring, or glamorous, but his postmodern flair is always put in the service of beautifully constructed, luxurious clothing. Today, his shows for both Louis Vuitton and Marc Jacobs are some of each season's most highly anticipated.

Right Marc Jacobs,
Fall/Winter 2011/12

Photo by firstVIEW.

"The idea of couture doesn't hold that thing for me. It's archaic—in my opinion. I mean, I am really interested in the craftsmanship behind couture. But I can explore all that in ready-to-wear."

Left Louis Vuitton,
Spring/Summer 2012

Donna Karan

1948– (United States)

A native New Yorker, Donna Karan was born into fashion, her mother a model and her father a tailor. While still a student at Parsons in the late 1960s, she started working with the American sportswear doyenne Anne Klein. On Klein's death in 1974, Karan stepped into the top spot, which she would share with Louis Dell'Olio. Karan brought her own ideas to the brand and created the bridge collection Anne Klein II. After a decade, with the support of her husband, Stephan Weiss, she launched her own company.

The first collection in 1985 introduced the world to the Seven Easy Pieces system of dressing. This wardrobe of essential garments—bodysuit, blouse, wrap skirt, leggings, blazer, coat, and dress—could be mixed and matched to create ensembles appropriate for any occasion or time of day. Her layered designs were urban and sophisticated, usually in black, and accented by statement accessories and shoes. She favored fabrics like cashmere and jersey for soft, unstructured garments. Like Claire McCardell before her, she knew that women, real women with real bodies, would be empowered by the freedom and confidence of wearing comfortable, stylish clothes.

In 1988, inspired by a daughter who was always raiding her closet, she launched DKNY, a collection of lower-priced designs aimed at a younger, easy-going customer. She also introduced hosiery, fragrance, jeans, menswear, and home furnishings lines. The brand began to struggle financially in the late 1990s, which paired with Weiss's battle with lung cancer, prompted the couple to sell the business to LVMH, though Karan remained on as designer. In 2001, she opened the Donna Karan New York flagship store on Madison Avenue as "a serene escape from the city's chaos," reflecting a new direction in the life of the Karan woman.

Photo by Rose Hartman, Getty Images.

Above Donna Karan with her husband, New York, 1985

Photo by firstVIEW.

"'How does Donna Karan see New York?' I'd say, 'In a car.' Then they'd ask, 'How about DKNY?' And I'd say, 'In a subway or a bus.' That was the difference."

Left Donna Karan, Fall/Winter 2009/10

Calvin Klein

1942– (United States)

Bronx-born Calvin Klein designed simple, modern clothes and created controversial fashion images. After graduating from FIT, he worked for mid-price coat and suit manufacturers. Then in 1968, Klein formed his own company, financed by his childhood friend Barry Schwartz. Among the first to see his freshman collection of finely tailored coats and dresses was prominent retailer Bonwit Teller, which placed a substantial order and featured his designs in eight of their highly sought-after windows.

Throughout the next few decades, Klein developed a minimalist, sportswear-influenced aesthetic, with clean lines and a muted neutral-tending palette. His sophisticated collections favored easy separates, classics in quality fabrics, and uncomplicated day-into-night ensembles.

In 1976, among the looks Klein sent down the runway was a pair of slim-cut jeans with his name stitched on a back pocket, marking his first use of the label as a branding tool. The extraordinary success of his designer jeans line was secured in 1980 by a highly suggestive campaign shot by Richard Avedon using a teenaged Brooke Shields—and by the public outcry that ensued. In magazine ads, TV commercials, and billboard posters, Klein steadily pushed the boundaries of what the public would accept, most notoriously in 1995 when accusations of child pornography led him to pull images from his cK Jeans campaign. Klein's genius extended beyond marketing tactics to an early recognition of the appeal of gender fluidity, when he restyled men's underwear for women and offered gender-sharing fragrances.

Klein himself, and his lavish lifestyle, became part of the brand image. By the time he and Schwartz sold the company to Phillips-Van Heusen in late 2002, lucrative licensing deals for underwear, perfumes, and home goods had built a multibillion-dollar empire.

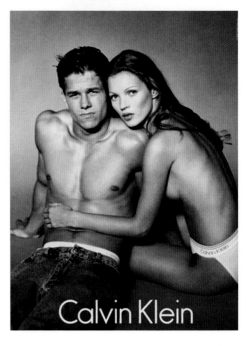

Above Calvin Klein, Fall/ Winter 1995/96 • *Right* Advertisement for Calvin Klein underwear, 1992

Photo by Jon Levy, AFP, Getty Images.

Calvin Klein

Photo by first VIEW.

"We're not doing outrageous fashion; I make sports clothes that are relatively conservative, clothes that everyone wears."

Left Calvin Klein,
Spring/Summer 1996

Karl Lagerfeld

1933– (Germany)

Responsible for the creative direction of three successful fashion labels, Chanel, Fendi, and his namesake collection, Karl Lagerfeld is a fashion phenomenon. He is multilingual, a voracious reader, a photographer and publisher, a collector and disposer of images, objects, and people—all of which feeds the forward momentum of his fashions. In his seventies, he designs eight major collections a year, plus resort and satellite collections.

Born to a wealthy Hamburg family, Lagerfeld moved as a teenager to Paris. He began working for Pierre Balmain in 1954 and for Jean Patou in 1958, training in couture techniques. Tired of what he saw as an old-fashioned system, in 1962 he left the world of haute couture and turned to ready-to-wear as a freelancer. He found an outlet for his talents designing for brands like Krizia, Mario Valentino, Max Mara, and Ballantyne, but especially for Chloé, where from 1963 to 1983 he created youthful, ultrafeminine dresses and coats (and to whose house he returned from 1992 to 1997), and for Fendi, where since 1965 he has been turning furs into lightweight, supple garments.

Lagerfeld has always displayed great stamina and the unique ability to become exactly the designer each house requires. This has never been more apparent than when the House of Chanel hired him in 1983 to revamp the moribund brand. Lagerfeld, always the scholar, soon realized that the house had no archive and began compiling one from which to draw. His irreverent reinterpretations of Chanel signatures, in modern materials and with a touch of the street, shocked the house back into life, and he has continued to make it relevant ever since.

Meanwhile, his eponymous collection, relaunched in 1997, affords him the freedom to experiment and reflects an edgier, often somber aesthetic closer to the look that he has cultivated for himself. Having celebrated nearly sixty years in fashion, he remains vital and his work is still evolving.

Photo by Karl Prouse, Catwalking, Getty Images.

Photo by Karl Prouse, Catwalking, Getty Images.

Above Left Fendi, Fall/Winter 2010/11 • *Left* Chanel haute couture, Spring/Summer 2011

"I think designers now have gotten used to putting themselves behind the label, the way Tom [Ford] has. It doesn't have to be 'my house, my name, my label, it will die with me.' That's not modern."

Left Chanel, Fall/Winter, 2011/12

Ralph Lauren

1939– (United States)

Not since Chanel has a designer marketed himself so thoroughly and successfully as Ralph Lauren. Born in the Bronx, the sartorially conscious Ralph Rueben Lifshitz changed his name at the age of sixteen. In 1968, he founded Polo Fashions, selling the wide ties that had already caught the attention of Bloomingdale's as well as suits and other menswear and, by 1971, clothing for women. Despite the financial crises behind the scenes, the Polo brand came to signal a certain lifestyle, and his logoed polo shirt became a staple of the preppy uniform. Hollywood helped to spread Lauren's vision to the masses: the glamorous nostalgia of his wardrobe for *The Great Gatsby* of 1974 and the men's styling of his clothes for Diane Keaton in *Annie Hall* of 1977.

Inspired by the thrift stores that he and his brother used to haunt, certain tropes have emerged, variations on moneyed American society: patrician New Englander, Western rancher, Wall Street businessman, country gentleman, equestrian club, yacht club, country club, ski lodge. In a tradition of timeless elegance, Lauren's collections return to certain items time and again: the oxford shirt, the Shetland sweater, the riding boot, the safari shirt, the prairie skirt, the romantic top, the bohemian skirt, the dress in white or dark florals, the tailored suit, the coat in camel or tweed, the velvet blazer.

Every aspect of every line under the Lauren umbrella, and there are many, relies on consistent presentation and packaging. Marketing campaigns have been carefully crafted, beginning in the late 1970s with a series of print ads shot by Bruce Weber, vignettes that linked all the Ralph Lauren products into one fantasy scenario into which anyone could buy. Lauren fully realized his total lifestyle concept, and redefined fashion retailing, when he bought and restored the Rhinelander Mansion at 867 Madison Avenue, which he opened in 1985 to showcase his lines in their properly imagined settings. Today, a second mansion at 888 Madison provides the backdrop for his women's collections.

Photo by Karl Prouse, Catwalking, Getty Images.

Opposite Page Right Ralph Lauren, Spring/Summer 2010 • *Far Right Above* Ralph Lauren, Fall/Winter 2011/12 • *Far Right Below* Ralph Lauren, Spring/Summer 2002

"I don't design clothes. I design dreams."

Photos by first VIEW.

Claire McCardell

1905–58 (United States)

Known for fashions that were both democratic and chic, Claire McCardell was one of the greatest American sportswear designers. Born in the small town of Frederick, Maryland, she left in the late 1920s to study fashion illustration at the New York and Paris campuses of Parsons. Later, the designer for whom she worked, Robert Turk, brought her along when he joined New York manufacturer Townley Frocks as lead designer in 1931; when he suddenly died the following year, she stepped in.

McCardell was expected to take her cues from Paris, but knew that American women sought an ease and comfort that European fashions lacked. She began introducing elements of her own: brass hook-and-eye closures, spaghetti string ties, wrap waists, and the then radical idea of a five-piece system of interchangeable separates. In 1938, she had astonishing success with the Monastic dress, an unfitted trapeze style that could be belted or not. But in financial distress from battling knock offs of McCardell's hit, Townley closed shop. The designer worked briefly for Hattie Carnegie, but her aesthetic didn't suit the Francophile customers. When Townley reopened in 1940 she returned, now designing under the label Claire McCardell Clothes by Townley. (She would become a partner in 1952.)

McCardell aligned high style with the requirements of mass production. She became known for the easy elegance of her dresses and coats and the youthful appeal of her playsuits and unlined bathing suits. Her designs were functional and innovative, eliminating corsetry, shoulder pads, and back zippers and adopting utilitarian details. She could even make housework appealing, as she did in 1942 with the Popover, a wrap dress with large patch pockets (and oven mitt) designed to be worn at home. She also had an affinity for common fabrics like denim, calico, even mattress ticking, and for fabrics that were stain resistant, washable, and stretchy. Her designs were meant to move from work to leisure, from day into night.

In 1990, decades after her untimely death in 1958, *Life* magazine named McCardell one of the 100 most important Americans of the twentieth century.

Right Claire McCardell for Dancing Twin Nylons, 1947
• *Far Right* McCardell, swimsuit, *Vogue*, May 1953

Photo by John Rawlings.

"I've always designed things I needed myself. It just turns out that other people need them, too."

Left McCardell, hostess dress, *Vogue*, June 1947 ▪ *Below* McCardell on the cover of *Time*, May 1955

Alexander McQueen

1969–2010 (United Kingdom)

East Londoner Lee Alexander McQueen ushered the fashion world forward with collections that crossed the borderlines of art and fashion; he was a master of technique with a magician's imagination to match.

McQueen left school at sixteen and began work as a tailor's apprentice at Anderson & Sheppard on Savile Row. After two years, he moved down the street to Grieves & Hawkes, then to a theatrical costumer. After a brief stint with avant-garde designer Koji Tatsuno, he went to the Milan studio of Romeo Gigli. Through all his training, he perfected six methods of pattern cutting, drawing from the sixteenth century to the present. Applying to teach pattern cutting at Central Saint Martins, he was instead offered a place in its design program. In 1992, fashion editor Isabella Blow, who would go on to become a friend and muse, purchased his entire graduate collection.

As Alexander McQueen, he started his own label in 1993 and immediately pushed at the limits of expression, creating provocative garments, like the drop-waist pants and skirts called bumsters, and just as shocking fashion shows. Dark meditations on the dynamics of power, his collections—like Highland Rape of 1995, which enacted the English ravaging of Scotland but led to accusations of eroticizing violation—were always deeply personal and meant to tell a story.

After just four collections, Bernard Arnault of LVMH approached McQueen to replace John Galliano at the House of Givenchy. From the artisans there, he learned the soft draping that would become a foil for his austere tailoring, but the designer was ill at ease in the confines of French haute couture. He left Givenchy in 2001, having the previous December sold a controlling interest in his own business to LVMH rival, the Gucci Group. The savvy business move gave him the funds to show in Paris, open stores, and launch a menswear line and diffusion line, McQ.

He and his team continued to produce clothing that was uncompromising, fantastical, and technologically advanced. With an affinity for the broken and the brutalized, McQueen found beauty in places from which most people shy away. He changed the fashion paradigm, and in 2010 he took his own life.

Right Alexander McQueen, Fall/Winter 2006/07 • *Far Right* Alexander McQueen, Fall/Winter 2010/11

Photo by Xavier Rossi, Gamma-Rapho via Getty Images.

"I want to be the purveyor of a certain silhouette or a way of cutting, so that when I'm dead and gone, people will know that the twenty-first century was started by Alexander McQueen."

Left Alexander McQueen, Fall/Winter 2003/04

Paul Poiret

1879–1944 (France)

Paul Poiret, the first to embody the idea of fashion designer as public arbiter of taste, came from a solidly respectable bourgeois family in Paris. He was selling his design sketches to *maisons de couture* such as Chéruit and Paquin when, in 1896, prominent couturier Jacques Doucet took him on. Designing evening coats and theatrical costumes, Poiret advanced to become head of the *tailleur*. In 1901, the House of Worth, whose founder had died several years earlier, hired him as an assistant designer. Although commercially successful, his stylish garments conflicted with the conservative standards of the house and resulted in his dismissal.

When he opened his own house in 1903, former clients such as the actress Réjane soon followed. His marriage in 1905 to the waiflike Denise Boulet gave him a muse who would greatly influence the direction of his work. Publication of the deluxe volume *Les Robes de Paul Poiret* of 1908, gorgeously rendered by Paul Iribe and printed in the color-saturated pochoir method, revealed a radical departure from belle époque fashions. Harking back to the Directoire, his long and narrow silhouette, with a high waist and low neckline, was meant to be worn without a corset. Poiret would pick up the orientalism of Léon Bakst's 1910 costumes for the Ballets Russes, in voluminous cocoon wraps and sheer evening dresses with overtunics that were awash in bold patterns and vivid colors. He also commissioned Raoul Dufy to design many of his textiles.

Though forever associated with the novelty of his hobble skirts and harem pants, Poiret's greatest contributions to fashion lay in his conception of the modern industry. A master of marketing, he used flamboyant window displays and spectacular parties to attract attention to his work, including his lavish 1,002nd Night costume ball of 1911. He hosted trunk shows, led promotional tours, and sent models to the opera dressed in his latest creations. Poiret understood that couture was the engine that drove the sale of other products. In 1911, he became one of the very first couturiers to introduce a fragrance, Rosine, and he expanded his brand to include home goods created at Martine, a school he established to train girls in the decorative arts. By 1925, a simpler aesthetic prevailed, however, and Poiret, having lost the rights to his name, closed his business for good in 1932.

Right Poiret dinner dress and coat, drawn by Georges Lepape, 1912

LASSITUDE
Robe de dîner, de Paul Poiret

SERAIS-JE EN AVANCE ?
Manteau de théâtre de Paul Poiret

LES COLOMBES
ROBE DU SOIR, DE PAUL POIRET

Nº 8 de la Gazette.

Année 1924. — Planche 41

Modèle déposé. Reproduction interdite.

"One must not suppose that each new fashion is the consecration of a definite type of garment, which will replace for ever that which is being abandoned: it is simply a variation."

Above Poiret evening dress, drawn by André Marty, 1924 ■ *Right and Far Right* Poiret gown as sold at Gimbel Brothers, and walking suit as sold at Wanamaker's, 1914

Miuccia Prada

1949– (Italy)

Once termed the "aristocommunist," Miuccia Prada produces work that expresses contradiction. Her unconventional path to the fashion industry led first to a doctorate in political science and five years training as a mime before, in 1978, she joined the luxury goods company that her grandfather, Mario Prada, had founded in 1913. In 1985 with Patrizio Bertelli, her business partner, mentor, and future husband, she introduced a collection of bags and backpacks constructed of rugged black nylon adorned only with the company logo on a small triangular metal plate. By the early 1990s, resonating with an understated current within fashion, they would become one of the most coveted accessories of the day.

In 1988, the company showed its first ready-to-wear collection in Milan. In 1992, the brand further expanded with a less expensive but more personal collection, both sensual and eccentric, to which Prada gave her nickname, Miu Miu. Menswear and sportswear lines followed. In the late 1990s and 2000s, the Prada Group began buying and selling stakes in other fashion companies, including Gucci, Fendi, and, notoriously, rivals Jil Sander and Helmut Lang. Prada began also to rethink the experience of shopping, launching innovative "epicenters," the first in New York's Soho designed by Rem Koolhaas, and, more recently, introducing salon-style gatherings in the Miu Miu stores.

In the northern Italian tradition of quality industrial manufacturing, Prada has eleven in-house production houses and a team of talented designers to draw on. She has built a strong reputation for eccentric but wearable clothing and accessories, with an offhand sense of luxury. Her approach to materials is imaginative; her color schemes improbable; and her proportions, awkward. Designing for the many different identities a woman might choose to express, and inspired most by the things that repel her, Prada pairs bad taste with refinement, staidness with provocation, ugliness with beauty. Making no effort to be fashionable, she is an intelligent interpreter of her times and a forecaster of trends.

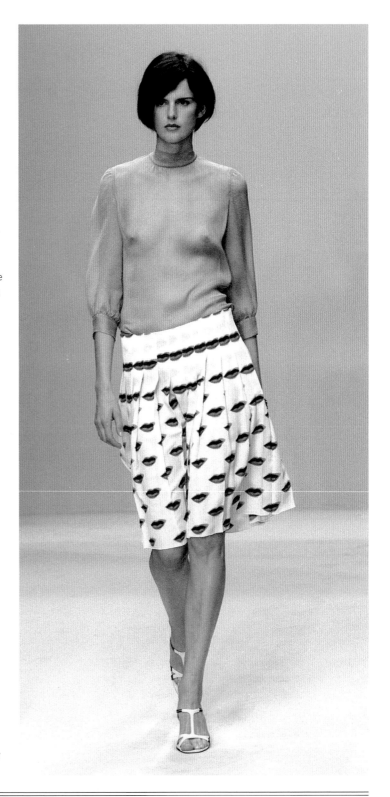

Right Prada, Spring/
Summer 2000

"I have always thought Prada clothes looked kind of normal, but not quite normal. Maybe they have little twists that are disturbing, or something about them that's not quite acceptable."

Left Prada, Prada, Fall/Winter 2011/12 • *Below* Miu Miu, Fall/Winter 2011/12

Yves Saint Laurent

1936–2008 (Algeria)

Moving between the classical and the subversive, Yves Saint Laurent was a pivotal force in twentieth-century fashion. He found success at a very young age. Introduced to Christian Dior in 1955, sketches in hand, he was hired on the spot, serving as an assistant and soon collaborator. When the couturier died suddenly in 1957, the twenty-one-year-old Saint Laurent became the head of the world's most important fashion house. His aesthetic was more modern than Dior's, however, and his collections began to introduce street-style elements like black leather jackets, which enraged the more conservative clientele. In 1960, the owners of the house allowed him to be drafted into the French army in Algeria. Hospitalized for a nervous breakdown, he was rescued by his companion, Pierre Bergé.

Upon his return to Paris, the two opened the House of Saint Laurent in December 1961, joined by staff and seamstresses from Dior. After several up-and-down years, he received a standing ovation in 1965 for his Mondrian dresses, whose strict cut and color blocking were a surprise. The collection was the first of many to use artists and writers as the catalyst for inspiration. The designer soon created a distinctive YSL style with recurrent themes and signature garments: tunics, smocks, jumpsuits, safari jackets, see-through dresses and blouses. He refined street and proletarian styles (pea coats, duffel coats) and ethnic costume (the African dresses, the Spanish and Chinese collections) into luxurious expressions of the craft of the couture salon. Starting in 1966, he reinterpreted a masculine wardrobe for women, with pantsuits and tuxedo jackets, which he called *le smoking*—especially radical for the evening.

Sensitive to changes in the industry, in the early 1970s Saint Laurent would put African and Asian models on the predominantly white catwalk. But his most prescient move came in 1966 when he opened the Rive Gauche boutique to bring his streamlined high-end ready-to-wear collection to a younger woman, more receptive to the future of fashion. A decade later, after suffering another collapse, Saint Laurent suddenly reversed direction in advance of the opulent 1980s. The ornate theatrical fantasy of his Opéra–Ballets Russes collection of 1976 was credited with making haute couture once more relevant. Yet from this point on, the designer became increasingly reclusive and fragile and his work never again as transporting. Saint Laurent showed his final haute couture collection in 2002 and died in 2008.

Right Saint Laurent see-through dress, Spring/Summer 1968 • *Far Right* Saint Laurent *le smoking*, Spring/Summer 1967

Photo by Bill Ray, Time & Life Pictures, Getty Images.

Photo by Reg Lancaster, Getty Images.

Photo by Alex Lentati, Daily Mail/Rex, Alamy.

"That's why my style is androgynous. I'd noticed that men were more confident in their clothes, and women didn't have much self-confidence. So I tried to give them this confidence and to give them a figure."

Left Potpourri of Saint Laurent designs inspired by artists • *Below* The designer with Betty Calroux and Loulou de la Falaise dressed in his safari look, 1969

Photo by John Minihan, Getty Images.

Elsa Schiaparelli

1890–1973 (Italy)

Shocking is the name of the fragrance that Elsa Schiaparelli introduced in 1937. But it is also an apt descriptor of her endlessly inventive designs and her own way of life. Born in Rome to a family of scholars and minor nobility, "Schiap" as her friends knew her, moved early on in a circle of intellectuals and artists. In 1924, raising her daughter on her own in Paris, she met couturier Paul Poiret, who encouraged her to try her hand at design. In 1927, she presented her first collection of trompe-l'oeil sweaters. Published in *Vogue* they became a hit in America, establishing a relation with manufacturers there that would always remain strong.

The Schiaparelli label thrived in the 1930s. In 1930 she designed the first wrap dress; in 1931, she introduced a broad padded shoulder into her collections, which became increasingly sharp and geometric. In 1935, she started using colorful dyed-to-match metal zippers in both her sportswear and eveningwear. Adopting hot pink as the signature of her bold brand, she experimented with innovative textiles such as acrylic, cellophane, Jersela (rayon jersey), Fildifer (rayon with metallic threads), and Rhodophane (a new plastic).

By mid-decade, she began to collaborate with many of the great surrealist and dadaist artists of her day: Man Ray, Jean Cocteau, Meret Oppenheim, Alberto Giacometti, Elsa Triolet, Leonor Fini, and especially Salvador Dalí, with whom she designed a chest-of-drawers suit and lobster and "tear" dresses. The eccentric designer literally turned fashion on its head with whimsical accessories like her high-heeled-shoe hat, and played masterfully with witty prints, concept jewelry, and decorative closures in the shape of paper clips, cicadas, or candlesticks. She might even be said to have launched technocouture, with her music-box belted gown of 1938. Beyond the garments, Schiaparelli pioneered the concept of themed collections (Zodiac, Circus, Pagan) and transformed the traditional *défilé* into an event that integrated music, lighting effects, and various stunts.

For all their flamboyance, Schiaparelli's clothes were always a commercial success. During the Occupation, she moved to New York; her couture house remained open though she wasn't designing. She returned to Paris in 1945, but disinclined to adapt to the postwar shift in fashions, her work became less popular, and in 1954 she closed the doors to her salon.

"Dare to be different."

Left Schiaparelli
embroidered dress with
a figure by Jean Cocteau,
holding a cellophane
handkerchief, drawn by
Cocteau for *Harper's
Bazaar*, July 1937

Schiaparelli

A grey linen dress embroidered
with Cocteau's design — hair golden,
lips pink, eyes peacock blue,
and a blue Cellophane handkerchief.

Robe de Schiaparelli - 1937.

dmé par Jean Cocteau.

40

*Opposite Page Far
Left* Schiaparelli pants
and jacket drawn by
Eric, 1937 • *Center Left*
Schiaparelli evening
gowns, *Vogue*, October
1947 • *Left* Advertisement
for Shocking perfume,
illustrated by Marcel
Vertés, 1949

Valentino

1932– (Italy)

An icon of elegance, Valentino Garavani represents the refinement of a craft and the persistence of an idea about what is chic. As a teenager, he studied fashion illustration in Milan. In 1950, he moved to Paris to study haute couture at the schools of the Chambre Syndicale, then worked for seven years in the ateliers of couturiers Jean Dessès and Guy Laroche. He returned to Italy in 1959 to open a couture house in Rome at a time when many film stars and jet setters had begun to congregate there. In 1960, he met the man who would become his companion and business partner. Giancarlo Giammetti's innovative approach would build worldwide recognition for the Valentino brand and its licenses, presciently putting the *V* logo on their products and introducing themed spreads for print ads.

The precise tailoring and luxuriousness of Valentino's early work won him recognition and a devoted following of wealthy socialites. In 1968, at a moment of crisis for haute couture, he opened a boutique in Paris and produced a couture collection that truly went global. From this sophisticated all-white collection came Jackie Kennedy's dress for her marriage to Aristotle Onassis. Like many of his contemporaries, he created a ready-to-wear line in 1969 and a few years later a menswear line. In 1976, he began to hold his ready-to-wear shows in Paris, where in 1989 he would move his couture presentations as well.

The suave, impeccably turned out Valentino embodied the celebrity designer living the same jet-setting *dolce vita* as his rich clients. An aesthetic of refined femininity remained the hallmark of his career. With strategically placed bows, ruffles, and ruching, he made opulently glamorous clothing that moved beautifully on the body—often in his signature Valentino red, a vibrant orange-crimson.

In 1998, after some financial struggles, he and Giammetti sold the company, though the designer remained on as creative director. Amid rumors of retirement, in July 2007 Valentino celebrated his legacy with a three-day extravaganza in Rome; in September, he showed his final collection. In 2011, the couple launched the downloadable Valentino Garavani Virtual Museum, using immersive 3-D technology to present fifty years of collections to a new generation on their own terms.

Right Valentino at an exhibition of his work, Museo dell'Ara Pacis, Rome, 2007 • *Far Right* Valentino, Spring/Summer 2004

Photo by Alberto Pizzoli, AFP, Getty Images.z

Photo by Pierre Verdy, AFP, Getty Images.

Photo by Jean-Pierre Muller, AFP, Getty Images.

"I love beautiful clothes, so when fashion became about grunge and minimalism I never followed. I think those trends were very offensive for women. I always say I am here to make women look beautiful and not like fools or crazy fashion victims."

Left Valentino haute couture, Spring/Summer 2001

Gianni Versace

1946–97 (Italy)

Gianni Versace represented the unrestrained, extroverted face of Italian fashion throughout the 1980s and 1990s. In his mother's dressmaking establishment in Reggio di Calabria, he learned as much about glamour as about construction. In 1973, he moved to Milan, where he freelanced for the Callaghan, Genny, and Complice labels. In 1978, he founded his own label with his brother Santo; his sister, Donatella, served as muse. From his first ready-to-wear collections for women and men, he successfully translated the image of the brand into diffusion lines as well as accessory, jewelry, fragrance, cosmetics, and home furnishings lines. In 1989, he began to show a couture collection in Paris.

Versace paired a solid foundation in fine tailoring and a preference for the bias cut with a taste for unconventional fabrics, dazzling color, boldly juxtaposed pattern, and elaborate combinations of texture and decorative detail. Whether his references came from the baroque or abstract modernism or the ancient Greek and Roman motifs that had surrounded him in southern Italy, his extreme styling resulted in a distinctively gilded aesthetic. Versace made classic clothes look sexy in the way he reshaped the body. The more brazenly sexual attitude of many of his designs, often perceived as an affront to good taste, was exactly what his large clientele of the young, the rich, and the extravagant were seeking.

Versace also showed a flamboyant knack for promotion, with an astronomical amount spent on publicity and advertising. He triggered the supermodel phenomenon of the early 1990s when he paid well-known editorial models like Linda Evangelista, Christy Turlington, Naomi Campbell, and Cindy Crawford enormous fees to walk his runways en masse. He was also the first designer to pack his front rows with celebrities, rock stars, and film goddesses.

Adopting an aristocratic pose—aware that he and his family embodied the dream his brand was meant to fulfill—the designer lived in opulent splendor in Milan, Como, New York, and Miami. When Versace died in 1997, shot on the steps of his Miami mansion, Donatella, who designed the Versus line, assumed creative direction over the company.

Photo by Pierre Verdy, AFP, Getty Images.

Above Versace Atelier, Spring/Summer 1995

"*I am not interested in the past, except as the road to the future. I want to be a designer for my time. I love the music, the art, the movies of today. I want my clothes to express all of this.*"

Left Naomi Campbell in Versace, Los Angeles, 1991

Madeleine Vionnet

1876–1975 (France)

Called an "architect among dressmakers," Madeleine Vionnet may have been the greatest creator of garments in the twentieth century. Born in a Parisian suburb, she became a dressmaker's apprentice at age eleven and, at the century's end, for five years interpreted Paris couture for the London house of Kate Reilly. In 1900, she returned to France and became the *première* to Marie Gerber at the House of Callot Soeurs, who innovatively applied the kimono sleeve to Western patternmaking. It was here that Vionnet learned to relate clothing to the natural form of the female body. In 1907, she became a designer at the House of Doucet, but her radical proposal of corsetless *déshabillés* to be worn in public met with rejection. Vionnet opened her own couture house in 1912, but closed it two years later at the onset of World War I and headed to Rome. After the war, she reopened her business, moving in 1923 to premises on the avenue Montaigne whose interiors harmoniously balanced the classical and the modern.

Working on a reduced-scale dress form, Vionnet approached each garment in its full three-dimensionality, seeking to enhance the dynamics of movement. She experimented with wrapping techniques from the Orient and classical antiquity. Most revolutionary, she elevated cutting on the bias—against the grain of the material—to create clothing that clung to and moved with the body like a second skin. She had textiles, especially supple new fabrics like silk crêpe, woven 2 yards (1.8 m) wider than then commonly available, which increased their

elasticity and reduced the number of seams a garment required. To maintain this pliancy, she eliminated foundations and linings and avoided darts. The freedom she accorded to the fabric liberated the woman as well. Some Vionnet signatures like cowls and loops resulted from this quest for fluidity. She believed that ornamentation ideally should arise from the construction of a garment, from reconfigurations of the fabric such as fagoting and drawn thread work, fringing, or pleating and tucking.

Vionnet actively supported copyright protection for designers. Her thumbprint on the label of her garments certified their authenticity. She was also far ahead of her time in labor practices, offering her employees holiday pay, maternity leave, child care, and medical and dental care. In 1939, then in her sixties, Vionnet retired.

Far Left Vionnet day dresses, drawn by Jacques Haramboure, *Femina*, 1930
• *Left* Vionnet, two-piece evening dress drawn by Eric, French *Vogue*, October 1938

"*Insofar as one can talk of a Vionnet school, it comes mostly from my having been an enemy of fashion. There is something superficial and volatile about the seasonal and elusive whims of fashion which offends my sense of beauty.*"

DE LA FUMÉE
ROBE DE MADELEINE VIONNET

N° 2 de la Gazette du Bon Ton.   Année 1922. — Planche 13

Above Left Advertisement for Vionnet's establishments, logo by Thayaht, 1925 • *Left* Vionnet dress, drawn by Thayaht, *Gazette du Bon Ton*, 1922

Vivienne Westwood

1941– (United Kingdom)

Vivienne Westwood is a self-trained genius of impudent, "heroic," as she would say, British fashion. A schoolteacher from Derbyshire, she met the impresario Malcolm McLaren in 1965; after a brief romance, they entered into a professional partnership. In 1971, she began making Teddy Boy–revival clothes for their new King's Road boutique, Let It Rock. The shop underwent numerous incarnations, as Westwood produced confrontational fashions that drew from biker culture (leathers, T-shirts), underground sex clubs (bondage and fetish wear), and the emergent punk scene (the DIY aesthetic of the destroyed and pieced together). It was in Westwood's Seditionaries clothing that the Sex Pistols, whom McLaren managed, exploded onto the stage.

In 1981, she presented her debut catwalk show in Paris with the dandified genderless Pirates collection, the first in which she turned to historical rather than subcultural references. Splitting from McLaren in 1984, she moved deeper into historical exploration, seen to inventive excess in 1985 with her minicrinis, short crinoline skirts worn with platform "rocking horse" shoes. Against the prevailing silhouette of the power suit, Westwood continued in a more structured, feminine direction, introducing the corset into her Harris Tweed collection of 1987. This collection also marked her fascination with traditional British dress, which she would parody, but also modernize through innovative tailoring, in eclectic presentations she has referred to collectively as Britain Must Go Pagan as well as in her Anglomania collection of Fall/Winter 1993/94.

Westwood's historicist drive dominated her work in the 1990s, whether drawing on seventeenth-century slashed costume, eighteenth-century dress as painted by Gainsborough and Watteau, nineteenth-century bustles, or mid-century New Look tailoring. Threaded through all these collections was a rousing eroticism and a call to dressing up as way of thinking about status, heritage, and power. In the new millennium, sartorial extremism gave way to an attention to cut and the manipulation of fabric, and for a period at least, she put the past aside. With a diversified range of lines—Red Label (ready-to-wear), Gold Label (custom), Anglomania (diffusion), Man, and bridal—the cheeky Westwood became a Dame of the British Empire in 2006.

Photo by David Montgomery, Getty Images.

Above Westwood and McLaren at World's End, the final iteration of their shop, with models in the Spring/Summer 1982 collection

Photo by Pierre Verdy, AFP, Getty Images.

Above Vivienne Westwood, Spring/Summer 1996

"In order to see the future, you have to understand what's been done, what's still worth keeping, and what could be done."

Left Vivienne Westwood, Fall/Winter 2011/12

Yohji Yamamoto

1943– (Japan)

Yohji Yamamoto is the rare philosopher-designer who enlarges the conception of fashion. Raised in Tokyo by his widowed dressmaker mother, he studied law at her request before pursuing his true passion. With prize money he received from Bunka Fashion College, he headed to Paris in 1969 just as ready-to-wear was taking hold. Not finding work, he returned to Tokyo. After a period freelancing, he started his Y's line for women in 1972, adding menswear four years later. His debut runway show in Tokyo in 1977 played with ideas about the Japanese worker's uniform.

In 1981, he arrived back in Paris with compatriot Rei Kawakubo, invited to show among the official ready-to-wear collections. Yamamoto's designs, which had startled in Japan, sent shock waves through the audience. In contrast to fashion's dominant figure of hard stilettoed glamour, his models came out in voluminous layers of dark, seemingly tattered garments, wearing flat shoes and little makeup. The collection contained key elements that would continue to define his aesthetic: the shades of black that foreground form; the humanly imperfect asymmetry; the beauty of the distressed and damaged; the oversized layers that obscure and protect; the androgyny that conveys both sensuality and power. In 1984, the designer expanded the high-end Yohji Yamamoto label with a menswear collection of soft, loose-fitting suits.

In the 1990s, Yamamoto began to embrace a wider palette of color, and his clothing became more structured than it had been early in his career, although he continued to play with unusual proportions and dramatic scale. His mastery of tailoring revealed a deep intelligence in search of the essence of each garment. In his investigations of the feminine silhouettes of the Victorians or the couture flourishes of the New Look, a lyric romanticism emerged, held in tension by his innate rebelliousness. A particularly evocative moment came in his wedding-themed Spring/Summer 1999 collection when the bride appeared dressed in a plain hoop-skirted wedding gown. From zippered pockets within the hoops, she pulled out the rest of her ensemble: sandals, mantle, hat, gloves, and bouquet.

Yamamoto, whose eye is always turned to the reality of what people wear, collaborated with Adidas on a shoe collection in 2001. Its success led to Y-3, a partnered sportswear line that has diversified his customer base. In 2009, Yamamoto's company file for bankruptcy protection, and later that year Integral Corporation purchased the brand. Yamamoto remains in place as head designer.

Right Yohji Yamamoto, Spring/Summer 1999 • *Far Right* Yohji Yamamoto, Fall/ Winter 2006/07

"I want to achieve anti-fashion through fashion. That's why I'm always heading in my own direction because if you're not waking up what is asleep, you might as well just stay on the beaten path."

Left Yohji Yamamoto menswear, Spring/Summer 2012

Artisans & Innovators

352

Artisans & Innovators

An artisan in fashion design is a steward of the practice, charged with keeping a legacy of rare skills alive. To produce artful work of consummate quality requires commitment and discipline. Many are the channels through which these traditions and techniques can be transmitted and mastered, from the careful study of the historical archive to the ideal model of apprenticeship. The clothes that are crafted always bear the hand of their creators.

An innovator in fashion design is a pioneer grappling with the assumptions that underlie the practice at any given time or place. Questioning received notions of history, gender, beauty, and function, they seek to modify or reinvent how clothing is constructed, produced, disseminated, and worn, which requires them to conceive of new tools, techniques, and technologies. Their independence, if not irreverence, may lead to revolutionary shifts in the industry, and sometimes helps to redefine a society's self-image.

Comme des Garçons, Fall/Winter 2012/13
Photo by Alexander Klein, AFP, Getty Images.

Haider Ackermann

1971- (Colombia)

Long on the radar of the cognoscenti, Haider Ackermann has in the last few years caught the attention of the fashion world at large. Born in Bogotà and adopted by a French couple, the designer spent a peripatetic childhood in Chad, Iran, Ethiopia, and Algeria, before his family moved to the Netherlands when he was twelve. In 1994, he went to Antwerp, where he studied at but dropped out of the Royal Academy of Fine Arts. His debut show in Paris in 2002 led to his appointment as designer for two seasons of the experimental "research" line produced by the Italian leather company Ruffo. As his own collections matured, Ackermann's name began to be heard frequently: In 2009, he was offered, but turned down, the top spot at Maison Martin Margiela upon the founder's retirement. In late 2010, Karl Lagerfeld spoke of the designer as his preferred eventual successor at Chanel. And in 2011, he was considered in the running to replace John Galliano (for whom he once interned) at Dior.

Ackermann is a master draper with a modern sensibility. Working with sumptuous, living fabrics—silks, cashmeres, supple leathers, and suedes—he folds, twists, loops, and layers his garments in utterly new ways. He is also a virtuoso colorist. Into the dark, moody palette of northern Europe, he has injected the rich tones of the African continent, in extraordinary combinations of cobalt and copper, pumpkin and marigold, emerald and teal. Certain elements recur: cropped jackets, sleeves pushed above the elbows; long, narrow skirts or soft pants; billowy tops; belted or peplummed waists; elegantly exposed skin. Seen to best effect in movement, Ackermann's clothes flow along the body with sinuous grace. His collections are both intellectually rigorous and emotionally resonant. Modest and louche, sensual and intelligent, Old World and contemporary, these are designs for a woman who captivates while she eludes.

Photos by first VIEW.

Above Left Haider Ackermann, Fall/Winter 2010/11 • ***Left*** Haider Ackermann, Spring/ Summer 2012

Photo by Nathalie Lagneau, Catwalking, Getty Images.

"These collections are, for me, in many ways like writing a book. You make one chapter after the other and hope the reader is going to be excited and want to read the next chapter."

Left Haider Ackermann, Fall/Winter 2007/08

Azzendine Alaïa

ca. 1940– (Tunisia)

Azzedine Alaïa designs for the body, not for the season. He began to develop his understanding of the human form at fifteen, studying sculpture at the École des Beaux Arts in Tunis and helping to copy French haute couture for a dressmaker in the city. In 1957, he moved to Paris, where for five days he worked alongside Christian Dior. He then honed his tailoring skills during two years in the atelier of Guy Laroche. Timely introductions led to private commissions by influential members of Parisian society, and in 1960 he became housekeeper/dressmaker for the Comtesse de Blégiers. In 1965, he opened a tiny couture salon catering to an elite clientele, though by the 1970s he was moving toward ready-to-wear.

Alaïa came to international attention in 1981 with his first fashion show, a collection of body-conscious knitwear that was simultaneously sober and erotically charged. Over the next decade, his figure-revealing garments, in wovens and leathers in addition to the knits, earned him the monikers "titan of tight" and "king of cling." Yet his work has never been vulgar; instead, his muted palette and lack of adornment emphasize the purity of form. Alaïa achieves these deceptively simple second skins with complex pattern work and meticulous construction techniques, with inventive seaming and stitching adopted from corsetry, always draping on a live model. He is a perfectionist who works closely with textile manufacturers. He creates each prototype himself and hand finishes every garment in his collections.

Preferring to work at his own speed, to perfect rather than reinvent each season, in 1993 Alaïa stopped showing on the established fashion calendar. He came back in 2000 with financing from the Prada Group, but left again in 2003. In July 2011, he presented an haute couture collection, his first such show in eight years. Although his approach has meant less coverage in the fashion press, an incredibly loyal clientele eager for his designs now follows his timetable. Meanwhile, Alaïa is forming a foundation to preserve both his own archives and his world-class collection of haute couture.

Above Right Pieces from Alaïa's haute couture, Fall/Winter 2006/07 collection
• *Right* Azzendine Alaïa, Fall/Winter 2009/10

Photo from exhibition, Museum of Fine Arts, Boston.

Photo by Andrew Lamb, Catwalking, Getty Images.

"Today I believe that designers are asked to do too much, too many collections. It's inconceivable to me that someone creative can have a new idea every two months. Because if I have one new idea in a year, I thank heaven."

Left Azzendine Alaïa, Fall/Winter 2007/08

Fukuko Ando

1964– (Japan)

Fukuko Ando is a poet of fabric and form. Having received a degree in literature, she studied fashion at the Mode Gakuen in Nagoya. To better understand the Western conception of the clothed body, she moved to Paris in 1991 to continue her education at the École de la Chambre Syndicale de la Couture Parisienne. Her career has led her to successful collaborations with the *maisons de couture* of Christian Dior and Christian Lacroix. Since 1995 she has been creating unique couture garments.

Ando forgoes patterns and traditional geometries. She drapes and sews each piece directly on a dress form, using a mirror to verify the evolution of the garment according the natural shape of the body. Moreover, her manipulation of the fabric into a three-dimensional object always obeys the material's inherent properties and the movement given by her hand. Whatever her technique—knotting, gathering, ribbing, pleating, crocheting, embroidering, or beading—she seeks a harmonious balance of sculptural shape and surface effect.

Her practice nurtures a very personal vision of fashion that extends into other art forms. Her interest in the way that no two human bodies are exactly alike gave birth to the Pleiades project of 2005, a collection of 140 one-of-a-kind dolls inspired by the seven sister stars that form the constellation (twenty variations of each sister). She presented her Spring 2007 Golden Promise collection as a performance by fifteen dancers from the Ballet de l'Opéra de Paris.

Ando sees her clothing as having a soul. As a designer, she enters into a conversation between the fabric and the body, in an attempt to awaken the wearer as a human being. Like the garments of Madeleine Vionnet, who has deeply inspired her philosophically, Ando's work is timeless and ageless.

"My dress is neither prêt-à-porter nor haute couture. It's a sensation."

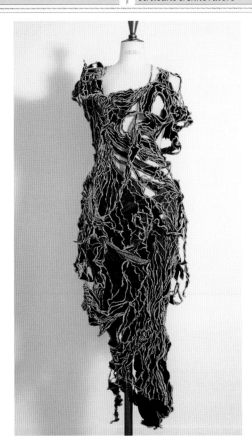

Photos courtesy of Fukuko Ando.

Above Left and Left Fukuko Ando, On Wings of Light, hand-made embroidery dresses• *Below* Ando, knotted Eden dress

Photo by firstVIEW.

Manish Arora

(India)

Manish Arora brings to a global fashion arena a pop sensibility rendered in the exuberant colors and elaborate embellishments of his native India. Three years after graduating from New Delhi's National Institute of Fashion and Technology in 1994, he launched his own label based in India. In 2000, he showed at the inaugural India Fashion Week in New Delhi. He launched Fish Fry, a diffusion line, in 2001, which led to a partnership with Reebok in 2004 to market a line of colorful sportswear. This would be the first of many collaborations for products from cosmetics to housewares, accessories to beverages. He went on to show at London Fashion Week in 2005. With his Spring/Summer 2008 collection debuting in Paris, he became the first Indian designer to find success in France.

Arora's design aesthetic is founded on Western silhouettes that he transforms into playful, eclectic garments with a riotous application of brilliant colors, kitschy patterns, and traditional Indian craftwork such as beading, embroidery, and appliqué. His maximalist approach is leavened by his impeccable execution. To this vibrant mix he adds avant-garde styling and campy runway presentations. A confident fashion showman, he takes his audience on a singular journey each season.

Arora was hired to helm the relaunch of Paco Rabanne in 2011 and put on a superbly theatrical debut show. But despite the affinity of his work's level of craftsmanship and its futuristic strain, he departed from the label after two collections.

Photo by Pierre Verdy, AFP, Getty Images.

"Fashion should be dramatic—what's the point of wearing something black and getting lost in the crowd?"

Above Left Manish Arora, Fall/Winter 2011 • *Left* Manish Arora, Spring/Summer 2011

Zowie Broach & Brian Kirkby

1966– & 1965– (United Kingdom)

Boudicca is an idea-driven design practice that uses fashion to explore issues of contemporary life, entwining the social, the political, and the personal. Zowie Broach and Brian Kirkby founded their fashion label in 1997, naming it for the warrior queen who died in A.D. 60 defending Britons from the Roman invaders. In the first four years of the partnership, they showed their work in the context of art galleries and other exhibition spaces. Their rigorous tailoring and distinct silhouettes then brought them an invitation to show at London Fashion Week in 2001 and a sponsorship from American Express in 2003. The conceptual nature of many of their designs, together with Broach and Kirkby's intentionally limited production, kept the business small. Yet the bold sophistication of their dark, edgy, feminine garments made the designers among the most watched in Britain.

In late 2006, the Chambre Syndicale invited Boudicca to show as a guest member during the haute couture collections. Their work already had a couturelike quality, superbly constructed in the finest fabrics with intricate piecing and unique detailing. Paris, for three seasons, gave Broach and Kirkby a place to refine their vision at the highest level. They also kept up their ready-to-wear output and in 2008 released Wode, a perfume in a spray can that goes on blue—an homage to ancient British war paint—then fades to leave only the scent.

Boudicca's designers continue to reinterpret modes of dressmaking to produce work that responds to issues of culture and identity, always imbuing their collections with a narrative context meant to provoke dialogue. Broach and Kirkby no longer participate in the official fashion weeks; instead, they look to new ways of engaging their audience, from short films like 2011's *Motion Capture Sequin Dress* to their evocative website, Platform 13.

"It's an unspoken language, that garments have; more function than just covering the body . . . not clothes as escapism, but of expression."

Photo by firstVIEW.

Photo by Antonio de Moraes Barros Filho, WireImage.

Above Left Boudicca, Fall/Winter 2006/07 • *Left* Boudicca haute couture, Spring/Summer 2008

Photo by Mark Von Holden, Getty Images.

Maria Cornejo

1962 (Chile)

Maria Cornejo designs spare but easy clothing that she calls "minimalism with a heart." Her family came to Manchester, England, as political refugees from Chile, and her work has always carried a quality of the outsider in the fashion world. Her first design effort after graduating from Ravensbourne College of Design and Communications in 1984 was the short-lived Richmond Cornejo collection, which was aimed at London club kids. She went on to act as creative consultant for a number of retail brands, including Joseph, Jigsaw, and Tehen. Following time in Tokyo, Milan, and Paris, in 1996 she and her husband, photographer Mark Borthwick, relocated to New York. She opened her Nolita boutique Zero + Maria Cornejo in 1998, making her clothes in the back. "Zero" was to represent a departure point: something neither positive nor negative, but rather, balanced. In 2006, the Cooper-Hewitt gave Cornejo a National Design Award for excellence and innovation in fashion.

Known as a modernist, she designs clothing both architectural and feminine. Cornejo bases her work on how simple geometric shapes and volumes (circles, squares, triangles, tubes) drape on the body. She often constructs a garment from a single piece of fabric, and certain motifs, like curved-seam patterns or cocoon shapes, as well as the theme of identity, reappear from one collection to the next. More recently, she has introduced quirky digital prints (a close-up of fur, a friend's bookshelf), frequently from photos taken with her iPhone. The evolution of her collections is one of subtle fine-tuning and distillation, not radical change. Even as her brand grows—to date, she has three New York boutiques and shows her collection each season in both New York and Paris—her work remains timeless and intimate, real fashion for intelligent women.

"I love the luxury of knowing that I can design what I want to wear."

Above Right Zero + Maria Cornejo, Spring/Summer 2010 • *Right* Zero + Maria Cornejo, Fall/Winter 2011/12

Hussein Chalayan

1970– (Cyprus)

Hussein Chalayan, hailed as one of the twenty-first century's most visionary designers, pushes the boundaries of fashion to create bridges between different cultures and different disciplines. A Turkish Cypriot, Chalayan was born in Nicosia, today the world's last remaining divided city. He grew up moving between there and London, and ideas about isolation and borders are never far from his work. For his 1993 graduate collection at Central Saint Martins, which addressed life and decay, attraction and repulsion, he buried his garments with magnetized iron filings, exhuming them shortly before their presentation. The following year, he began his eponymous label and by the mid-1990s became associated with a deeply thoughtful minimalist aesthetic. From 1998 to 2001, he collaborated with luxury cashmere company TSE, twice won Designer of the Year at the British Fashion Awards, and debuted in Paris with his Spring/Summer 2002 collection.

From the first, Chalayan's collections evinced a preoccupation with themes of homelessness, migration, metamorphosis, speed, spatial systems, disembodiment, demarcation, and cultural identity. His Between collection for Spring/Summer 1998 addressed the way belief systems are used to define one's territory and featured six models wearing chadors of varying lengths, the first naked but for a short yasmak over her face. His Afterwords collection for Fall/Winter 2000/01 dealt with displacement and the plight of refugees. Within a domestic tableau, models converted the furnishings into garments; chairs became tailored dresses (and suitcases), a coffee table became a skirt.

Chalayan has also worked at the crossroads of fashion and technology, even while suggesting the human tendency to submit to the machine. He showed his first remote-controlled, mechanically animated dresses in his Echoform and Before Minus Now collections in 1999. In his breathtaking One Hundred and Eleven collection for Spring/Summer 2007, he introduced a suite of computer-operated transformer dresses, which morphed through over a century of silhouettes. The next season's Airborne collection, which explored climate change and lifecycles, debuted an LED dress and other delicate mechanical dresses. His appointment in 2008 as creative director of two Puma lines has allowed him to realize some of his technological ideas in actual streetwear.

In the 1990s, Chalayan pushed the art of the show to the pinnacle of creativity with his intimate, human-scale stagings and performances more often seen in the art world. With Temporal Meditations, shown in June 2003 at the Pitti Uomo, he was among the first designers to produce a film as an alternative to a live runway show, a practice he continues. Beyond the theatre and the theory, the clothes themselves are often subtly sensual and elegant.

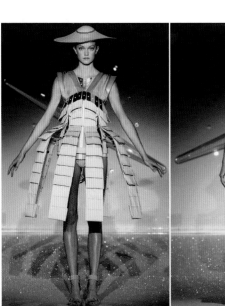

Photo by Pierre Verdy, AFP, Getty Images.

Photo by Snead Lynch.

Far Left Hussein Chalayan, Spring/Summer 2007 ●

Left Hussein Chalayan, Fall/Winter 2000/01

"I think of modular systems where clothes are like small parts of an interior, the interiors are part of architecture, which is then part of an urban environment. I think of fluid space where they are all part of each other."

Left Hussein Chalayan, Fall/Winter 2012/13 •
Below Hussein Chalayan, Fall/Winter 2011/12

Ann Demeulemeester

1959– (Belgium)

Ann Demeulemeester creates clothing with a warrior soulfulness, from the very first using her own body and that of her husband as the basis of her investigations of form. In 1987, with fellow graduates of Antwerp's Royal Academy of Fine Arts she headed to London for the British Designer Show, as a result of which the New York boutique Charivari bought her first collection. In 1988, she added an accessories collection, and in 1991 she made her Paris runway debut.

The hallmark of a Demeulemeester garment is its play of contrasts. Her modern yet romantic designs combine toughness and tenderness, a sharp strength and a slouchy insouciance. A signature look pairs the military-tailored lines of a long coat with softly draped asymmetrical pieces, sturdy boots with delicate feather jewelry. Her designs unite supple fabrics like rayon, silk, and even linen painter's canvas with harder materials like leather and fur. Her primary palette of black and white, with occasional interjections of other deep shades, pulls out the nuances of form, texture, and detail.

The poetic power of Demeulemeester's style, in fact, comes from a carefully considered creative process, approaching the imperfect human form with a concern for proportion and movement. Her deconstruction of traditional patternmaking, her sometimes complex layering, wrapping, and strapping is in search of a balance that feels honest to the wearer.

Her ideas of femininity and masculinity are fluid. From 1996 until 2005, she showed her men's and women's collections together on the Paris runway, and her choice of models has only underlined the way the cut of her clothing allows these gender markers to flow freely from one to the other.

Demeulemeester prefers to avoid the spotlight, working out of a studio in her Le Corbusier–designed house in Antwerp. Indifferent to trends, in 2008 she debuted Collection Blanche, an edition of highlights from her twenty-year archive, all without identifying dates, untethered from any but their own time.

Right Ann Demeulemeester, Fall/Winter 2012/13

"Fashion has a right to exist, because it permits the people to define themselves over and over again."

Left Ann Demeulemeester, Fall/Winter 2011/12 •
Below Muse Patti Smith walking Demeulemeester's menswear show, Fall/Winter 2006/07

Alber Elbaz

1961– (Morocco)

The affable Alber Elbaz has built a reputation for his commitment to, and success in, making his women look and feel beautiful. Raised outside of Tel Aviv, he studied fashion design at Shenkar College before moving to New York. In 1989, he began a seven-year mentorship with American couturier Geoffrey Beene, from whom he learned the importance of drape and fit. In 1996, the House of Guy Laroche hired the little-known designer to rejuvenate its collections. Two years later, Yves Saint Laurent wooed him away to design his Rive Gauche line. The Gucci Group's takeover at YSL, however, put the designer out of a job in 2000. In 2001, Elbaz found his perfect fit at Lanvin, where for the last decade he has rebuilt and redefined the legendary house.

Elbaz is a master of flow and volume, sculpting garments into something lighter than air. That he has absorbed the lessons of Old World tailoring and dressmaking is clear from the complexity and precision of his seamless draping and pleating and from his fine attention to detail and finishing. At the same time, his clothes are very contemporary. He modernizes classical forms with exposed industrial zippers; he weathers opulent fabrics like satin and taffeta or leaves their edges raw; and he gives his collections youthful styling with his signature ballet flats and eye-catching jewelry.

The designs of an unabashed romantic, his clothes convey joy but also, in their womanly femininity, the depth of a life really lived. Elbaz's approach evokes Iribe's original mother-and-daughter logo for Jeanne Lanvin: timeless, chic clothing being passed from one generation to the next and relevant to both.

Photo by François Guillot, AFP, Getty Images.

Left Lanvin, Fall/Winter 2011/12

"Perfection is never interesting to me, but the search for perfection . . . is."

Left Lanvin, Spring/Summer
2011

Carla Fernández

1973– (Mexico)

Carla Fernández belongs to a new generation of designers as agents of social change. Her label, Taller Flora, not only produces fashion-forward and functional garments, but also helps to improve the lives of the indigenous peoples of Mexico. Her purposeful work on ethical fashion earned Fernández the United Kingdom's Young Fashion Entrepreneur of the Year award in 2008.

Her process starts with collecting and cleaning cotton, spinning yarns, and hand weaving them into fabric on a backstrap loom. Fernández designs with geometric pattern pieces, primarily squares and rectangles. Much like traditional Mexican garments, such as *huipiles* (tunics) and *rebozos* (shawls), her clothing is constructed to minimize, if not entirely eliminate, the need to cut the fabric. Instead, she uses strategically placed folds, darts, tucks, and pleating to tailor a garment to the body. Her approach to patternmaking and construction both reduces waste and serves as an homage to native tradition. Far from folk costumes, though, Fernández's interpretations for the modern consumer range from softly draped silhouettes to boldly architectural ones.

To fully comprehend the principles of making contemporary clothes with ancient techniques, Fernández travels throughout Mexico in her mobile laboratory, collaborating with many Mexican artisans and often reacquainting them with their own cultural heritage. She also empowers locals through workshops and cooperatives by teaching them self-sustainable skills. A respect for history and a sense of responsibility for the environment and indigenous communities all contribute to Fernandez's long-term vision for fashion.

Above and Right Carla Fernández, Fall/Winter 2011/2012

Photos courtesy of Carla Fernández.

"All this creativeness comes from who we are as a people, what we have become, and how we want to be seen in the future."

Helmut Lang

1956– (Austria)

Helmut Lang's entrée into the fashion world came in the late 1970s through a made-to-measure business based in Vienna, Austria. Experience with the bespoke process set a strong foundation for a design practice that concerned itself primarily with minimalism and deconstructivism. The purity and practicality of his austere aesthetic might also be attributed to a kind of essentialism.

His first international fashion presentation took place in Paris in 1986. His second, in 1987, included a menswear line. Even as his work gained momentum, Lang began to break with the conventions of the fashion industry and build bridges to the art world. As early as 1988, he rejected traditional fashion shows and initiated collaborations with sculptress Louise Bourgeois and conceptual artist Jenny Holzer to create installations called *séances de travail* (working sessions).

Lang expanded his business throughout the 1990s, adding accessory and jeans lines and, by decade's end, relocating to New York. Making good use of technological advances in the domain of textiles, he introduced many new high-tech materials, including latex-bounded laces, thermal and holographic fabrics, and lacquered silks. Lang was also the first designer to stream his collection online in 1998.

A fundamental respect for the craft of couture and the need for artistic experimentation defined him as a designer and explained the creative direction of his collections. Lang transitioned into the art world after retiring from fashion in 2005 after the Prada Group acquired his label in 2004.

"You have to work hard and you have to recognize when [fashion] evolves into something interesting and be able to let go of it when the work is interesting enough to fight you back."

Photo by firstVIEW.

Left Helmut Lang, Spring/ Summer 1997

Nicolas Ghesquière

1971– (France)

Combining computer-age vision, historical reverence, and commercial savvy, Nicolas Ghesquière has become one of fashion's most influential designers. Raised in a provincial town in the Loire Valley, he never received a formal education in fashion design. At fifteen, he started as an intern first for Agnès B., then for Corinne Cobson, before joining Jean Paul Gaultier for two years in 1990. In 1995, he took a job at Balenciaga designing knitwear, wedding dresses, and mourning clothes for a Japanese license. The company recognized Ghesquière's raw talent, and when the position of creative director came open in 1997, he was promoted. Under his direction, Balenciaga has become a major brand, with capsule collections (Pants, Knits, Silks) and lines for menswear, perfume, and highly sought-after accessories.

If in his first several collections, the designer was more muted, by 2000 he had found his voice, which became only stronger once he gained access to the Balenciaga archives when the Gucci Group acquired the brand in 2001. Ghesquière's cutting-edge work defies easy categorization. It is cerebral and sexy, strange and chic, from another galaxy and consummately French. In a complex collage of textures, colors, and materials, suggesting references that can't quite be pinned down, he redefines familiar garments and, whether cropping a torso or broadening a shoulder, gives a new proportion to the human body. Indeed, Ghesquière treats his runway collections like a research lab. His passionate commitment to experimentation has produced an unending stream of innovative fabrics, techniques, finishes, shapes, and volumes, all imbued with his cool techno-urban sensibility.

Ghesquière's respect for the timeless work of Cristóbal Balenciaga is clear: In 2004, he introduced the Edition collection, reissued pieces from the house's vast archives, executed with great precision and authenticity. But it is through his own futuristic, abstracted take on what he finds in the archives that he introduces entirely new proposals for what to wear in the twenty-first century.

Above Left Balenciaga, Spring/Summer 2007
• *Left* Balenciaga, Fall/Winter 2010/11

Photos by firstVIEW.

"I have no idea what I would do for my own collection. I give so much of myself for Balenciaga that today if you put me in a room and said, 'Okay, let's try to do a Nicolas Ghesquière project,' I wouldn't be able to do it."

Left Balenciaga, Spring/Summer 2011 • *Below* Balenciaga, ad for Spring/Summer 2012

Viktor Horsting & Rolf Snoeren

1969– & 1969– (Netherlands)

The Dutch design duo known as Viktor & Rolf turn their powers of imagination and their considerable tailoring skills toward an ironic critique of the fashion industry. Horsting and Snoeren met as students at the Academy of Arts in Arnhem. In 1992, they moved to Paris to look for jobs in the world's fashion capital. Unsuccessful on that front, they collaborated on a small collection reconstructed from menswear, which they presented in 1993 at the Salon Européen des Jeunes Stylists in Hyères to win grand prize.

Commenting on society at large and the world of fashion in particular—the hype, the preciousness, the banality—their conceptual presentations found a natural home in the art gallery. In 1996, they created a limited-edition scentless perfume whose bottle could not be opened; it sold out at Colette in Paris. From 1997 to 2000, Viktor & Rolf developed their work as haute couture, the first collection underwritten by the Dutch government and the Groninger Museum. In 1999, invited to show on the official haute couture calendar despite their nonconforming status, the designers presented the surreally beautiful Russian Doll collection in which they dressed a single model in nine successive layers of clothing, like a nested matryoshka. The doll has been a leitmotif of Viktor & Rolf's work. For their retrospective in 2008 at the Barbican Art Gallery in London, the pair not only showed their garments on life-size porcelain mannequins, but also re-created every one in miniature for dolls populating a gigantic dollhouse. The designs themselves are characterized by an appetite for disorientation and displacement, with distorted proportions and exaggerated silhouettes that often engulf their models.

Masters of the art of marketing, the mirror-imaged duo tapped into their commercial potential, turning to ready-to-wear in 2000 and introducing a menswear line in 2003. In 2004, they launched a wearable perfume, Flower Bomb (albeit in a grenade-shaped bottle). Even here, they turned the catwalk into a space of spectacle. For their Fall/Winter 2002/03 collection, the cerulean blue elements of each ensemble became a bluescreen for projected moving images. If the performance sometimes obscures the craft, their wit offers memorable images (the carved-out tulle of the "credit crunch" dresses for 2010) and their more understated tailoring provides pieces of real elegance.

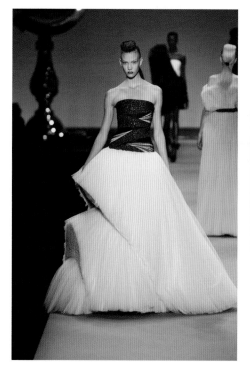

Right Viktor & Rolf, Spring/ Summer 2010 • *Far Right* Viktor & Rolf, Spring/ Summer 2011

"It's always about escaping reality, so in that sense the clothes are meant to show beauty first. Beauty and hope. Because cynicism, you know, kills everything."

Photos by firstVIEW.

Left Viktor & Rolf, Fall/Winter 2010/11

Rei Kawakubo

1942– (Japan)

Rei Kawakubo has consistently challenged conventional notions of fashion with collections that often discomfit, frequently inspire, and always confound. Raised in postwar Tokyo, she studied art and literature at Keio University, graduating in 1964. Initially, she took an advertising job at an acrylic textiles company. She then worked as a freelance stylist. Dissatisfied with the designs she was given, she began to make her own, selling them in 1969 to small boutiques around Tokyo under the label Comme des Garçons. She showed her first collection in 1975 and the following year opened her first shop, which was mirrorless to encourage customers to choose pieces according to how the clothes felt rather than looked.

In 1981, Kawakubo brought her avant-garde aesthetics to the West. Her Paris debut overturned the dominant standards of beauty and femininity with darkly monochromatic designs, voluminous, asymmetrical layers of distressed fabrics that enfolded rather than contoured the body. Ever since, she has found original ways to approach clothes making, whether deconstructing classic tailoring to produce half-finished garments or garments that fuse masculine and feminine components, or manipulating fabric—wrapping, twisting, bunching it—into sculptural or architectonic forms. Along the way, she has offered up a new, liberated relationship between clothing and body, most famously in her Body Meets Dress, Dress Meets Body collection for Spring/Summer 1997, whose padded protuberances deformed the usual silhouette. However disorienting, her designs are always meant to be worn, though the designer is clear that they may not always sell.

Kawakubo's outside-the-box thinking has nevertheless proved very successful. Her creative efforts have extended beyond her clothes to her store environments. Her retail operation expanded quickly and has embraced many radical strategies. Starting in Berlin in 2004, Kawakubo and her husband, Adrian Joffe, became early proponents of the pop-up shop, making guerillalike incursions into marginalized neighborhoods. That same year, they opened the eclectic Dover Street Market in London, selling not only the various Comme lines (including her eccentric perfumes) but also other cutting-edge brands, both big and small. In creative collaborations, such as with Paris boutique Colette and über-brand Louis Vuitton, Comme des Garçons has approached the retail space as a laboratory.

Above Comme des Garçons, Spring/Summer 1997 • *Right* Comme des Garçons menswear, Fall/Winter 2011/12

Even as Kawakubo continues to produce her enigmatic collections, she nurtures young designers who share her vision of the possibilities for fashion, since 1992 extending the Comme des Garçons brand as a protective umbrella to designers Junya Watanabe, Tao Kurihara, and Fumito Ganryu.

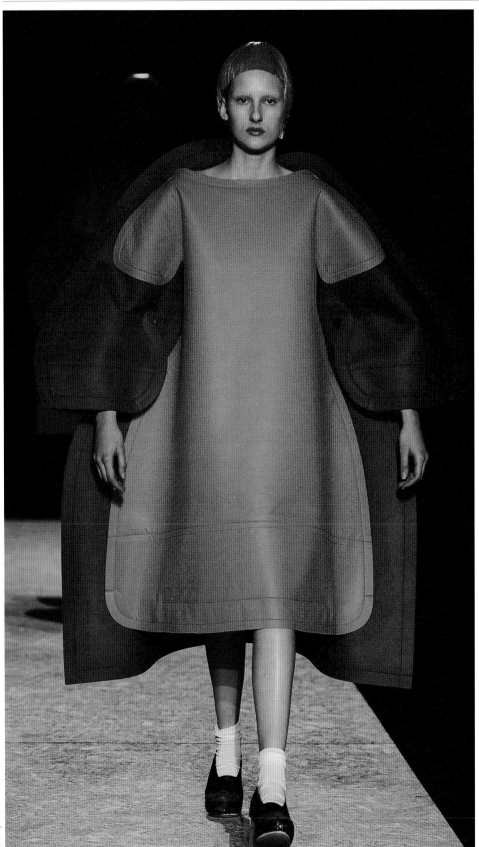

"I think that pieces that are difficult to wear are very interesting, because if people make the effort and wear them, then they can feel a new form of energy and a certain strength."

Left Comme des Garçons, Fall/Winter 2012/13 •
Below Comme des Garçons, Fall/Winter 2009/10

Lie Sang Bong

(South Korea)

From of a fusion of French elegance and Korean artistry Lie Sang Bong has created his own poetics of fashion. The designer studied broadcasting and drama at the Seoul Institute of the Arts and spent time in the theatre before shifting to the Kookje Fashion Academy. He started designing womenswear in 1985, but it was the success of his 1993 runway debut, entitled the Reincarnation, that brought him national recognition. Six years later, the strength of his commercial enterprise and the high level of his aesthetics led him to be named Korea's Best Designer of the Year.

In 2002, he presented his first Paris show, the Lost Memoir. The collection of chic predominantly black ensembles with touches of white and cinnabar red established him as an international designer, and he now moves between Seoul and Paris. His magnetic garments have since caught the attention of fashion adventurers like Lady Gaga and Rihanna.

Lie's designs tap equally into European history (Napoleon and Josephine) and art movements (cubism, the Bauhaus) and Korean traditions (calligraphy, pottery, *dancheong*, the decorative painting of architectural forms). He translates this blend of styles, eras, and cultures through intricate construction techniques and exquisite surface treatments, as well as a rich spectrum of color and patterning. The result is a language serenely energetic and sweetly edgy.

Above Lie Sang Bong, Spring/Summer 2008 •
Right Lie Sang Bong, Fall/Winter 2011/12

"One good thing about being a fashion designer is that you can live in different ages."

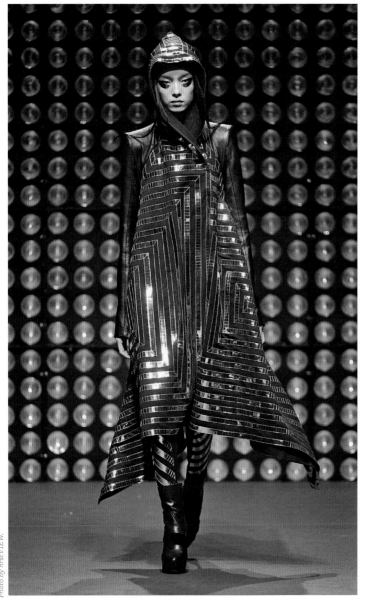

Photo by first VIEW.

Above Gareth Pugh, Fall/
Winter 2011/12 • *Below*
Gareth Pugh, Spring/
Summer 2011

Gareth Pugh

1981– (United Kingdom)

Gareth Pugh is a swiftly rising star of the English avant-garde. Born in Sunderland in the northeast, the designer studied dance as a boy, then spent the summer of 1995 working in the costume department of the National Youth Theatre in London. In 2003, his degree collection for Central Saint Martins, with its inventive use of balloons, landed him the cover of *Dazed and Confused*. In 2004, he interned for Rick Owens at furrier Revillon, where he caught the attention of Michèle Lamy, Owen's wife and head of his label. In 2005, Fashion East in London invited Pugh to participate in its cutting-edge group show. In February 2006, he debuted at London Fashion Week and by year's end received backing from Lamy, to whom he would sell a percentage of his company.

Pugh's vision of fashion is an extremely personal one. He approached his early shows as sensationally surreal performances, a carnival filtered through the London club scene. His monochromatic, predominantly dark palette and hard-edged construction often conjured an armoring of the body. His obsessive experimentation with textiles and bold architectural silhouettes, especially an alien articulation of form, fed a futuristic sci-fi aesthetic.

Although considered a creative genius, Pugh had yet to produce anything to sell to the public, and the fashion press had began to question his commercial viability. But in the summer of 2007, his designs, mostly manufactured in Italy, became available through high-end high-concept specialty stores. Then in 2008, the designer relocated to Paris. In 2009, he introduced a men's line that shares the catwalk with his women's collection; his shows also received the financial backing of LVMH.

While Pugh has continued to treat the runway as a theatrical unfolding, his garments have evolved in a softer, more fluid direction, with sinuous lines added into the mix. The shift has been well captured in his collaborations with SHOWstudio filmmaker Ruth Hogben on a number of mesmerizing shorts shown to audiences in lieu of or to enhance his runway presentations.

Photos courtesy of Gareth Pugh.

"We have to sell the dream before we can sell the clothes."

Maison Martin Margiela

1957– (Belgium)

For twenty years, one of the most innovative and influential of designers, Martin Margiela remains an enigmatic figure in the world of fashion. He was adept at removing himself from the public eye—no photographs, no face-to-face interviews, no runways bows—stressing that the work, the collaborative result of a design team, should speak for itself. What is known is that the Flemish native graduated from Antwerp's Royal Academy of Fine Arts in 1979. He then worked for Jean Paul Gaultier as a design assistant from 1984 to 1987. Remaining in Paris, in 1988 he debuted his first collection under the label Maison Martin Margiela.

Margiela's elusiveness was fundamental to the house's antimarketing stance, taken at a time when a designer's name or personality often held more interest than the designs. The label on his clothes was anonymous, a blank white tape tacked to the garment, the stitches usually left exposed on the outer surface. When a second label appeared in 1997—a circled number from 0 to 23 denoting one of the various lines—the name of the brand was still omitted. The issue of (non) identity carried through to the *blouses blanches* of the staff, the laundry bag as packaging, the plural "we" in all correspondence, and the often obscured faces of the models.

The fundamental project of the house under Margiela was the reworking of existing forms, an idea that challenged the fashion system with its own brand of antifashion. He disassembled and reconstructed clothes, fraying hems, displacing pockets, collars, and lapels, turning linings and seams to the outside of the garment. He experimented with scale, from the distortions of doll-size clothing made large to the exaggerated proportions of an Italian size 68. The Artisanal line recycled old garments and accessories (and other discarded objects such as car seats or luggage), transforming them into entirely new creations. The Replica pieces exactly reproduced found garments, each label citing type, provenance, and period: "Man's shirt, Italy, 1970." Items from one collection repeated in the next, like the many incarnations of the tabi boot or shoe.

Margiela was in fact a master craftsman, a skill acknowledged by heritage house Hermès. From 1997 to 2003, he served as creative director of the women's collection, stripping the luxury brand's tailoring to its essentials. The designer stayed fashion's invisible man to the end. Amid much speculation, in 2009 Renzo Rosso, the founder of Diesel who had acquired a majority stake in Maison Martin Margiela in 2002, confirmed publicly that Margiela had left the house.

Photo by firstVIEW.

Photo by Chris Moore, Catwalking, Getty Images.

Above Left Maison Martin Margiela semicouture, Fall/Winter 1997/98 • *Left* Maison Martin Margiela, Fall/Winter 2007/08

Photo by Pierre Verdy, AFP, Getty Images.

"It may be considered that a designer expresses a viewpoint and approach through his or her own work and the work of all the other members of the team that surrounds them. It is also true that the many others working on the garments and for a house—assistants, pattern-cutters, tailors, commercial staff—also express their expertise and sensitivity through the work of a designer."

Above Maison Martin Margiela haute couture, Fall/Winter 2006/07

• *Right* Maison Martin Margiela tabi boots, 1990

Collection of the Museum of Fine Arts, Boston.

Issey Miyake

1938– (Japan)

Issey Miyake has fused tradition and technology to develop new ways of conceiving and constructing garments. Born in Hiroshima, he was seven when he witnessed the atomic bomb's devastation of the city; he gravitated toward fashion as a creative force that was, by contrast, something "modern and optimistic." After studying graphic design in Tokyo, he attended the École de la Chambre Syndicale de la Couture Parisienne. Graduating in 1965, he stayed in Paris to assist first Guy Laroche, then Hubert de Givenchy. In 1969, he moved to New York to work with Geoffrey Beene. In 1970, he returned to Tokyo, where he founded the Miyake Design Studio, and by the following year Bloomingdale's was featuring his work. With the institutionalization of *prêt-à-porter* in 1973, he was invited to show alongside other designers in Paris. From the start, he grasped the relationship between two-dimensional cloth and three-dimensional human body. Wrapped and layered, Miyake's garments asked that the wearer actively engage with them.

Working with textile director Makiko Minagawa, and later with Dai Fujiwara, Miyake strove to identify new ways in which fabrics could be manipulated and made into garments. He first began to explore the dynamics of pleating in the late 1980s and in 1993 introduced his Pleats Please line. Reversing the usual order, polyester fabric is first cut and sewn in the desired shape, two to three times larger than the final size, then pleated, and between sheets of paper fed into a heat press. The garments retain their knife-edge pleats but when worn assume forms that float or expand with the body's movement.

After over twenty years of experimenting with the concept, in 1999 Miyake debuted his revolutionary A-POC (A Piece of Cloth) collection. Computer-programmed machines produce tubes of knit jersey into which are integrated the basic outlines of complete garments (dress, shirt, skirt, socks, hat). The customer is entrusted with the final step: cutting out and modifying the seamless garments as she sees fit. The process is ideal for mass production, requires no sewing, and considerably reduces waste.

Although officially retired in 1999, Miyake still oversees the direction of each collection produced under his name. Long known for his collaborative involvement in the art world—his was the first fashion design to appear on the cover of a major art magazine and one of the earliest to show in the context of the art museum—in 2007 he spearheaded the creation of 21_21 Design Sight, Japan's first design museum/research center.

Photo by Waring Abbott, Michael Ochs Archives, Getty Images.

Photo by Lyndon Douglas.

Above Grace Jones performing in Miyake's red plastic bustier, 1980 ●
Left A-POC installation, Barbican Art Gallery, London, 2010

Photo by Pool Arnal/Garcia, Gamma-Rapho via Getty Images.

"From the beginning I thought about working with the body in movement, the space between the body and clothes... The clothes are for people to dance or laugh."

Left Issey Miyake, Spring/ Summer 1994 • *Below* Miyake's rattan bodice and nylon polyester skirt, cover of *Artforum*, February 1982

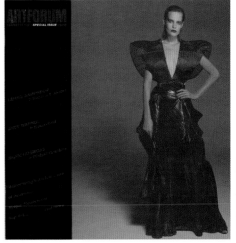

Photo by Eiichiro Sakata.

Kate Mulleavy & Laura Mulleavy

1979– & 1980– (United States)

Kate and Laura Mulleavy create idiosyncratic, wildly imaginative garments using both couture techniques and their own inventive twist on construction. Born in Oakland, California, the sisters studied art history and English literature, respectively, at U.C. Berkeley. The self-trained designers produced their first collection from their parents' home in Pasadena. Calling their label Rodarte (their mother's maiden name), the Mulleavys captured the attention of the fashion press with paper-doll replicas of their first ten-piece collection, which they debuted in New York in 2005. The following year, they set up a small design studio in downtown Los Angeles, where they remain based.

Delicate goddess dresses with cascades and pinked edges became a Rodarte signature, as did their cobwebby sweaters. Their starting points are multilayered and eccentric, veering in one recent collection from Disney's *Sleeping Beauty* to Vincent van Gogh to the Mount Wilson Observatory. The designers favor unconventional, sometimes baroque, combinations of materials—for Spring/Summer 2010 nine different types in one garment alone—any of which they might encrust with beads, crystals, or appliqué. In addition to collaging, pleating, and dyeing their fabrics, they have shredded, sandpapered, and burnt them. Although considered ready-to-wear, nothing is mass produced. The sisters instead work the garments meticulously hand.

This level of craft makes the clothes expensive, and Rodarte has faced criticism for its limited reach. Looking for ways in which to expand their compass (beyond capsule collections for the Gap in 2007 and Target in 2009), the Mulleavys have begun to incorporate more accessible daywear and outerwear pieces into their collections. At the same time, their experimental approach led to a National Design Award in 2010 and an invitation to show at the Pitti Uomo in Florence in 2011. Not surprisingly, they have also turned their efforts toward costume design, such as for the film *Black Swan*. The sisters continue to evolve their fashion vision, taking risks even as they refine their talent.

Above Left Rodarte, Fall/Winter 2011/12 • *Left* Rodarte, Spring/Summer 2011

Photos by firstVIEW.

"*I always say we're story-tellers. Sometimes the stories are very abstract, and sometimes I don't think the meaning is really clear for either of us. The medium that works for us is fashion.*"

Left Rodarte, Spring/
Summer 2010

Rick Owens

1962– (United States)

Paris-based California native Rick Owens has cultivated an aesthetic of poignant, broken-down beauty. Raised in an agricultural town north of Los Angeles, he headed to Otis-Parsons in 1979 to study painting, but left after two years to learn patternmaking. He spent fours years working at various knockoff houses before being hired in 1988 as a pattern cutter for a sportswear company owned by Michèle Lamy, whom he would eventually marry. In 1994, Owens began selling his distressed garments through top L.A. retailers. Five years later, Barneys was carrying his label. In 2002, he showed his first runway collection at New York Fashion Week and won the CFDA's Perry Ellis Award for Emerging Talent. In 2003, Revillon invited him to Paris where for three years as creative director he brought an edgy relevance to the French furrier.

Owens has founded his reputation as a fashion renegade on a casual grungy glamour, equal parts raw and refined. Early on, his long clingy T-shirts, asymmetrical bias-cut skirts, and narrow draped jackets conveyed a life-of-excess romance. He gave all his clothes a worn edge; for example, machine washing and drying the leather for his jackets. He continues to find the perfect gesture to express imperfection, relying on expert if unconventional craftsmanship and rich materials. With his pared-down palette, a certain austere discipline complements his subversive tendencies such as his signature long skirts for men. The designer creates clothes for people who have experienced life, and from season to season, he imbues his urban tribe with a tough shadowy grace.

Owens has built his rock'n'roll via Vionnet style into an extremely successful business, extending the brand with his Lilies (diffusion), DRKSHDW (denim), and Hun (furs, conceived with Lamy) lines as well as a supersized furniture collection that resonates with the clothing.

Above Left Rick Owens, Spring/Summer 2009
• *Left* Rick Owens, Fall/Winter 2011/12

Photos by first VIEW.

"I had always hoped that my clothes would propose a primitive but disciplined elegance. I don't think an elegant discipline would be a bad direction to the world."

Left Rick Owens
meanswear, Spring/
Summer 2012

Ralph Rucci

1957– (United States)

Over the last thirty years, Ralph Rucci has been quietly honing his skills as a couturier of the highest caliber. The Philadelphia-born designer studied literature and philosophy at Temple University before being inspired to enroll at FIT. After graduation, he worked briefly for Halston. Although he showed his first collection in 1981, in 1994 he relaunched his business under the label Chado Ralph Rucci. The name references a Japanese Buddhist tea ceremony of 331 precise steps, evoking respect, control, and tranquility. The designer worked under the radar until 2002 when the Chambre Syndicale invited him to show as a guest member during the haute couture collections in Paris—the first American to receive such an honor since Mainbocher in the 1930s. Although he did not remain in Paris, his designs from this point on became lighter and more experimental.

Rucci focuses his distinct point of view on utterly refined occasion dressing that balances contemporary design and superb craft. With a level of devotion to couture comparable to Balenciaga, every piece is worked by hand in his New York City atelier, considered among the best in the world. To make each collection as individual as possible, he draws on traditional artisanal specialties like embroidery, stitching, beading, and featherwork, as well as techniques he and his team have conceived and developed (cutting apart and repiecing fabric "suspended" from knots, quilting silk moiré along the pattern lines). What appears as the epitome of simplicity is, in fact, the result of complex construction and intricate detail. On a Rucci gown, every seam has a purpose, an integrity of craftsmanship that he describes as "invisible luxury." To create his exquisite wearable sculptures, the designer uses the most sumptuous of materials (double-faced cashmere, Mongolian lamb, silk gazar, paper taffeta). He also designs his own prints, inspired by Asian culture or contemporary art or taken from his own abstract paintings, and works closely with textile mills to create custom fabrics.

Rucci's couture is stupendously expensive, and he has never displayed any interest in offsetting it with lucrative accessory or fragrance lines. Now, however, he is reaching out to a new client with a line of luxury sportswear that he hopes will bring the same response as the standing ovation that met his Spring 2012 show.

Above and Left Ralph Rucci, Spring/Summer 2012

"I am adamant and almost rude about my expectations that editors and also buyers have an encyclopedic knowledge of our profession to qualify them to judge. How can you possibly talk about satin structure or jersey draping unless you know who Charles James and Madame Grès were?"

Left Ralph Rucci,
Fall/Winter 2010/11

Jil Sander

1943– (Germany)

Jil Sander is one of fashion's ultramodernists, creating designs of austere but luxurious purity. Trained as a textile engineer at the Krefeld School of Textiles in 1963, she worked as a fashion editor in both the United States and Germany, then opened a boutique in Hamburg. In 1969, she launched her label. In 1975, the designer showed to a Paris not yet ready to embrace her reductivist aesthetic, but by 1989, a year after her Milan catwalk debut, her company's listing on the Frankfurt stock exchange proved a spectacular success. Over the next decade, she would help to define a new direction for women's fashion.

Sander was concerned foremost with structure, shape, and proportion, keeping a strict palette of neutrals—white, gray, brown, blue, black—and stripping away anything extraneous, including all references to the past. The economy of her streamlined silhouettes was the result of highly refined tailoring. Their opulence came from quality fabrics, often taken from menswear but also made from her own blends of rich fibers. The uncompromising beauty of her suits, dresses, and coats earned her a loyal following of powerful independent women who wished to express a liberated femininity without frills.

Sander expanded into menswear in 1997 and the following year began to collaborate with Puma on a footwear line. In 1999, the Prada Group purchased a 75 percent stake in Jil Sander. Six months later, following disputes with CEO Patrizio Bertelli, the designer resigned and the label lost direction. She came back in 2003, embracing a softer look, only to terminate her relationship again in late 2004. After four years away from the fashion spotlight, she returned as a consultant to the Japanese brand Uniqlo. From 2009 to 2011 she focused her disciplined vision on +J, an affordable line for men and women produced by the fast fashion retailer. Then, in February 2012, the Japanese apparel group that has owned Jil Sander since 2008 announced that she would once again helm the company that bears her name.

Above Jil Sander, Fall/Winter 1996/97

"The more masterful you get, the lighter you can be, the more you can take away and still have purity in the form."

Left Jil Sander, Fall/Winter 2000/01 • *Below* Jil Sander, Fall/Winter 2004/05

Raf Simons

1968– (Belgium)

Raf Simons has led an extraordinary course from self-trained icono-clastic designer to head of one of fashion's most iconic houses. In the early 1990s, he studied industrial and furniture design at the Institute of Visual Communication in the Belgian city of Genk, but following an internship with Walter Van Beirendonck, he turned his attention to men's fashion and in 1995 debuted a collection of narrow-shouldered suits. From the first, the designer successfully rethought menswear, merging sartorial refinement and tradition with the energy and individuality of street culture. His designs also took advantage of new technologies in textiles. In 2000, Simons shut down his Antwerp-based business to reevaluate his brand and accepted a position as head of the fashion department at the University of Applied Arts in Vienna (where he remained until 2005). He returned to the runway in 2001 with a small staff and a clear direction.

Although his Spring/Summer 2004 collection had included six wom-enswear looks, in 2005 Simons might have seemed an unlikely choice for creative director at Jil Sander, which was faltering after Sander had again left the company. Yet under his care, the brand flourished. While maintaining its core values, the clean lines and understated sophistication, Simons added his own flair, a vision of minimalism enriched by bright color and pattern, asymmetry and fresh propor-tions. Moreover, he introduced a greater sensuality to the collections, from Spring 2011 interpreting anew the feminine lines of mid-century haute couture.

After six and a half years at Jil Sander, Simons was suddenly dis-missed. The delicate modernity of his final show, however, met with thunderous applause. Two months later, in April of 2012, the designer became the new artistic director of Dior. His haute couture debut was a tour de force that looked to the past and to the future.

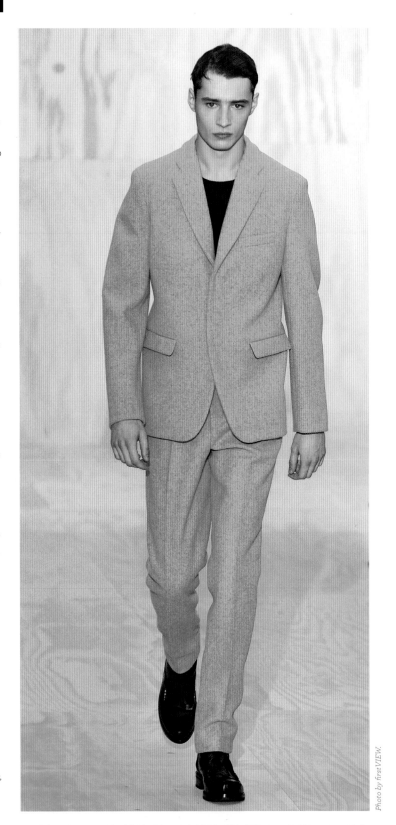

Right Jil Sander menswear, Fall/Winter 2011/12

Photo by firstVIEW.

"Dress codes and gestures and attitudes have always inspired me."

Left Jil Sander, Fall/Winter 2012/13 • *Below* Jil Sander, Fall/Winter 2011/12

Yeohlee Teng

1955– (Malaysia)

Yeohlee Teng has long referred to her clothing as shelter or, in the title of an early exhibition, "intimate architecture." She came to New York from Penang in the 1970s to study at Parsons and stayed in the city to establish her label, Yeohlee, in 1981. Her first collection included a hooded cape cut from a single piece of fabric and incorporating all the material. This zero-waste design, versions of which she continues to sell, immediately signaled her approach to patternmaking. She lets the properties of her fabrics (weight, texture, wear resistance) inform the overall silhouette, style lines, and finishing techniques.

Strongly resonate with the built environment (referencing practices as varied as Greene & Greene, Luis Barragán, Rudolph Schindler, Antoni Gaudí, Bernard Tschumi, and SANAA), Yeohlee's work uses geometries, from circles to cubes to parabolas to möbius strips, and construction techniques, such as suspension, more often associated with engineering than fashion. More recently, she has drawn from the structure of energy and sound. Yet, however intellectually sophisticated her process, there is a simplicity to the garments themselves that derives from Yeohlee's deep commitment to functionalism. Her clothes are seasonless, easy to move in, easy to maintain, and adaptable to different contexts. The confident urban nomad for whom she designs might be any age or size.

Yeohlee is highly respected within the art and larger design communities. In 2004, she received the Cooper-Hewitt's National Design Award for Fashion, and to a remarkable degree throughout the last three decades, her work has been exhibited at museums and galleries worldwide. At the same time, she has been actively dedicated to the economic sustainability of New York's fashion industry. In 2010, Yeohlee became the first designer to open a store in the Garment District.

"I think the reason I get drawn to one-size-fits-all is that I am fascinated by proportions and how you can make something look terrific on somebody that is 5 feet 2 inches and a size 4 and have it work on somebody who is 5 feet 9 inches but a size 12 or 14."

Photo by Stefan Gosatti, Getty Images for IMG.

Photo by Steven A. Henry, Getty Images.

Opposite Page Yeohlee
Teng, Fall/Winter 2010/11
• *Above* Isabel and Ruben
Toledo, New York, 2011

Isabel Toledo

1961– (Cuba)

Isabel Toledo brings a rare alchemist's touch to fashion, marrying an instinct for the mood of a garment to "the maths behind the romance." She learned to sew as a girl and took classes at both Parsons and FIT. But working alongside Diana Vreeland from 1979 to 1984 as a restorer at the Metropolitan Museum of Art's Costume Institute marked the real beginning of her education in the techniques of the leading couturiers. Though she had previously staged small, sometimes impromptu shows in New York club venues, with interest in her work growing, in 1985 she presented her first collection of hand-sewn ensembles to rave reviews.

With an undisputed mastery of draping and complex pattern work, Toledo transforms geometry into glamour. Whether the ingenuity of her construction produces liquid falls or origami folds, the clothes are feminine, refined, and idiosyncratic. She works in close creative partnership with her husband, the illustrator Ruben Toledo. To realize her designs, she explains a garment's feel—both physical and emotional—for Ruben to sketch. The two go back and forth until the result satisfies Isabel. At times, new ideas emerge from imperfections in the drawings.

The couple grew up in New Jersey in a community of Cuban émigrés and something of the tenacity and enterprise of the immigrant has informed their approach to the fashion business. As independent entrepreneurs, without financial investors and the attendant marketing, they have remained small scale, catering to private clients and a select group of retailers. In 1991, Toledo began showing on the fashion calendar in New York and, for a few years, in Paris as well, but in 1998, she stopped holding seasonal runway shows, instead, creating collections on her own schedule. Everything is designed, prototyped, and produced in New York.

A recipient of the Cooper-Hewitt's 2005 National Design Award for Fashion, and long a favorite of industry insiders, Toledo secured global recognition in 2009 when Michelle Obama attended her husband's presidential inauguration in the designer's wool lace dress and overcoat in an optimistic shade of lemongrass yellow.

"I was always fascinated by clothing patterns; that was architecture to me."

Olivier Theyskens

1977– (Belgium)

From high to low, Olivier Theyskens possesses an innate ability to dress the female form in clothing that is enchanting, elegant, and cool. Knowing from an early age that he wished to be a couturier, he attended the prestigious visual arts school La Cambre in 1995, but dropped out after two years. In 1997, he showed his first goth-inflected collection in Paris, refusing to sell any of the garments despite an offer from Barneys for the entire line. For five years, he produced strong, dark collections that thrilled the fashion press. In 2002, having lost his financial backing, he shuttered his company.

Almost immediately, Theyskens was appointed creative director of Rochas. Tasked with redefining the fabled fashion house for a whole new generation, he revealed a flair for a delicate and restrained femininity. His work applied the meticulous techniques and quality fabrics of haute couture to what was now a ready-to-wear label. Though his collections were a critical success, his refusal to compromise on expenses together with his resistance to designing marketable accessories were seen as contributing factors in the house's closure in 2006. That same year, Theyskens received the CFDA's International Award, and in November he accepted the post of creative director of Nina Ricci. His romantic collections with a disheveled edge and muted palette appealed to a young clientele, but once again proved too costly for them. In 2009, he was abruptly let go before the end of his contract.

In 2010, Andrew Rosen, founder of the contemporary clothing label Theory, approached the designer to create a capsule collection. Theyskens presented long, loose silhouettes with an urban grittiness not seen since his first eponymous collections. The collaboration proved so successful that the company extended the Theyskens' Theory line and named its creator artistic director for the entire brand. Theyskens now gives affordable American sportswear a twenty-first-century twist on chic.

Photos by *firstVIEW.*

Above Olivier Theyskens, Spring/Summer 1999 • *Left* Theyskens Theory, resort, 2012

Photo by Judith White, Bloomberg via Getty Images.

"I look to create the right clothing at the right place for the right moment. I am not a different person in all my adventures."

Left Nina Ricci, Fall/Winter 2007/08 • *Below* Theyskens Theory, Fall/Winter 2011/12

Photo by firstVIEW.

Riccardo Tisci

1974– (Italy)

Raised by his widowed mother alongside eight older sisters, Riccardo Tisci is at home in the feminine world, though it's one to which his clothes give a slight masculine energy. His parents were from Taranto in the south, but he grew up in Como. In 1991, he headed to London and eventually secured a scholarship that allowed him to attend Central Saint Martins. After graduating in 1999 with a Fellini-inspired collection that was picked up by one of the city's edgier boutiques, he returned to Italy, working for a series of Italian brands as well as briefly for Ruffo Research before it was disbanded. In 2004, encouraged by his friend Mariacarla Boscono, he presented his own work, not on the typical Milan runway but in a warehouse with models in *tableaux vivants* with demolished cars. In this and a second collection that drew on the iconography of his Catholic upbringing, his designs were raw, sensual, and deeply gothic.

In 2005, LVMH approached Tisci to helm the House of Givenchy, a job that he took to support his family. At Givenchy, he focused on rebranding a *maison* that had gone through three designers since the retirement of its founder in 1995 and that was still associated with the classy chic of Audrey Hepburn. His collections have projected a darker romanticism, mixing a moody eroticism and a glamorized street style into the traditions of elegance and sophistication. His tailoring comes through in bold, almost architectural silhouettes and his eye for detail in the intricate layering of fabrics, patterns, and embellishments. He constantly offers new imaginings of hard and soft, such as crocodile scales separated and sewn on tulle for a recent form-fitting haute couture gown.

His direction for the house may have been questioned at first, but Tisci has succeeded critically and financially, making garments to be worn as much as desired and dramatically increasing the number of haute couture clients. Yet he is never too far from the transgressive, especially when playing with gender paradigms. Even in the most ethereal of garments, his women are dynamic and powerful. When he took on the menswear collection in 2008, he showed that his male is tough enough to embrace hot pink lace. Transgender model Lea T, a longtime assistant whom he first put on the catwalk and in ad campaigns in 2010, embodies perfectly the in-between of masculine and feminine that Tisci's clothing suggests.

Photo by firstVIEW.

Left Givenchy, Fall/Winter 2011/12 • *Below Left* Givenchy, Spring/Summer 2011 • *Below* Givenchy haute couture, Spring/Summer 2012/13

Photos by Karl Prouse, Catwalking, Getty Images.

Photo by Givenchy.

"I am very attracted to the feminine world, because I love the strength and romanticism."

An Vandevorst & Filip Arickx

1968– & 1971– (Belgium)

The husband and wife team design team of An Vandevorst and Filip Arickx pursue theoretical investigations to generate innovative clothing of striking urban glamour. The two met in 1987, on the day they began their studies at the Royal Academy of Fine Arts in Antwerp. Upon graduating in 1991, Vandevorst joined Dries Van Noten as an assistant designer, while Arickx became a freelance designer after training with Dirk Bikkenbergs. As A.F. Vandevorst, they presented their first collaboration in Paris in 1998. They were awarded the Venus de la Mode after their second collection, which they showed on models awaking from hospital beds. A year later, they were selected as Ruffo Research designers for 2000/2001.

Their logo is a red cross, evocative of both the military nurse uniforms that were an early influence and the "social sculpture" of the late German artist Joseph Beuys, who continues to be muse of sorts. The duo's aesthetic relies on the refined juxtaposition of opposites: constrained and liberated, stiff and soft, masculine and feminine, formal and sporty, wearable and conceptual, played out in unexpected combinations of textiles, imaginative uses of balance and asymmetry, and the pairing of lingerie-inspired elements with clever tailoring such as their signature reworked button-downs and variations on the trench.

The designers have extended their label to include Fetish, a shoe collection, and Nightfall, a lingerie collection, as well as a more affordable line called A. Friend by A.F. Vandevorst. In 2005, they curated "Katharina Prospekt: The Russians" for MoMu in Antwerp and in 2011 created the installation "Dreaming" for the Armhem Mode Biennale. The interventions around Belgium from 2009 to 2011 of their Aktion guerilla shops, followed globally in 2012 by the Smallest Travelling Store in the World (TSTSITW)—reviving the idea of a hospital-room setting—have further captured the bold spirit of their brand.

Photo by firstVIEW.

Above A.F. Vandervorst,
Fall/Winter, 2011/12

"This is the most important thing for us; to see fashion not as something that is superficial but to probe as deep as possible."

Walter Van Beirendonck

1957– (Belgium)

Walter Van Beirendonck approaches fashion as a kind of storytelling, offering his collections as ultimately optimistic, if sometimes disconcerting, guides for a better world. He started his menswear line in 1983, three years after graduating from Antwerp's Royal Academy of Fine Arts. In 1987, he was among the six alumni of the fashion program to take London by storm at the British Designer Show, solidifying his reputation as a talented maverick. From 1993 to 1999, in conjunction with the German jeans company Mustang, he designed high-end street-style clothing under the label W.&L.T. (Wild and Lethal Trash), experimenting with high-tech, innovative materials. He followed with aestheticterrorists by walter, before returning to his eponymous collection in 2004.

Van Beirendonck's avant-garde collections are instantly recognizable for their innovative cuts, vibrant color combinations, and bold graphics, all of which draw on his recurring fascination with language and ritual, gender and fetishism, aliens, shamans, and avatars. His collections are narrative in character and evidence his sense of humor and whimsy—his shows often resemble a carnival in atmosphere—even while addressing tough topical issues from ecology to HIV/AIDS to racism to consumer society. (He named his Fall/Winter 2006/07 collection Stop Terrorising Our World.) Inspired by how different ethnic tribes use their bodies as expression, the designer repeatedly pushes at the frontiers of masculine beauty, sexuality, and identity.

Seeding the discourse on fashion, politics, and culture, Van Beirendonck has curated numerous exhibitions and publications, including *Mutilate*, on the power of self-transformation, and *Patterns*, a manual for copying his designs. As part of his commitment to supporting pioneering fashion design, in 1998 he opened Walter, a concept boutique in Antwerp that showcased other practices in addition to his own. In February 2012, his store filed for bankruptcy. He continues to mentor young designers at his alma mater, however, where he has taught since 1985 and directed the fashion department since 2007.

Right Walter Van Beirendonck menswear, Spring/Summer 2012

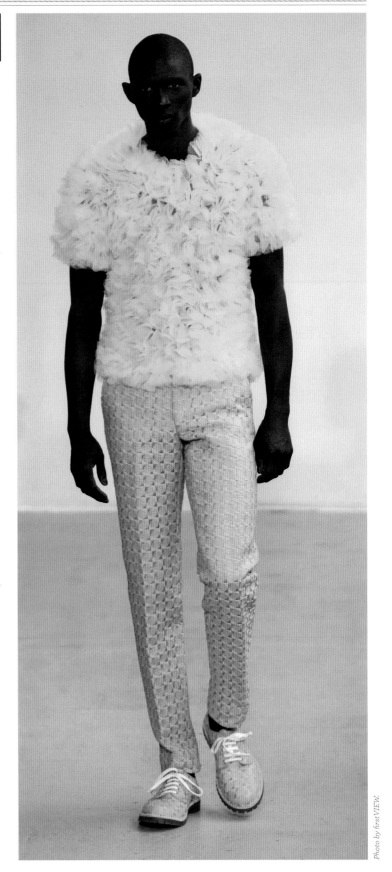

Photo by firstVIEW.

"I really did try to do [the work] in an unconventional way and come up with new propositions. I hope that I will be remembered for that and also that I changed some boundaries. That's really important for me because it's ultimately what I want to do as a fashion designer."

Below Walter Van Beirendonck menswear, Fall/Winter 2010/11

Photo by Victor Boyko, Getty Images.

Dries Van Noten

1958– (Belgium)

Dries Van Noten is fashion's master of elegantly unexpected juxtapositions of color, texture, and pattern. Born into an Antwerp tailoring family, with a father who owned an upscale fashion emporium, he benefitted from an early experience with the technical and commercial aspects of the industry. He launched his label in 1985 and shortly thereafter opened the first of his carefully designed boutiques. In 1987, the designer attracted international attention when he presented his menswear collection at the British Designer Show along with fellow graduates of the Royal Academy of Fine Arts. He went on to debut his collections in Paris, menswear in 1991 and womenswear in 1993.

The immediate visual impact of his clothes is often that of a bohemian exoticism. His work has encompassed a world tour of textile history and artisanal techniques, moving through India, Afghanistan, Turkey, Morocco, Romania, Thailand, and Japan, to name a few points of embarkation. More recently, his inspirations have come as much from the art world; yet even when conveying an ethnic or historical tone, his designs have been nonchalantly modern.

Van Noten employs unusual textiles, most of which will not be found outside his garments. Sometimes, he overprints motifs onto patterned fabrics. He also plays with scales of pattern, from exploded to minute, and with tactile mixtures, such as crisp cotton against the cool sheen of snakeskin. Onto a collage of prints he might add opulent embellishments of beading or embroidery. Finally, with an insouciant touch, he will layer the pieces themselves, perhaps a skirt over trousers.

Van Noten has never compromised his artful aesthetic, no matter the prevailing trends. Though he brings an attention to the craft of his clothing worthy of haute couture, he remains resolutely committed to ready-to-wear. His label has thrived while his company has stayed fiercely independent.

Right Dries Van Noten, Fall/Winter 2010/11

Photo by first VIEW.

Photo by *firstVIEW.*

Above Dries Van Noten, Fall/Winter 2011/12 • *Right* Dries Van Noten, Fall/Winter 2012/13

"I'm part of the fashion system, but I don't want to follow all the rules. I don't want to be contrarian—I just want to do my own things, which are most honest and correct to do."

Photo by Victor Virgile, Gamma-Rapho via Getty Images.

Junya Watanabe

1961– (Japan)

Junya Watanabe turns his technical expertise to the endless invention of extraordinary hybrid garments. The Tokyo native graduated from Bunka Fashion College in 1984 and immediately went to work as a pattern cutter at Comme des Garçons. He soon became a protégé of founder Rei Kawakubo, designing her Tricot line. In 1992 he introduced his own collection under the Comme des Garçons umbrella, which he debuted in Paris for the Spring/Summer 1994 season. In 2001 he began to design the Comme des Garçons Homme collection as well.

Watanabe is a master of complex draping and tailoring techniques (from unexpected seaming, darting, and zipper placement to origami folding and honeycomb forms). His sourcing of materials is unpredictable. He has gained a reputation as a techno-couturier for his unusual application of high-performance fabrics, such as in the waterproof evening gowns of his Spring/Summer 2000 collection, and his early adoption of cutting-edge fibers including glass, plastic, metals, laminated paper, and fluorescents. But he has also worked ingeniously with traditional materials, whether humble like denim or refined like lace.

His aesthetic often involves deconstructing utilitarian garments like the trench or army jacket, then redesigning them into something altogether different. He will also incorporate seemingly unrelated parts of disparate garments into one new form. In both his men's and women's collections, Watanabe displays a profound interest in fashion's codes and totems—his many transformations of iconic garments is almost a signature of his work. Interweaving high and low, couture's history with subcultural style, for instance, he perfectly reimagined the leather biker's jacket through Dior's hourglass silhouette for Fall/Winter 2011/12. Even when referencing the past, his clothes look forward, mining the terrain between the serene and unsettling, the romantic and probing.

In 2005, having benefited from Kawakubo's mentorship, Watanabe was instrumental in helping his own protégé, Tao Kurihara, to launch her label within the Comme des Garçons family.

Above Junya Watanabe, Spring/Summer 2010

Photo by François Guillot, AFP, Getty Images.

Photo by firstVIEW.

"*Sometimes I cannot achieve what I really want to do in just one collection, so in the following collection I do it again. There are certain things I've been working on for three years.*"

Above Junya Watanabe, Fall/Winter 2011/12 • *Right* Junya Watanabe, Spring/Summer 2012

Photo by Chris Moore, Catwalking, Getty Images.

Future of Fashion

"That's the future of fashion. If you can be really exclusive and it's at a price point that everybody can handle, that's genius." *Robert Duffy, 2010* "When one says 'feminine', it brings up a vision of ruffles and fussy ornamentation. Interesting is a better word, for that is what clothes are becoming." *Edward H. Molyneux, 1927* "I don't think the menswear look is over, and I don't think women will ever give up wearing pants." *Marc Bohan, 1967* "Fashion in the future will keep changing. We will see innovative body art, as well as come-backs from key style pieces from the past. Fashion is a roller coaster. . . . At the end of the day, it will continue coming around." *Laura Panter, 2011* "I see the future of fashion weeks around the world as not only a physical schedule

struction of fashion." *Sonia Rykiel, 1978* "The young women of our day cannot stand anything annoying her, for example, she has given up her grandmother's stays. . . . She requires practical clothes that allow her to move with freedom, ease and harmony." *Jean Patou, 1924* "A new American fashion is emerging, one not obsessed with the past, and the good news is that the evolution is open to all. The past is taken; the future is up for grabs." *Russell Simmons, 2003* "I think we're on the cusp of something so major. I really think conscious consumerism is where it's at." *Donna Karan, 2010* "I believe we are already experiencing major changes in the industry. Keyword: Web; more specifically, social networks and blogs." *Simona Frasca, 2011* "I think in the future, there

"A CREATION WHICH GOES AGAINST THE TENDENCIES OF ITS PERIOD CAN NEVER BE SUCCESSFUL: AND IF FASHION CHANGES MORE QUICKLY NOWADAYS THAN IT USED TO DO THIRTY OR FIFTY YEARS AGO, THAT IS ONLY BECAUSE LIFE, TRAVEL, AND EVENTS THEMSELVES HAVE TAKEN ON A NEW RHYTHM." Célia Bertin, 1956

will be a complete elimination of all the little gadgets. You are the gadget that communicates. I think that technology-based fashion, both for fun and purpose, is on the cusp." *Francesca Rosella, 2010* "Maybe I won't see it in my lifetime, but

"IT'S A NEW ERA IN FASHION—THERE ARE NO RULES. IT'S ALL ABOUT THE INDIVIDUAL AND PERSONAL STYLE, WEARING HIGH-END, LOW-END, CLASSIC LABELS, AND UP-AND-COMING DESIGNERS ALL TOGETHER." Alexander McQueen, 2010

of shows, but also as a calendar of fashion experiences online, which bridge the industry and consumer experience." *Nick Knight, 2010* "I've taken clothes as far as they can go. Now it is the démodé, or de-

there will come a day when it will be quite common to see a black face on the cover of *Harper's Bazaar* or *Vogue*." *Naomi Sims, 1970* "I think it will be very difficult for a lot of magazines, because now you see so many things on the Internet right away and you cannot be as quick as the Internet. Maybe some magazines will stay, but they have to be very beautiful, like collector's items." *Carine Roitfeld, 2011* "The future of fashion seems to be hanging on the fabrics." *Suzy Menkes, 2010* "Fashion will last forever. It will exist always. It will exist in its own way in each era. It's interesting to know the old methods. But you have to live in the present moment. The evolution today is in the machinery." *Azzedine Alaïa, 2011* "I think we're about to

"I THINK THAT THE NEXT FASHION REVOLUTION SHALL COME FROM THE CHEMIST'S TUBE."
Geoffrey Beene, 1988

enter into an extremely creative time, and I don't think it's going to be as much about a façade and excess and all of that. It's going to be about things that really matter, that have quality and a lot of integrity." *Julie Gilhart, 2010* "The commercial magazines may be replaced, because the Internet is a better place for commerce and immediate information. The Internet is a chance for magazines because it forces them to really explore what they are. . . . But a true creative fashion magazine can't be replaced by a true creative fashion site because it doesn't exist and it won't exist. You don't want to look at a fashion shoot on your screen, do you?" *Olivier Zahm, 2010* "[Marc Jacobs]—who is both credited with setting more trends than almost anybody else and accused, because of his incessant referencing, of never inventing anything original—

declared that what is new is simply what is now; that anything can be new, given a fresh context." *Stefano Tonchi, 2011* "Simplicity survives

"THE FUTURE OF FASHION IS SIX MONTHS." Karl Lagerfeld, 2010

the changes of fashion. Women of chic are wearing now dresses they bought from me in 1936. Fit the century, forget the year." *Valentina, 1947* "It is rather easy to imagine and create wildly fantastic clothing with no regard to the realities of the world. The true avant-garde sensibility, though, is one that acknowledges reality while simultaneously providing a glimpse of the solutions and surprises that tomorrow will surely bring." *Yohji Yamamoto, 2010* "I think that the next fashion revolution shall come from the chemist's tube." *Geoffrey Beene, 1988* "The whole idea is to find this kind of harmony between newness and tradition, between yesterday and today. It's not just about being modern and high-tech

"THE HARDEST THING TO REALIZE IN FASHION IS THAT THE FUTURE LIES IN THE PAST. THE SECOND HARDEST THING IS TO FORGET THE PAST."
Cathy Horyn, 2012

and going forward. In order to go forward you have to have some base, you have to come from somewhere." *Albert Elbaz, 2010* "The future has to be bright. It is the nature of fashion to evolve, only this time it might evolve more than ever, with seat belts optional." *Hedi Slimane, 2010* "That's also what the future is going to be about, it's going to be all crossovers, everywhere, finally." *Raf Simons, 2008*

Recommended Reading

The following titles are a subjective list of favorites. In addition, we highly recommend the databases of the Berg Fashion Library, Oxford Art Online, and Women's Wear Daily (WWD) Online as well as the journals *Costume* (Costume Society of Great Brtain), *Dress* (Costume Society of America), *Fashion Practice: The Journal of Design, Creative Process, and the Fashion Industry* (Berg), and *Fashion Theory: The Journal of Dress, Body, and Culture* (Berg).

Photo by Claire Zellar Barclay and Iping Hsieh.

Teri Agins, *The End of Fashion: How Marketing Changed the Clothing Business Forever* (New York: William Morrow, 1999).

Norberto Angeletti and Alberto Oliva, *In Vogue: The Illustrated History of the World's Most Famous Fashion Magazine* (New York: Rizzoli, 2006).

Juliet Ash and Elizabeth Wilson, *Chic Thrills: A Fashion Reader* (London: Pandora Press, 1992).

Bettina Ballard, *In My Fashion* (New York: David McKay, 1960).

Barthes, Roland. *The Fashion System*, trans. Matthew Ward and Richard Howard (Berkeley: University of California Press, 1990).

Célia Bertin, *Paris à la mode*, trans. Marjorie Deans (New York: Harper, 1957).

Dilys Blum, *Shocking!: The Art and Fashion of Elsa Schiaparelli* (Philadelphia: Philadelphia Museum of Art, 2003).

Christopher Breward, *Fashioning London: Clothing and the Modern Metropolis* (Oxford: Berg Publishers, 2004).

Breward and Caroline Evans, eds., *Fashion and Modernity* (Oxford: Berg Publishers, 2005).

Breward and David Gilbert, eds., *Fashion's World Cities* (Oxford: Berg Publishers, 2006).

Leslie Hoffmann, ed., *Future Fashion White Papers* (New York: Earth Pledge, 2007).

Laura Eceiza, ed., *Atlas of Fashion Designers* (Beverly, Mass.: Rockport Publishers, 2008).

Edmonde Charles-Roux, *Chanel and Her World: Friends, Fashion, and Fame* (New York: The Vendome Press, 2005).

Christian Dior, *Dior by Dior* (London: V&A Publishing, 2007).

Christian Esquevin, *Adrian: Silver Screen to Custom Label* (New York: Monacell Press, 2008).

Caroline Evans, *Fashion at the Edge: Spectacle, Modernity, and Deathliness* (New Haven: Yale University Press, 2003).

Evans and Minna Thornton. *Women and Fashion: A New Look* (London: Quartet, 1989).

Akiko Fukai et al., *Fashion: The Collection of the Kyoto Costume Institute: A History from the 18th to the 20th Century* (Köln: Taschen, 2005).

John Harvey, *Men in Black* (Chicago: University of Chicago Press, 1995).

Elizabeth Hawes, *Fashion is Spinach* (New York: Random House, 1938).

Mark Holborn, *Issey Miyake* (Köln: Taschen, 1995).

Anne Hollander, *Seeing Through Clothes* (Berkeley: University of California Press, 1993).

Hollander, *Sex and Suits: The Evolution of Modern Dress* (New York: Kodansha International, 1995).

Pamela Golbin, *Balenciaga Paris* (Paris: Les Arts Décoratifs, 2006).

Golbin, *Madeleine Vionnet* (Paris: Les Arts Décoratifs, 2009).

Nancy L. Green, *Ready-to-Wear and Ready-to-Work: A Century of Industry and Immigrants in Paris and New York.* (Durham, NC: Duke University Press, 1997).

Yuniya Kawamura, *The Japanese Revolution in Paris Fashion* (Oxford: Berg Publishing, 2004).

Betty Kirke, *Madeleine Vionnet* (San Francisco: Chronicle Books, 1998).

Harold Koda, *Poiret* (New Haven: Yale University Press, 2007).

Suzanne Lee, *Fashioning the Future: Tomorrow's Wardrobe* (London: Thames & Hudson, 2005).

Joel Lobenthal, *Radical Rags: Fashions of the Sixties* (New York: Abbeville, 1992).

Alice Mackrell, *Art and Fashion: The Impact of Art on Fashion and Fashion on Art* (London: Batsford, 2005).

Maison Martin Margiela (New York: Rizzoli, 2009).

Richard Martin, *American Ingenuity: Sportswear, 1930s–1970s* (New York: Metropolitan Museum of Art, 1998).

Peter McNeil and Vicki Karaminas, eds., *The Men's Fashion Reader* (Oxford: Berg Publishers, 2009).

Patricia Mears, *American Beauty: Aesthetics and Innovation in Fashion* (New Haven: Yale University Press, 2009).

Mears, *Madame Grès: The Sphinx of Fashion* (New Haven: Yale University Press, 2007).

Caroline Milbank, *Couture: The Great Designers* (New York: Stewart, Tabori & Chang, 1985).

Milbank, *New York Fashion: The Evolution of American Style* (New York: Abrams, 1989).

Alexandra Palmer, *Dior* (London: V&A Publishing, 2009).

Phillippe Perrot, *Fashioning the Bourgeoisie: A History of Clothing in the Nineteenth Century*, trans. Richard Bienvenu (Princeton: Princeton University Press, 1996).

Paul Poiret, *King of Fashion* (London: V&A Publishing, 2009).

Bradley Quinn, *Techno Fashion* (Oxford: Berg Publishers, 2002).

Quinn, *Textile Futures: Fashion, Design, and Technology* (Oxford: Berg Publishers, 2010).

Aileen Ribeiro, *Dress and Morality* (Oxford: Berg Publications, 2004).

Geoffrey Aguilina Ross, *The Day of the Peacock: Style for Men 1963–1973* (London: V&A Publishing, 2011).

Penelope Rowlands, *A Dash of Daring: Carmel Snow and Her Life in Fashion, Art, and Letters* (New York: Atria Books, 2005).

Elsa Schiaparelli, *Shocking Life* (London: V&A Publishing, 2007).

Sabine Seymour, *Fashionable Technology: The Intersection of Design, Fashion, Science, and Technology* (Vienna: Springer-Verlag, 2009).

Valerie Steele, ed., *The Berg Companion to Fashion* (Oxford: Berg Publishers, 2010).

Steele, *Fashion, Italian Style* (New Haven: Yale University Press, 2003).

Steele, *Paris Fashion* (New York: Oxford University Press, 1988).

Dana Thomas, *Delux: How Luxury Lost Its Luster* (New York: Penguin, 2008).

Diana Vreeland, *D.V.* (Cambridge, Mass: Da Capo Press, 2003).

Jonathan Walford, *Forties Fashion: Siren Suits to the New Look* (London: Thames and Hudson, 2008).

Linda Welters, and Abby Lillethun, eds., *The Fashion Reader*, 2nd ed. (Oxford: Berg Publishers, 2011).

Claire Wilcox, ed., *The Golden Age of Couture: Paris and London, 1947–1957* (London: V&A Publishing, 2007).

Elizabeth Wilson, *Adorned in Dreams* (London: I.B. Tauris, 2003).

Robert Violette, ed., *Hussein Chalayan* (New York: Rizzoli, 2011).

Yohji Yamamoto, *My Dear Bomb* (Antwerp: Ludion, 2010).

Kohle Yohannan and Nancy Nolf, *Claire McCardell: Redefining Modernism* (New York: Harry N. Abrams, 1998).

Bettina Zilhka, *Ultimate Style: The Best Dressed List* (New York: Assouline, 2004).

Index

Alicia Kennedy is a design editor and writer and teaches twentieth-century fashion history at Lasell College. She was cofounder and coeditor of the award-winning *Assemblage: A Critical Journal of Architecture and Design Culture.*

Emily Banis Stoehrer is a fashion educator and heads the Fashion Program at Fisher College in Boston. She was formerly a curatorial research associate in textiles and fashion at the Museum of Fine Arts, Boston.

Photos by Lisa Kessler.

Jay Calderin is director of creative marketing at the School of Fashion Design in Boston. He founded and was executive director of Boston Fashion Week. He is the author of *Form, Fit, and Fashion* and *Fashion Design Essentials.*

Photo by Tracy Aiguier.